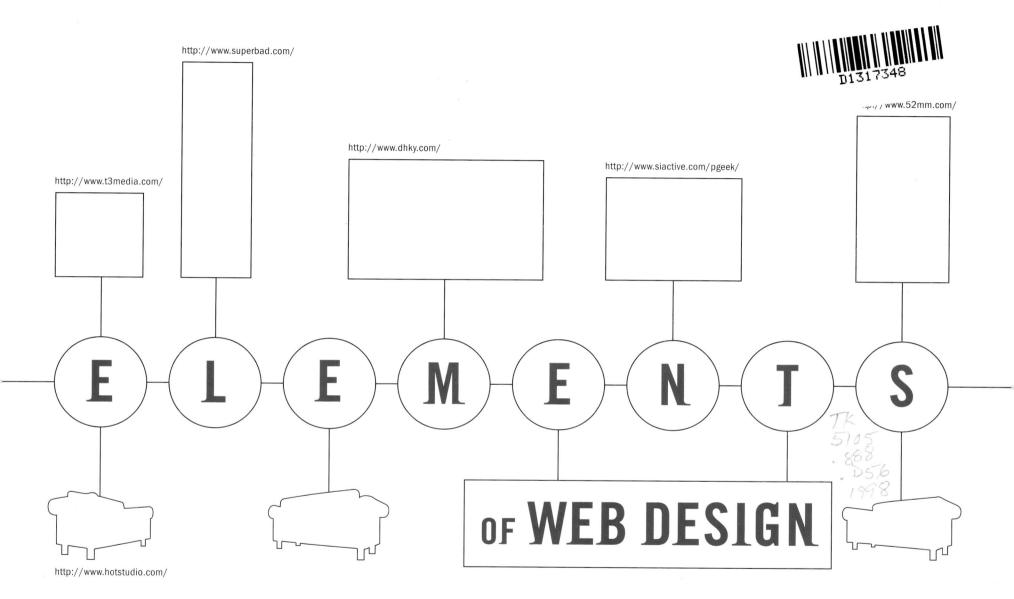

http://www.superbad.com/

http://www.52mm.com/

http://www.dhky.com/

http://www.t3media.com/

http://www.siactive.com/pgeek/

E L E M E N T S

OF **WEB DESIGN**

http://www.hotstudio.com/

Darcy DiNUCCI with Maria **GIUDICE** & Lynne **STILES**

Elements of Web Design, 2nd Edition

Darcy DiNucci, Maria Giudice, Lynne Stiles

Peachpit Press
1249 Eighth Street
Berkeley, CA 94710
510/524-2178
800/283-9444
510/524-2221 (fax)

Find us on the World Wide Web at http://www.peachpit.com/

Peachpit Press is a division of Addison Wesley Longman

Editor: Simon Hayes
Cover and interior design: Maria Giudice, Lynne Stiles, Ben Seibel, and Renee Anderson
Copyeditor: Tema Goodwin
Technical reviewer: Stefan Fielding-Isaacs
Production coordinator: Kate Reber

We would like to thank all the Web designers who shared their knowledge and opinions with us as their thinking and the Web evolved, especially those who are quoted throughout this book and profiled in the "Who's Doing Web Design?" chapter. Thanks also to Ted Nace, founder of Peachpit Press, for the chance to do this book and to Nancy Ruenzel, Peachpit's publisher, for giving us the opportunity to try to do it even better the second time. Special thanks to Matthew Butterick, of Atomic Vision, for loaning the spinning couch to HOT for inclusion on its Web site, http://www.hotstudio.com/.

Colophon

This book was created with QuarkXPress 3.3, Adobe Illustrator 7.0, and Adobe Photoshop 4.0 on Macintosh computers. The fonts used were Franklin Gothic and Beach. Final output was on a CREO Platesetter, and it was printed on 80# Influence Soft Gloss at GAC/Shepard Poorman in Indianapolis, IN.

ISBN 0-201-69698-3

9 8 7 6 5 4

Printed and bound in the United States of America

Introduction

The World Wide Web fired a fuse under the Internet, transforming it from a mysterious buzzword to one of the hottest topics in business and the media. It offers worldwide distribution. It's interactive. It can include sounds, movies, and animation, in addition to text and graphics. And starting from nowhere a few years ago, it's now the fastest-growing medium on Earth.

The jump to electronic publishing—distributing magazines, marketing communications, books, and other materials in electronic form—has been predicted for ages, but now, with the advent of the World Wide Web, it has become a reality. Whether they're putting out personal e-zines or the *New York Times,* publishers see it as a way to widen their distribution at a very low cost. Businesses from one-person home offices to Sony and Disney use it as an efficient way to reach customers and sell products. Others look to it for office "intranets," taking advantage of the cross-platform compatibility and easy navigation of Web publishing to distribute information within corporations. The Web bypasses the barriers of paper and distribution costs, allows unlimited updates, and puts information in front of its audience instantly.

For designers as well as for publishers, the World Wide Web is a great business opportunity. Any company that hasn't built a Web site or an intranet yet is planning one now—and that includes your current and prospective clients. As businesses throughout the world rush to establish their presence on the Web, they need professional designers to help create striking and effective electronic interfaces.

Designing for the Web isn't hard. You probably already have most of the software you'll need—an image editor, an illustration program, a word processor. The popularity of the Web has prodded software companies to introduce easy-to-use Web-authoring features into mainstream design and office software, and more specialized tools are often quite inexpensive and easy to learn. Thanks to these innovations, delving into multimedia, scripting, and other aspects of leading-edge Web design is becoming easier every day. And renting space on a Web server for your own Web presence can be unbelievably cheap. Many Internet service providers offer their customers Web page space on their servers for free.

There's no better time to get your feet wet than now. This book has been created to give designers a grounding in the world of the Web, guided by Web design professionals who have set the current high-water mark for innovative and effective use of the medium. We'll help you understand how and why design for the Web differs from design for print, how to assemble the team you'll need, how to think about interface design for the new medium, how to use different kinds of media, and how to keep up in the ever-changing world of the Web.

Special features throughout the book help you navigate:

as a way to download images (→**106**), has attributes specially designed for this task.)	A number preceded by an arrow directs you to a page where you can find more about the topic at hand.
supports a work-alike scripting it calls **JScript**.) Visual Basic Script, popular browser support.	Terms you'll need to know are highlighted in red, defined in the margin next to their use, and gathered in a glossary at the end of the book.
START TAG **\<OBJECT\>**	HTML quick-reference boxes show the codes you'll use to create the effect we discuss in the adjoining text and illustrations. At the end of the book you'll find an alphabetical list of the most useful HTML tags.
stop and download things. page and hear a voice and except you will be able to SABINE MESSNER, HOTWIRED	Quotes from our panel of expert Web designers point out tricks and pitfalls.
http://www.sandia.gov/sci_compute/elements.html http://www.netscape.com/ **Shockwave** http://www.macromedia.com	References to online sources at the end of each chapter show where you can find out more.

Table of Contents

What Is the Web?

It's Based on Hypertext

It Supports All Kinds of Media

It Can Be Interactive

Its Pages Can Be Designed

You don't need to know a lot about the technical underpinnings of the World Wide Web to design great Web pages. It will help, however, to have a little grounding in just what the Web is, how it's related to other parts of the Internet, and what a few of the terms mean that you'll run across in your work. Here's a brief introduction.

The first thing you need to know is that the World Wide Web is just one of several services available through the **Internet**, a worldwide, informal agglomeration of connected computers, linked by high-capacity lines that stretch across the country and under the oceans.

Unlike smaller networks, the Internet (often just called "the Net") isn't located in any single place, isn't based on any central computer, and isn't overseen by any network manager. It was started in the 1960s as an experiment by the U.S. Department of Defense, as a way to communicate with its contractors and researchers at large universities. The government laid cables between its contractors and created a **protocol**, called **TCP/IP**, that defined the way computers on the network would talk to one another. To ensure that the important communications taking place over the

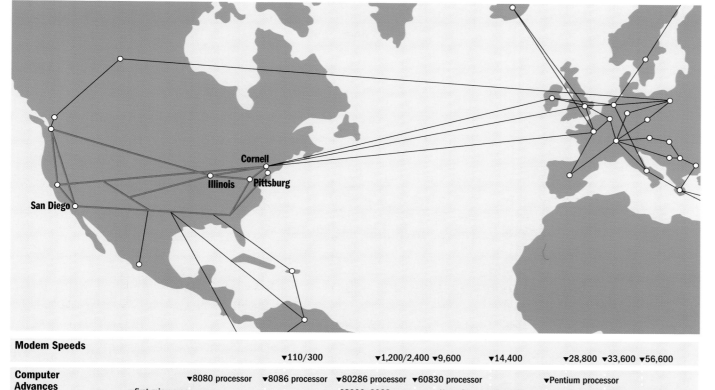

HIGH-CAPACITY BACKBONES carry Internet traffic between major hubs throughout the world. (The U.S. locations named here are the hubs of NSFNET, the National Science Foundation network that provided the skeleton of the early Internet.) Millions of individual computers are connected to these backbones by modem or cable connections.

Labels on map: Cornell, Illinois, Pittsburg, San Diego

Modem Speeds	▼110/300	▼1,200/2,400 ▼9,600	▼14,400	▼28,800 ▼33,600 ▼56,600

Computer Advances

	▼8080 processor	▼8086 processor	▼80286 processor ▼60830 processor	▼Pentium processor
▼first microprocessor			▼68000, 8088 processors ▼HyperCard ▼QuickTime	▼PowerPC processor
▼Unix OS	▼hard disk ▼Apple founded		▼SGI founded ▼Macintosh released	▼first laptop computer
▼floppy disk	▼Microsoft founded		▼IBM PC/DOS ▼Microsoft Windows	▼Windows 3.0 ▼Windows 95
▼Pong, the first video game			▼Apple Lisa (first graphical user interface)	

Computers on the Internet	▼4 ▼23	▼100	▼1,000 ▼10,000	▼100,000 ▼1,000,000	▼10,000,000

Internet History

▼ARPAnet commissioned		▼NSFNET created (56Kbps)	▼Web TV
▼Telnet ▼TCP/IP established		▼NSFNET upgraded to 1.5Mbps	▼InterNIC created
▼first international connections to ARPAnet		▼EUNet connects European cities	▼NSFNET upgraded to 44.7Mbps
▼FTP specification ▼e-mail specification		▼ARPAnet stops	▼AOL founded ▼Microsoft Internet Explorer
▼first BBS			▼NSF allows commercial use of Internet
▼Usenet newsgroups established			▼WWW invented ▼Netscape Navigator
▼CompuServe founded ▼domain name servers introduced			▼Mosaic ▼AOL offers Internet access

9 **1970** 1 2 3 4 5 6 7 8 9 **1980** 1 2 3 4 5 6 7 8 9 **1990** 1 2 3 4 5 6 7 8 9 **2000**

Internet
A worldwide computer network that links thousands of smaller networks.

protocol
A set of rules for exchanging information between computers over a network or via a modem connection.

TCP/IP
Stands for Transmission Control Protocol/Internet Protocol, the protocol developed for communications over the Internet and now supported by most computer systems.

Internet Services

E-mail
Short for "electronic mail," e-mail is sent over computer networks, such as those inside businesses or the Internet, from one user to another. Each user has a unique "mailbox," in which personal messages are stored.

FTP
Stands for file transport protocol, a method of sending files over the Internet.

Gopher
A protocol used to create hierarchical menus, allowing users to move through information by moving through the directory structure until they find the file they need. (Named in honor of the school mascot at the University of Minnesota, where the protocol was developed.)

Newsgroup
On the Internet, a collection of information on a certain topic, automatically compiled from messages sent by individual users. Newsgroups are available on just about any topic, from the Internet itself, to highway traffic laws, pets, and, of course, sex.

Telnet
A protocol that allows one machine on the Internet to run programs stored on another computer on the network, or a program that puts that protocol into effect.

WAIS
Stands for Wide Area Information Service, a protocol used to build indexes of text pages on the Internet, allowing quick searches for information within the indexed content.

World Wide Web
The World Wide Web supports multimedia pages that are connected by a system of hyperlinks. The Web is based on HTTP, the Hypertext Transfer Protocol.

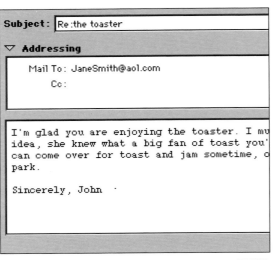

E-MAIL

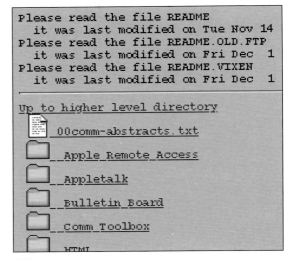

FTP

EACH INTERNET SERVICE offers a different way of publishing and viewing information on the Internet.

NEWSGROUP

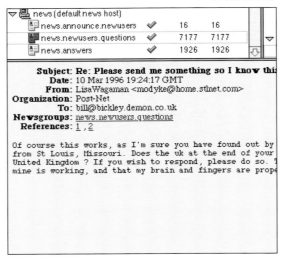

WORLD WIDE WEB

HEATH STALLINGS
http://www.crashsite.com/Driverbox.cgi

Internet could not be interrupted by an enemy attack, TCP/IP was designed to create a decentralized system, in which any computer on the network can talk to any other, and messages on the network can be rerouted as needed, depending on what lines are free.

Software was quickly developed for communicating over the Net, through services like e-mail and newsgroups. Over the years, new methods of storing and retrieving information were added one by one. Telnet let remote users log on to Internet computers as guests and run programs on them from their own machines; FTP let Internet users download files from remote computers; Gopher provided hierarchical menus for finding information; WAIS provided a search engine for finding what you needed anywhere in the world.

In 1991 a group of scientists at CERN, the European Physics Lab, came up with yet another system for accessing information on the Internet, called the World Wide Web, and this one turned out to be groundbreaking.

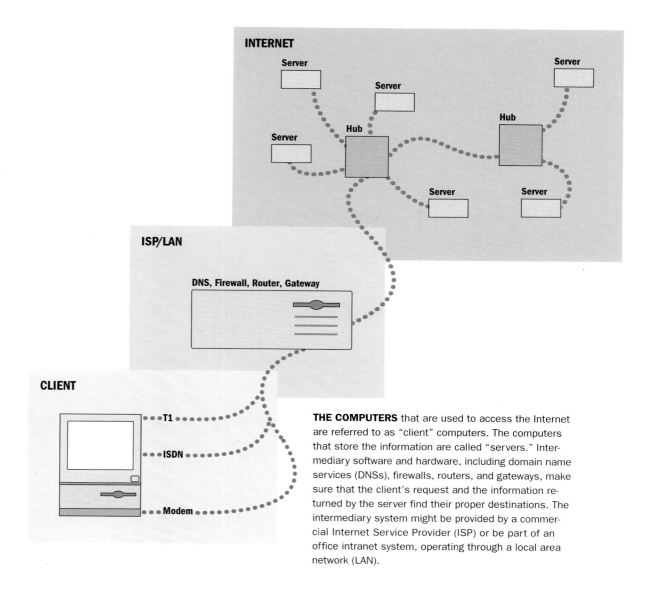

THE COMPUTERS that are used to access the Internet are referred to as "client" computers. The computers that store the information are called "servers." Intermediary software and hardware, including domain name services (DNSs), firewalls, routers, and gateways, make sure that the client's request and the information returned by the server find their proper destinations. The intermediary system might be provided by a commercial Internet Service Provider (ISP) or be part of an office intranet system, operating through a local area network (LAN).

One of our production managers said, "People talk about Web surfing, but it's really Web fishing. It's not about going somewhere, it's about casting out a line and trying to pull back what you need."

BARBARA KUHR, HOTWIRED

Like other Internet services, the World Wide Web is not based on a certain network or computer. Instead, it's a way or organizing information so that any computer around the world that operates according to the rules can access it. The rules that specify how to access and transfer files over the Web are called by the name HTTP, for Hypertext Transfer Protocol.

Hypertext Transfer Protocol

The Hypertext Transfer Protocol (HTTP) has been in use by the World-Wide Web global information initiative since 1990. HTTP is an application-level protocol with the lightness and speed necessary for distributed, collaborative, hyper media information systems. It is a generic, object-oriented protocol which can be used for many tasks, such as name servers and distributed object management systems, through extension of its request methods (commands). A feature of HTTP is the typing and negotiation of data representation, allowing systems to be built independently of the data being transferred.

News and Updates

- HTTP/1.1 and Digest Authentication become Proposed Standards New!
- HTTP 1.1 Internet draft 07 New!
- Minutes from the IETF HTTP-wg meeting

http://www.w3.org/pub/WWW/Protocols/

HTTP
Stands for Hypertext Transfer Protocol, the protocol on which the World Wide Web is based. HTTP sets rules for how information is requested and sent between Web servers and clients.

hyperlink
In a hypertext document, such as a Web page, an electronic link that calls up a related piece of information.

hypertext
An electronic information structure in which the reader controls how he or she moves through the information.

IN HYPERTEXT SYSTEMS, you can click on a hypertext anchor to call up linked information. In the example shown here, clicking on the word *HTTP* calls up a page describing the protocol.

It's Based on Hypertext

Like other Internet services, the World Wide Web is not a certain network, based on a certain computer. Instead, it's a way of organizing information so that any computer around the world that operates according to the rules can access it. The rules that specify how to access and transfer files over the Web are called **HTTP**, for Hypertext Transfer Protocol.

The Web was a breakthrough in many ways. Perhaps its most important feature, though, is its use of **hypertext**. Text and other content in a Web document can be made to link to any other document, anywhere in the world, that is saved on an HTTP server and connected to the Net. Let's say that you were reading the previous paragraph on line. On your screen you might see that the word HTTP was highlighted (in a different color, or underlined, for example). On a Web page, that means the word is a **hyperlink** to another page, and if you wanted to learn more about HTTP, you could just click on that word with your mouse, and another page, describing HTTP in more detail, would appear on your screen.

The text that appears may be something written by the same author and stored at the same site as the first page you were reading—or it could be stored in Switzerland or Beijing, written by someone the first author doesn't even know. To the reader, it makes no difference: Click, and you're there.

It Supports All Kinds of Media

Anyone who has worked with personal computers in any kind of collaborative project knows that sharing files can be a headache. Too often, you may try to share a file with colleagues or friends, only to find that they are on a different kind of computer or they don't have the software they need to read it. So how do publishers on the Internet provide files that might be read by anyone, anywhere in the world?

The one sure way is to rely on **ASCII**—pure text documents, with no formatting information. Or you could specify that everyone reading your files must get special software that reads the standard formats you'll be using for your online documents. Or you could use formats that are commonly used on many different platforms and readable by many different kinds of software. Publishers on the World Wide Web depend on a combination of all three of these tactics.

The basic format for text published on the Web is ASCII. (Really it's ASCII with a twist; the files contain certain "tags," referred to as Hypertext Markup Language, or **HTML**, that help them take on a bit of character when they're pulled up on the reader's screen.) The scheme also depends on the reader having special software, called a **browser**, that is specially made to retrieve and display HTML files and other commonly used formats and to help users navigate through the Web.

Any formats that can't be read by the browser—those belonging to particular applications or in a medium, say video, that the browser doesn't support—can be read by software, called **helper applications,** that launch alongside the browser to open those files. A special type of helper application called a **plug-in** can display files right inside the browser window. Special formats can also be displayed by programs based on ActiveX (→**192**) or Java (→**188**), which can add any type of new capability to the browser, including the ability to play additional formats.

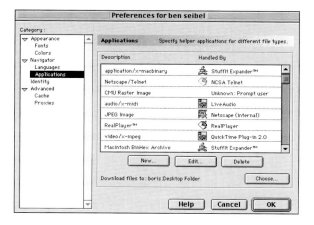

EACH FILE FORMAT and media type has an identification code called its MIME type, a two-part description (shown in the Description column here) used to identify it on the Internet. In most browsers (such as Netscape Navigator 4.0, shown here), you can specify which application you want to use for each each MIME type.

ASCII
Stands for American Standard Code for Information Interchange. ASCII files, sometimes called "pure text" files, can contain only text and no formatting information.

browser
Software designed to communicate with Web servers and interpret the data received from them. The two most common browsers are Netscape Navigator and Microsoft Internet Explorer.

helper application
An application launched by the browser to display files it can't read itself.

HTML
Hypertext Markup Language, a set of codes used to mark up World Wide Web documents with tags that describe the document's structure and allow for hyperlinks to other documents on the Internet.

plug-in
A helper application that displays non-standard formats inside the browser window.

EVERYONE WHO USES the Web must have a piece of software called a browser, which is responsible for fetching files from servers around the world and displaying the HTML file along with its associated graphics and other media.

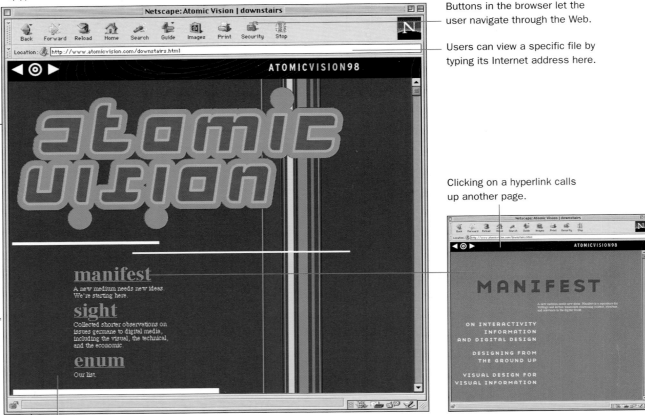

ATOMIC VISION
http://www.atomicvision.com/downstairs.html

Buttons in the browser let the user navigate through the Web.

Users can view a specific file by typing its Internet address here.

Clicking on a hyperlink calls up another page.

```
<HTML>
<HEAD>
<TITLE>Atomic Vision's eastern hub</TITLE>
</HEAD>

<BODY BGCOLOR = "#000080" BACKGROUND="pix/bg_stripes.gif" TEXT =
"#ffffff" LINK = "#80ff00" ALINK = "#00ffff" VLINK = "#ff0000">

<TABLE WIDTH = "580" BORDER = "0">
    <TR>
        <TD ALIGN = "center" COLSPAN = "3">
        <A HREF="../foyer.html" TARGET="_top"><IMG WIDTH = "561"
        HEIGHT = "255" VSPACE = "8" SRC = "pix/techno_av.gif"
        BORDER = "0"></A></TD>
    </TR>
    <TR>
        <TD ALIGN = "left" COLSPAN = "3"><IMG SRC = "pix/white.gif"
        HEIGHT = "5" WIDTH = "250" VSPACE = "6"></TD>
    </TR>
    <TR>
        <TD ALIGN = "left" COLSPAN = "3"><!--<IMG WIDTH = "323" HEIGHT =
        "18" VSPACE = "8" SRC = "pix/caption.gif"--></TD>
    </TR>
    <TR>
        <TD WIDTH = "100" ROWSPAN = "5"><IMG HEIGHT = "10"
        WIDTH = "100" SRC = "../gpix/pixel.gif" BORDER = "0"></TD>
        <TD COLSPAN = "2" ALIGN = "right"><IMG SRC = "pix/white.gif"
        HEIGHT = "3" WIDTH = "370"></TD>
    </TR>
    <TR>
        <TD VALIGN="top"><BR></TD>
        <TD WIDTH = "300" ROWSPAN = "3"><IMG HEIGHT = "10"
        WIDTH = "250" SRC = "pix/pixel.gif" BORDER = "0"></TD>
```

Most Web pages are saved in a format called HTML. Tags in the text file tell the browser how to display the page on screen.

HTML files are displayed directly in the browser window.

It Can Be Interactive

Unlike material printed in a book or brochure, Web publications can respond to input by the user. A Web site's visitors can communicate with the site's publishers and even order products online. Sites can play an animation when a user's pointer rolls over an onscreen graphic. Users can ask for exactly the information they need, interacting with databases on the server that send back customized responses.

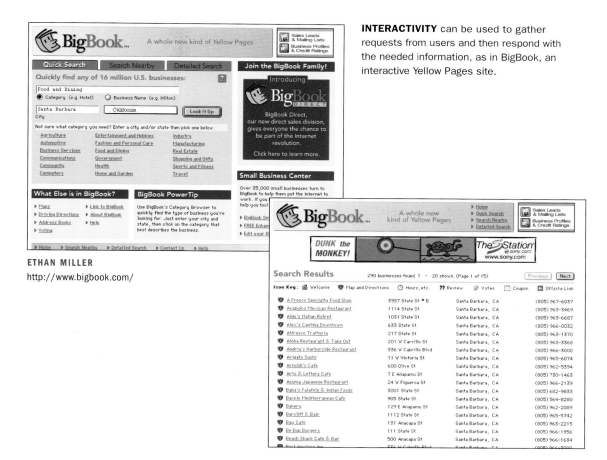

ETHAN MILLER
http://www.bigbook.com/

What online can give you that nothing else can is live information, throbbing information that is pouring from some source. On one end of it, users are pushing the buttons, and on the other end databases are spewing out all sorts of information.

MATTHEW BUTTERICK, ATOMIC VISION

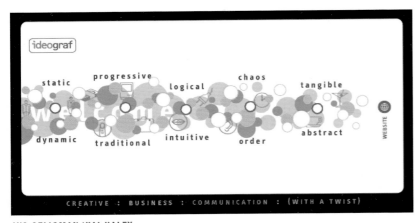

AYO SELIGMAN/KAI HALEY
http://www.ideograf.com/

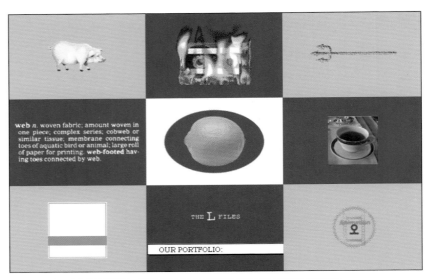

DAVID MOK/CHRIS POTTER/EVERETT RODRIGUEZ/MITCH LEUNG/LEMON
http://www.lemon.com.hk/

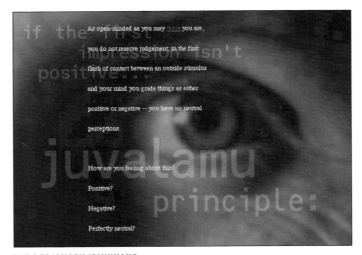

THE DESIGNORY/PINKHAUS
http://www.designory.com/jump.b.html

WEB PAGES can include full-color text and graphics, plus sound, animation, video, and almost anything else you can dream up, all in a hyperlinked environment that gives designers the opportunity to experiment with navigation as well as visual effects.

Its Pages Can Be Designed

Thanks to HTML and its ability to support graphics and other media, the World Wide Web is the first service on the Internet that lends itself to any kind of graphic design. That, perhaps more than any other attribute, is what made it the first service on the Internet to grab the attention of the public, publishers, and businesses. Thanks to its use of hyperlinks for navigation, it presents an exciting design problem that challenges designers to create fluid and friendly interfaces, as well as attractive graphic design, to help visitors find, scan, and enjoy the material published there.

In the next chapter we'll talk about the factors that influence what can and can't be done, design-wise, on the Web. After that we'll introduce you to some of the people and companies pioneering the field. Then, with the help of those pioneers, we'll guide you through the elements of Web design, one by one.

BEN BENJAMIN
http://www.superbad.com/

Online: What Is the Web?

Browsers
http://browserwatch.internet.com/browsers.html
http://www.microsoft.com/ie/
http://home.netscape.com/comprod/products/communicator/

General Information About the World Wide Web
http://www.excite.com/computers_and_internet/internet/
    beginner_guides/
http://www.yahoo.com/Computers_and_Internet/Internet/
    World_Wide_Web/

HTTP
http://www.w3.org/Protocols/

Plug-ins
http://browserwatch.internet.com/plug-in.html
http://home.netscape.com/comprod/products/navigator/
    version_2.0/plugins/

What is a Web site? It's television, it's a magazine, it's a brochure. A site for Con Edison is an information distribution vehicle for a large utility. For Carnegie Hall, it's a presence on the Internet and a way to buy tickets. These are different entities with very different information needs.

PETER SEIDLER, AVALANCHE

Possibilities and Limitations

The Web Is Nonlinear

Page Layout Is Not Necessarily Under the Designer's Control

HTML's Capabilities Are Changing All the Time

Download Time Sets the Standard

The Tools Are Improving—Quickly

The reputation of the Web among designers is that its design possibilities are practically nonexistent, but that isn't really so. In reality, the Web is quickly becoming one of the most exciting and flexible design media in history.

Layout options are, admittedly, still limited on the Web. On the other hand, the Web opens brand-new possibilities for inventive navigation schemes, a wide variety of media, and exciting interactivity, and its options for layout are growing fast. The key to satisfying and groundbreaking design on the Web—as in any other medium—is understanding the possibilities and limitations of the form. This chapter will help by explaining some important distinguishing features of design on the Web.

The Web Is Nonlinear

The first thing to remember about your site on the Web is that visitors access each page by hypertext links—from another page on your site or from anywhere else on the Web. You could lead the visitor through a controlled series of pages, but that's not what the Web is about; it's about letting the visitor choose his or her own path through the information. Your site will probably be just one among dozens the visitor will view in the space of several minutes. Visitors following a link from another site can land at any page of your site, may stay for just a few seconds, and then launch off to another site entirely.

In this context, you've got to make each and every page represent you or your client strongly; after all, it might be the only page of yours the visitor sees. Equally, every page should entice the visitor to explore your site further—and make it easy to do so.

How you accomplish this is wide open, of course; there's no single right way to do it. The challenge is finding the method that works best for the content you're presenting and the experience you want to invoke. One of the most exciting opportunities of design for the Web, especially in these early days, is to be one of the people finding new solutions and setting new standards for finding ways around cyberspace.

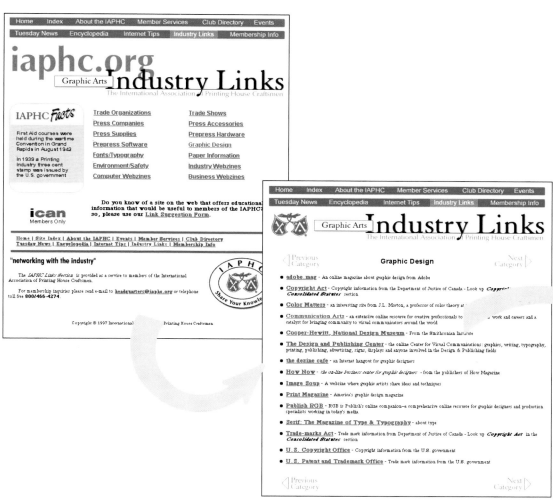

DAN MILLSIP
http://www.iaphc.org/

THE IDEA BEHIND THE WEB is to allow nonlinear access to information stored on sites all over the globe. Whatever else your design does, it must help visitors understand how to get to the information they're searching for. It must also establish an idiosyncratic identity among the dozens of sites the visitor may view in the space of a few minutes.

KHA HOANG
http://woodblock.simplenet.com/

**PATRICK COYNE/JEFF STAFFORD/
BONNIE SMETTS/GARY WIUM**
http://www.commarts.com/

FUNNY GARBAGE

http://www.luakabop.com/

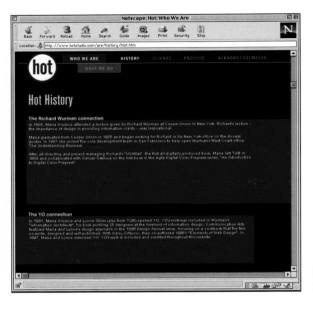

THE SAME HTML TAGS can result in different layouts in different browsers. Each browser uses somewhat different layout specifications for common tags, and not all browsers support all HTML codes. To make things more complicated, individual visitors can set their own layout preferences, changing the default typeface, the window width, or even choose to view pages without graphics. These illustrations show how the same HTML page looks in different browsers or with different user settings.

**ON MACINTOSH
IN NAVIGATOR 4.0**

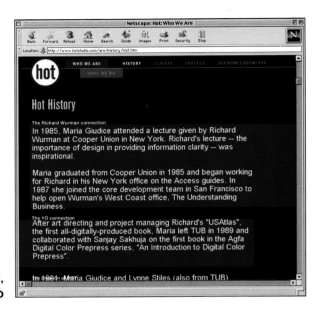

**ON MACINTOSH,
DEFAULT FONT CHANGED**

**ON PC
IN NAVIGATOR 4.0**

**ON MACINTOSH,
GRAPHICS OFF**

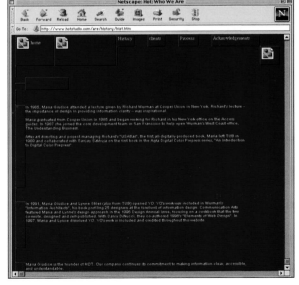

HOT
http://www.hotstudio.com/are/history/hist.htm

Page Layout Is Not Necessarily Under the Designer's Control

As we explained in the last chapter, most Web content is in the form of ASCII files, tagged with HTML, the Hypertext Markup Language. The HTML tags, which are simple codes placed between brackets within the file, label each element of the document—<P> for paragraph text or <H1> for a first-level heading, for example. The browser software interprets the codes and lays out the document on screen accordingly.

Designers who go back to the pre–desktop publishing era will recognize the idea at work here: It's very similar to the method used for old electronic typesetting systems. On the Web, as with such typesetting systems, the tags merely name the type of element; they don't specify its layout. The indentation, the type size and style, and other aspects of its appearance are determined by the specifications for each element programmed into the output system.

On the Web, though, designers have less control over how those codes are interpreted. In fact, until recently, they had no control at all. Instead, default specifications are programmed into the browser. For example, for paragraph text (marked with the HTML <P> tag), most browsers use 12-point Times with a line space above. First level heads (marked <H1>) are displayed as 16-point Times with a space above and below.

To make things more complicated, though, you can't even count on the defaults, because they can be changed by individual users. Users can pick another favorite font for their default face, and many users set a larger type size for easier reading on screen. Readers can also turn off graphics for faster downloading.

Pages also appear different depending on the browser they're viewed in. The two major browsers, Netscape Navigator and Microsoft Internet Explorer, use similar settings for most—but not all—tags, and the settings may vary even between different releases of the same browser.

Last but not least, pages will look different on different platforms. For example, type looks bigger on PCs than on Macs, and the resolution of the user's monitor can also make graphics and type appear larger or smaller. And not all browsers are on personal computers. Web surfers can now read pages on TVs, palmtop computers, text-only devices, and Braille readers.

Some control is being put back in the hands of the designer with advances such as style sheets (→**98**), which let designers attach their own specifcations to HTML tags. Unfortunately, though, style sheets can only be read by the latest browsers, and even style sheets can be overridden by the user's own settings.

All this means that, although a significant portion of your audience will see your pages just as you intended, another segment will not. Good Web design includes the art of creating pages that can be viewed successfully under a number of different conditions.

We have to make a best guess about exactly what users will see—it all depends on how they've got their browser configured, what type of computer and display system they have, all of that. In the end, we just have to test the page in every browser and on every platform we want to reach, and sometimes do some serious editing of the HTML to make it all work.

STEFAN FIELDING-ISAACS, ART & SCIENCE

HTML's Capabilities Are Changing All the Time

HTML's creators weren't thinking of blazing ground for a commercial Babel of online art magazines and corporate brochures when they defined the basic tags. What they were focusing on—and achieved supremely well—was a way of navigating through information on the Internet using a system of easy-to-use hyperlinks. The text styles included in the first revision of the language—six head levels, one standard and one monospaced font, numbered and bulleted lists, footnotes, indented quotes—provided a very basic set of elements for the straightforward text documents that, just a few years ago, were about the only kinds of documents found on the Internet.

The sudden popularity of the World Wide Web as a commercial publishing medium took the developers of HTML, like the rest of the world, by surprise. When the demands on HTML were noted, a standards committee was quickly formed to preside over and document the further development of the language. (The work, originally overseen by the Internet Engineering Task Force, or IETF, has more recently been headed up by a group called the **World Wide Web Consortium,** or **W3C**, composed of representatives from Internet software companies, academics, and other interested parties.) The working group's first task was to document the codes currently in use,

HTML 2.0

INLINE GRAPHIC

HEAD

DIRECTORY LIST/BOLD TYPE

UNORDERED LIST

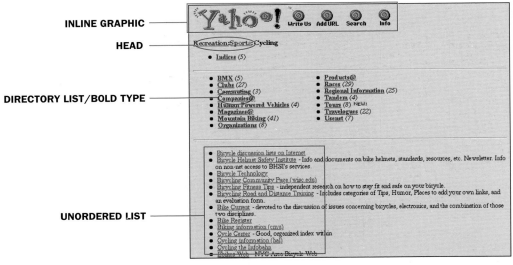

CKS PARTNERS
http://www.yahoo.com/

HTML 3.2

FRAMES

TRANSPARENT IMAGES

GIF ANIMATION

BACKGROUND GRAPHICS

CUSTOM-COLORED TYPE

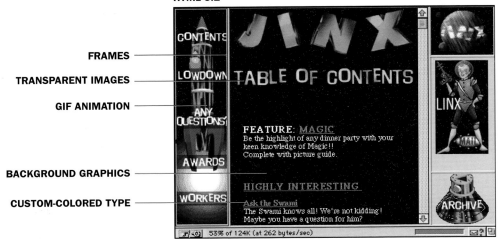

THE BUOYANT COMPANY
http://www.jinx.com/

a task that took until the fall of 1995 and resulted in a specification called **HTML 2.0**. Meanwhile, the consortium's academic and industry members began to suggest extensions to the language. **HTML 3.2**, the next standard version, included many additional controls, such as centering, text-wrap around graphics, and table (grid) layouts. Even more capabilities are added in the current version of the specification, called **HTML 4.0**, including style sheets (→**98**), which let designers specify fine points of layout, including type size and leading. And change won't stop there. As one version of the HTML spec is being codified, new additions are being proposed and hammered out in committee, and Microsoft and Netscape often add support for new HTML features to their browsers even before they are adopted by the W3C.

The advantages of this rapid growth are clear. Designers should also be aware of the other implication: The learning curve is constant, and to stay current and take advantage of new possibilities, designs may need to be updated often.

HTML 4.0

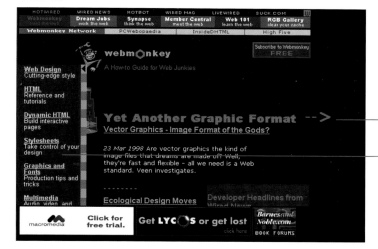

CASCADING STYLE SHEETS

DYNAMIC HTML

HOTWIRED
http://www.hotwired.com/webmonkey/

EACH NEW VERSION of HTML supports new layout capabilities.

HTML 2.0
The specification, finalized in September of 1995 by the HTML working group of the Internet Engineering Task Force (IETF), that codifies the basic set of HTML tags.

HTML 3.2
The second official HTML recommendation by the W3C, adding features such as tables and some style tags.

HTML 4.0
Currently, the latest version of the HTML specification, which introduces style sheets and other advanced features to HTML.

World Wide Web Consortium (W3C)
A group, composed of volunteers from Internet software companies, academics, and other interested parties, that oversees the development of Web technologies.

After years of struggling, we now have style sheets, and we're finally at a point where we can lay out a page using logical systems rather than hacks.

ERIC EATON, HOTWIRED

THE TIME IT TAKES to download a Web page varies with the kind of connection in use. Over the next few years, telephone and cable companies are expected to make high-speed connections widely available at affordable prices, but for now, designers need to understand that most home and small business users will be using 14,400 or 28,800bps modems. This chart shows the average times it might take to download this relatively complex graphic at different connection speeds.

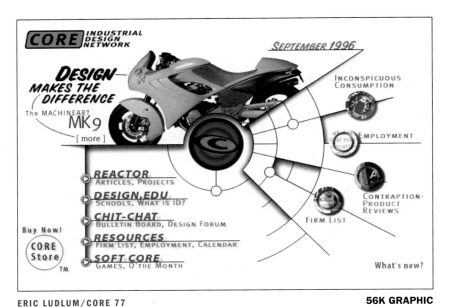

ERIC LUDLUM/CORE 77
http://www.core77.com/

56K GRAPHIC

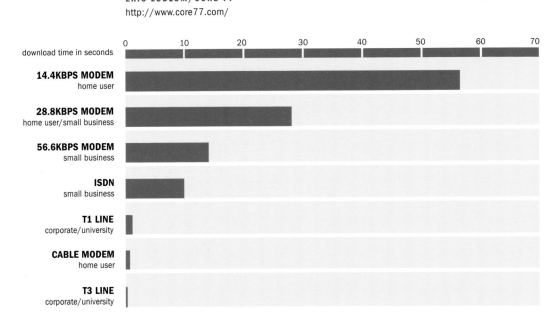

Download Time Sets the Standard

Theoretically, the Web is capable of all the multimedia fireworks associated with CD-ROM: immersive 3D graphics, animation, digital video. In reality, though, those types of experiences are pretty rare. The most important thing to remember about the Web is that eveything a user sees on screen needs to first be downloaded over a network connection, and rich media, with their associated large file sizes, usually make for unacceptably long download times. On the Web, file sizes must be kept as small as possible.

Designers working in print are used to seeing graphics files that weigh in at 20 megabytes (MB) or more. Successful Web designers, on the other hand, know to keep graphics to 30 kilobytes (K) or less. This takes into account the fact that lots of people who will view your work will be downloading it to their computer over a 28,800- or even 14,400-bit-per-second (bps) modem. In real terms that translates to about 1K or 2K per second—over a good connection—or as much as 30 seconds just to download that graphics file. This doesn't necessarily mean using thumbnail-size images throughout your site. The standard World Wide Web graphics formats—GIF and JPEG (→**121**)— are highly compressed, you can use lots of tricks to shorten download times (→**136**).

The problem is even greater when you consider time-based media such as animation, video, or sound, for which file sizes are substantially larger. New technologies for compressing multimedia files and delivering them to the user more efficiently are under development (→**151**), and new technologies, such as cable modems, will help speed connections and download times. But for now and the foreseeable future, the Web designer's greatest challenge is to execute ideas using the smallest possible file sizes.

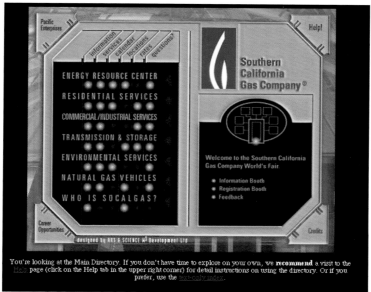

You're looking at the Main Directory. If you don't have time to explore on your own, we **recommend** a visit to the Help page (click on the Help tab in the upper right corner) for detail instructions on using the directory. Or if you prefer, use the text-only index.

ART & SCIENCE
http://www.socalgas.com/macro.html

THE GRAPHIC INTERFACE at left is created from four different graphics files (below), which many browsers can load simultaneously, significantly reducing download time. The center graphic is an animated GIF.

If users have to wait more than 15 or 20 seconds, they're gone.

FRED SOTHERLAND, CNET

People will look back at what we're doing now and think it's funny and primitive. But I remember the old days of television, when the TV would go blank or fill with static, and you'd see "Please stand by. We are experiencing technical difficulties." People didn't care; they stood by. That's the stage we're in now.

BARBARA KUHR, HOTWIRED

The Tools Are Improving— Quickly

Many designers are taking a "wait and see" attitude toward the Web, holding out until the tools and design possibilities become more sophisticated. If you're tempted to wait, though, think of what happened to those who waited until the Mac had proved itself for desktop publishing—and then think of what happened to those who jumped in early and started exploring its possibilities.

The Web is in a state similar to the state of desktop publishing in the mid '80s. It was clear that this new thing was going to be very, very big. It was also clear that it wasn't nearly capable of the kind of design and production values available in other media. Same with the Web.

The difference is that the publishing industry has learned from its experiences of the last decade, and the tools for Web publishing are developing at an astonishing pace. Leading software companies are working day and night to meet designers' demands. Today, mainstream graphics programs like Photoshop can save files as Web formats. Adobe, Macromedia, and other leading companies are creating WYSIWYG HTML layout tools that let designers create HTML pages using the kind of graphic tools they're used to in page layout programs, without seeing HTML at all, if they don't want to. It's going to take two or three years—not ten—for Web publishing tools to match—and surpass—those available for print and CD-ROM production.

Meanwhile, learning what you need to know to begin designing for the Web is a lot easier than you might think.

So our advice is, don't wait. Sure, the tools will change, and things will get easier, but there's lots to learn about this new medium. Here's your chance to blaze some new ground.

Online: Possibilities and Limitations

HTML Specifications
http://www.w3.org/MarkUp/

Microsoft Internet Explorer HTML Support
http://www.microsoft.com/workshop/author/default.asp

Netscape Navigator HTML Support
http://developer.netscape.com/docs/manuals/htmlguid/

Good Web design means good content, well organized, and speed over everything else.

FRED SOTHERLAND, CNET

Who's Doing Web Design?

Art & Science
Atomic Vision
Avalanche
CNET
Construct
HotWired
Organic
Studio Archetype
Vivid Studios

Many of the first Web design companies got their start with the Web itself, springing up to handle a medium that most existing design firms didn't feel equipped to handle. But now, as the medium becomes more familiar, the tools more sophisticated, and the demand ever greater, more and more traditional design businesses have taken on Web site design as part of the range of services they offer their clients.

The Web designers we profile in this chapter, and whose wisdom we quote in the rest of this book, were among the first to enter the new profession—in fact, you could say they actually invented it. They were some of the first people to see the Web's potential, and they jumped right in and began exploring a territory no one had worked in before, and now, four years later, they've logged countless hours experimenting with the business and technology of Web design.

The stories of how these pioneers started and how their businesses have grown and changed with the Web encapsulates a lot of information about the kinds of talents required in this new medium, the types of jobs available in Web design, and some of the many different ways to define a Web design business.

Art & Science

http://www.artandscience.com/

Founded in the fall of 1994, Art & Science has had in some ways a prototypical Web design history: a computer-literate nondesigner with an interest in hypertext and storytelling finds the Web, exploits its possibilities creatively, and makes it big.

Stefan Fielding-Isaacs, the company's president and chief information architect, graduated from a liberal arts education into work as a technical writer for Microsoft and other high-tech companies. As a freelance technical writer he worked for Taligent, Silicon Graphics, Sun, and other companies whose products would later be tightly tied to the Web, and where he first experimented with hypertext as a format for documentation.

This experience won him a job doing a Web site for RSA Data Security, a company for which he'd worked as a writer. Around that time, he also met the marketing director for Joe Boxer at a cocktail party, and the rest is history. The playful graphics and creative navigation system Art & Science built for Joe Boxer's site won the design firm notice just as Web fever was taking off in the business world. Recent projects include the Mercedes-Benz SLK230 Web site, HIVInsite, sites for Microsoft and Better Homes & Gardens, and ad work for Saatchi & Saatchi and Lowe & Partners/SMS.

Art & Science offers a full range of Web services. "We take a holistic approach to site design," says Fielding-Isaacs. "We want to see and understand everything from the marketing plan to the lowest level of the content." The staff of a dozen, consisting of artists, engineers, information architects, a creative director and a chief technology officer, is cross-trained, so each member has all the Web knowledge necessary to produce and manage a site. The broad knowledge, he says, is crucial in the collaborative world of Web design.

In the new field of Web design, Fielding-Isaacs sees the firm's relatively long history as a boon to its clients. "We've been careful to analyze our processes and codify them," he says. "Now each project team starts with a leg up, a knowledge base compiled from all our past experience."

We differentiate ourselves by our technical expertise. We've been programmers from day one, using "out of the box" thinking about technology to expand our creative possibilities. We don't let technical limitations hinder the creative process.

STEFAN FIELDING-ISAACS, PRESIDENT, ART & SCIENCE

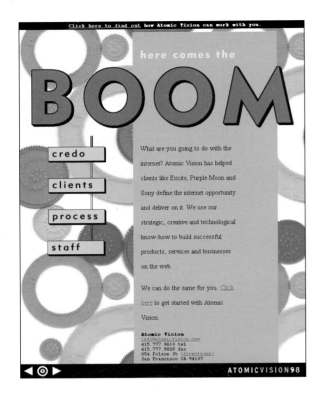

Atomic Vision

http://www.atomicvision.com/

In the two years between graduating from Harvard and founding Atomic Vision, Matthew Butterick was a type designer, working at Boston's Font Bureau on new and revival typefaces and contributing his own experimental typeface to Neville Brody's *Fuse* magazine. Butterick started Atomic Vision in Cambridge in late 1994, and in 1995 he moved the company to San Francisco.

"I could do type design, but people have been doing that for 300 years, and I'll never be one of the best," says Butterick. "With Web design, there's the opportunity to get in on the ground floor and make something happen. In the Web I get to use design and technology, and also the components of marketing and message and editorial. And it's all completely new."

Butterick practically boils over with energy and ideas as he describes Web design, his work with new navigation structures, and his plans for his company. "I don't want to do marketing brochures," he says. "I want to find ways to extend the new medium." To that end, he has targeted a niche that he describes as "companies whose business plans have an important Web component." Atomic Vision clients such as Excite, Netscape, Purple Moon, and VeriSign—all companies born with and based on the Internet—are examples of clients in his target market.

Now with a staff of 14, including designers, producers, programmers, and a marketing director, Butterick plans to keep his company small. "The ratio in terms of what a few people can turn out is much greater than with print," he points out. He also clearly enjoys wearing a variety of hats as head of his own small company. "I can do all this dabbling," he laughs. "I get to be this designer guy and marketing guy and programmer guy all at once."

I never refer to Atomic Vision as a Web design company. It's not about technology, it's about ideas. What we do is help companies on the Web be successful.

MATTHEW BUTTERICK, PRESIDENT, ATOMIC VISION

Avalanche

http://www.avsi.com/

Avalanche, an interactive agency in New York's Soho, had its start as Seidler Design, an eight-year venture also headed by Avalanche's president, Peter Seidler. After relaunching at the beginning of 1995, Avalanche now has 35 people and a client list that includes Warner Music Group, FAO Schwarz, and Sotheby's International Realty. "When we started, it was pretty clear that there was a lot of work to be done for the Web. Getting clients to understand that early on was more difficult. Even a year and a half ago, most people didn't know what the Web was," says Seidler.

Seidler describes the company's jobs as covering the breadth of interactive design, including the development of projects such as intranets, CD-ROM, and interactive press kits, but he admits that the Web is a large part of the business these days—and the culmination, as he sees it, of the short history of multimedia publishing, which he has been involved in from the start. "I always felt like there were so many things we wanted to do. Now the tools are starting to catch up to the vision." When the tools are wanting, Seidler sees it as part of his company's task to create them, whether it's new compression functions for media on CD-ROM or Java interaction for a Web site.

With both his company and the field exploding, much of Seidler's energy these days goes into trying to grow fast gracefully. "I interview constantly," he says. Since the pool of talent with Web and multimedia skills is small, he says he looks for people with a good conceptual design approach. One of the biggest challenges for a Web company like his, says Seidler, is riding the sudden tidal wave of interest in the Web without wiping out the team, a goal he describes as "trying to create our business in a way that's as beautiful as the sites we create." As part of that plan, Avalanche's crew is encouraged to pursue their own interests, developing projects with no immediate commercial market, a strategy that has led not only to numerous design awards, but also to ideas that later enrich projects for clients.

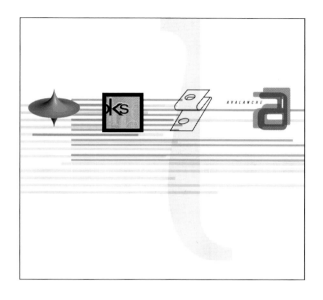

Our specialty is conceptual design, design derived from the nature of the content. We put a high value on the emotional content of a site, and we're never satisfied until we can say it's totally beautiful. But a large part of that is how it works conceptually.

PETER SEIDLER, PRESIDENT, AVALANCHE

CNET

http://www.cnet.com/

CNET.COM was originally conceived as an companion Web site for CNET Central, a television show launched by CNET in April 1994. Between the business plan and the launch, though, something happened; the Web caught fire. Now, CNET.COM and its companion Web sites, including SEARCH.COM, NEWS.COM, COMPUTERS.COM, and SNAP.COM, share the limelight with CNET's four television shows as key elements in the company's business plan.

As a site whose purpose is to provide timely technology news, CNET's challenge has been to create a staff and procedures that can support the ongoing addition of new content, a need that has led it to develop sophisticated database-driven publishing tools for updating the sites. And the need to deliver that news as quickly as possible puts extremely tight limits on file sizes.

"We want all our sites to look as great as possible, but we have to find the happy medium between custom design for each page and efficiency," says Fred Sotherland, CNET's senior vice president for creative services. To meet those challenges, Sotherland and Cotton Coulson, vice president for creative services, have split their staff (now numbering about 60 art directors, designers, and graphic production assistants) into two groups. The central creative services group develops design standards and templates for the company as a whole, while teams assigned to individual sites and sections design, art direct, and produce the individual Web sites.

CNET's overall design has remained remarkably consistent over the years, featuring a bright color palette, a standard graphic treatment, and a three-column layout. The reasons for that steadfastness are twofold, say Sotherland and Coulson. The first is a need to keep download fast and pages accessible. "In the past couple years, there haven't been any new technologies that haven't eaten into the page loading speed," explains Sotherland. Second is the comfort factor for users. "I think there's something to be said for not redesigning your site every year or so," says Sotherland. "There's an advantage for the user who comes to CNET.COM not having to figure out over and over again how to navigate the site. Another benefit: CNET's look and feel has become one of the the Web's most recognizable designs.

Our goal is to have the fastest loading site on the Internet.

FRED SOTHERLAND, SENIOR VICE PRESIDENT, CREATIVE SERVICES, CNET

Construct

http://www.construct.net/

The core group at Construct met at the Interactive Media Festival (IMF), an annual event (sponsored by Motorola) that brings together artists and businesses engaged in developing interactive electronic environments. Lisa Goldman, now Construct's president, was the festival's creative director. Mark Meadows, who explores new Web technologies and dreams up new applications as Construct's chief investigating officer, was the festival's webmaster. Annette Loudon, now Construct's webmistress, was in charge of online design.

"We built a Web interface for the festival, including a private jury chamber that held one of the first HTML conferencing interfaces," recalls Meadows. "When it was time to put the gallery online, I wanted to use something that was more interactive and more spatially accurate, so I started to look into to how to make it 3D." Thus began the group's fascination with, and expertise in, VRML (Virtual Reality Modeling Language), a format for creating 3D interfaces on the Web. To get help with the job, Meadows turned to the Net. Messages on the WELL (a Sausalito, California–based Internet conferencing service) rounded up a group of like-minded experimenters.

When the festival ended, the IMF group turned into Construct. Goldman says that calls for work began coming in almost immediately, from people who knew the team's work from the festival. The company incorporated in August of 1995, and its staff now numbers 16 full-timers. "Almost everyone has a design background," notes Meadows. "Even our tech director studied stage design—something we only realized after we formed the company."

Construct remains on the outer technical edges of Web design. Much of its work is still focused on interactive graphical environments of the type the group began exploring at the IMF. Its expertise with hardcore coding has also won the company work creating and testing new software code for Microsoft, Netscape, and other Internet software developers.

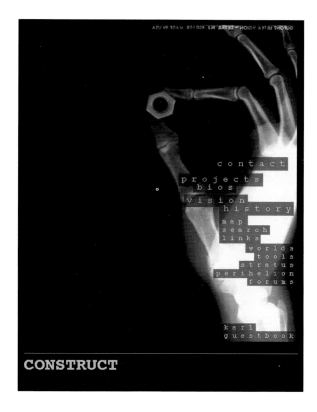

Construct is exploring shared data spaces, concentrating on the characteristics that define the online medium. We think that good Internet design welds together the aesthetic and the technical.

MARK MEADOWS, CHIEF INVESTIGATING OFFICER, CONSTRUCT

HotWired

http://www.hotwired.com/

As the first child of the marriage of ultra-hip *Wired* magazine and the World Wide Web, *HotWired* was under a lot of scrutiny when it launched in 1994. *Wired* had long been testifying about this revolution in communications, and *HotWired* was its Exhibit A.

In the spring of 1994, Barbara Kuhr and John Plunkett, the founding art directors of *Wired,* set about defining what a magazine might look like on the Web—a task that has continued through every day of its four-year history. It was a success. *HotWired* not only convinced the world that an online magazine can work, but along the way it pioneered ideas about what advertising might look like on the Web (*HotWired* was the first to use those ubiquitous, hot-linked ad banners), how content can be customized for each reader (providing a "Your View" for registered users), and how a site's content could be used to knit together communities of readers with chat and newsgroups.

Over the years, *HotWired*'s content has explored a variety of territories, from health to travel to cocktail recipes, to Web development, but, according to Kuhr, technical innovation remains at the core of its mission. It's a goal that requires intense collaboration across disciplines, she says, with editors, designers, engineers, and production specialists assigned to each project. In addition to Kuhr, we spoke to Sabine Messner and Eric Eaton, who are senior designers, and Jeff Veen, Wired Digital's interface director, who keeps an eye on upcoming technologies and develops the production and navigation systems that span the entire site.

HotWired's design is as much about experimenting with the technology as it is about creating compelling content on the Web.

BARBARA KUHR, CREATIVE DIRECTOR, HOTWIRED

Organic, Inc.

http://www.organic.com/

Jonathan Nelson, CEO of Organic Inc., remembers making cold calls on corporations in 1993 trying to convince their marketing departments that they needed Web sites, with no luck. Nelson, along with his brother Matthew (Organic's director of operations) and Brian Behlendorf (chief technology officer) had been offering Web design and networking services as a part-time business, keeping their day jobs until about the summer of 1994, when, says Nelson, those companies starting calling him back. "It was about the time that *Time* magazine put the Internet on the cover," he remembers. Nelson gave up the sound engineering he'd been doing to devote full time to the Web.

As one of the earliest companies to pitch the idea of communicating on the Web, Organic was perfectly poised to ride the first wave of commercial interest in the new medium. Behlendorf was an early web-master for *HotWired*, and its first clients were some of *HotWired*'s—and thus the Web's—first advertisers, including AT&T, Volvo, and Saturn.

Organic offers a range of Web design, marketing, and production services. Clients can take advantage of any or all of the company's services, from strategic planning up front; to the design, writing, programming, and production leading to the launch of a site; to online publicity and statistical and demographic analysis after the site is live. Most of Organic's clients keep their sites on its servers, says Nelson.

"If you would have told me a few years ago that we would be working with Nike and McDonald's, I would have thought you were crazy," says Nelson. "Now we say, OK, we've got Nike and McDonald's. Who don't we have?"

If you think of us as an HTML shop, you're missing the point. That's a handful of people in a company of 130. We do interactive communications. We develop content, special technologies, and marketing plans for strategic issues.

JONATHAN NELSON, CEO, ORGANIC

Studio Archetype

http://www.studioarchetype.com/

Formerly known as Clement Mok designs, Studio Archetype was founded in 1988. The band of designers, information architects, and multimedia professionals headed by Clement Mok quickly grew to be recognized as leaders in high-tech design, both because many of the firm's clients were based in the Silicon Valley and because the company was one of a handful doing new media projects such as CD-ROMs and show-floor kiosks in the '80s. As Studio Archetype, the name the business adopted in early 1996, the studio has continued to help clients build brand identities that span different media types, a type of design the company calls "identity and information architecture." By early 1998, the firm had branched out from its San Francisco headquarters to open offices in New York and Atlanta. The company's staff has more than doubled since the advent of the Web, now numbering 120.

John Grotting and Peter Merholz spoke for Studio Archetype in this book. Grotting is one of the company's five creative directors. Like the studio's other designers, Grotting moves back and forth between print and new media projects, a mix he sees as a definite advantage for the company. "It forces you to approach each project fresh," he says. Merholz is one of the studio's interaction designers, helping to ensure that the interactive interfaces that are now so important to Web design are as clear and usable as possible for Web site visitors.

Clients seek out Studio Archetype for its long history with new media (Mok helped launch HyperCard as creative director for Apple in 1986), its reputation for clean and colorful design, and it's stringent design process, which helps clients identify and then meet their projects' requirements for branding and information. The company has done some of the most high-profile sites on the Web, including the official site for the Nagano Winter Olympics; 24 Hours in Cyberspace; iQVC, the Internactive shopping Website; and a special site for IBM that tracked the Kasparov/ Deep Blue chess match.

It's the range of disciplines you get involved in that allows you to make connections and bring different experiences to the work. What we're really good at doing is being in many different spaces, and where we add value is making those connections between different industries and different media.

CLEMENT MOK, CHAIRMAN AND CHIEF INFORMATION ARCHITECT, STUDIO ARCHETYPE

Vivid Studios

http://www.vivid.com/

As a company specializing in multimedia and publishing, San Francisco based Vivid Studios has gone through myriad changes since its founding in 1990. In its earlier days, Vivid was known as a publisher of books focusing on computers and multimedia, including the popular titles *Multimedia Demystified* and *Careers in Multimedia,* and as a producer of CD-ROMs and interfaces for online services such as The WELL and Delphi. By 1994, it had delved full-time into Web design.

Vivid's original three-person staff consisted of Nathan Shedroff as creative director (he's still in that role), a programmer, and a marketing director—a constellation of skills that could be seen as a recipe for a successful Web design firm. Now about 50 strong, the company calls its business "Internet experience architecture." Vivid coined the term to communicate the idea that its site designs are created with the primary goal of serving the user. In keeping with that concept, Vivid's project teams are lead by interaction designers. "They own the experience," explains Shedroff. "They're in charge of being inspired."

Vivid's services range from creative and technical production to strategic planning and management, handled by a workforce split into four groups: "experience," engineering, client services, and operations.

"You've got to remember that your competition isn't other Web sites; it's everything else people might be doing: rollerblading, scuba diving, or watching TV," says Shedroff. Vivid's workday operations are designed to encourage both interaction and inspiration. Weekly design meetings keep all the firm's staff apprised of how others in the company are approaching design problems, and field trips to theater, sports events, and museums help generate new ideas.

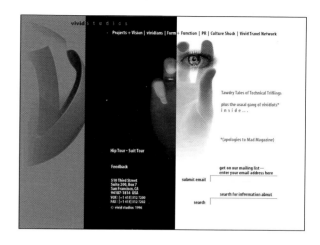

As a company, we are trying to concentrate on online experiences that are truly interactive.

NATHAN SHEDROFF, CREATIVE DIRECTOR, VIVID STUDIOS

The Process of Web Design

When approaching the Web or any other new medium, just remember: Underneath the mix of unfamiliar job titles, file formats, and terminology, the work still comes down to design, production, and distribution—the same tasks you'll find in any publishing venture. In this chapter, we'll describe what those steps entail in a Web publishing project and talk about ways some teams split up those jobs.

The World Wide Web is such a new medium that no models have really been established for who does what and how the team members interrelate. The situation is made harder to describe by quick changes in technology. Just as desktop publishing tools like PageMaker changed the role of print designers, new tools for HTML page layout and interactive scripting may quickly put some of the tasks usually handled by production engineers into the hands of Web designers. And as bandwidth improves and sites become more media-rich, producing a Web site could demand all the skills of producing a film, requiring professional video and sound production—even actors.

The Web Site Development Process

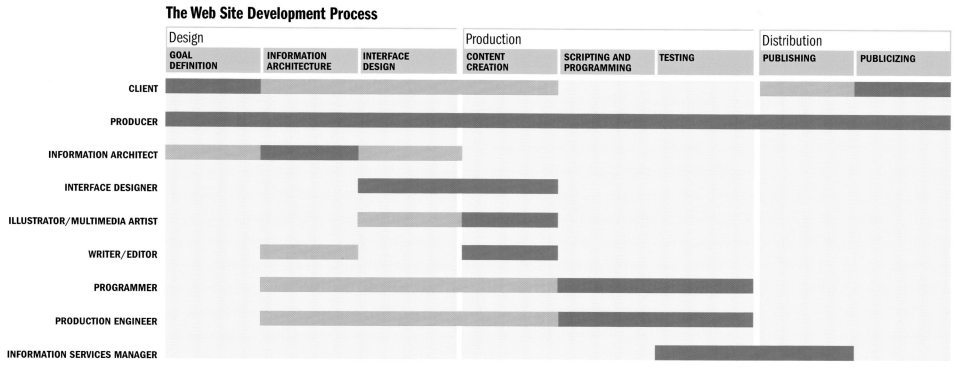

	Design			Production			Distribution	
	GOAL DEFINITION	**INFORMATION ARCHITECTURE**	**INTERFACE DESIGN**	**CONTENT CREATION**	**SCRIPTING AND PROGRAMMING**	**TESTING**	**PUBLISHING**	**PUBLICIZING**
CLIENT	███	░░░	░░░	░░░			░░	███
PRODUCER	███							
INFORMATION ARCHITECT	░░	███	░░░					
INTERFACE DESIGNER			███████					
ILLUSTRATOR/MULTIMEDIA ARTIST			░░░	███				
WRITER/EDITOR		░░░		███				
PROGRAMMER		░░░░░░░░░		███████				
PRODUCTION ENGINEER		░░░░░░░░░		███████				
INFORMATION SERVICES MANAGER					███			

WEB PUBLISHING IS COLLABORATIVE by nature, calling on the skills of a variety of team members. The dark bars here show the areas of each team member's main responsibility. The light bars show where those people play a consulting role. Of course, a single team member may wear several of these hats.

At HotWired, collaboration is crucial. Our team consists of project managers, editors, designers, production specialists, and engineers. Only with teamwork can we get things to work right.

SABINE MESSNER, HOTWIRED

As soon as we win a project, we take a deposit and do a detailed needs analysis. What the client really needs will quickly rise to the surface. We'll come back at them with a contract that includes a timeline and a statement of work that includes the deliverables, a staff list, and a creative brief. Everybody signs it, and we go.

JONATHAN NELSON, ORGANIC

Managing the Project

As in any publishing project, the job of pulling together the ideas and expertise of individual team members into a coherent plan is generally given to a single manager, usually called the producer. The job—perhaps the most important on a Web team—is to define the project, pull together an appropriate team, and, as the job progresses, oversee the project from a bird's-eye view, communicating the project plan to team members and making sure the project is implemented according to that plan.

If the job is being done for an outside client, an account manager may also be involved in order to represent the client's wishes to the team and communicate the team's ideas and progress back to the client.

On the Web, project managers often have a special challenge, created by the newness of the medium. Many clients have no experience with the Web, so even more than with other media, the manager will need to take special pains to help the client understand just what to expect from the process. Careful delineation of what you need from the client and what the client can expect from you will help smooth the road.

The Webmaster

One of the most common yet loosely defined roles in the world of the Web is "webmaster" or "webmistress." Depending on the site, it can mean the chief programmer, the head editor, the lead producer, the information services manager (the person who oversees the setup and maintenance of the server)—or just about anything else. It may be the title used for a jack-of-all-trades, who oversees every aspect of a Web site from mangement to writing to design. Often, it just means the person who was the first to take an interest in the Web at that particular company and who headed up the initial effort to launch a site. Given the history of the Web, that often means someone who has a background in Unix computers and network management.

Defining the Site's Goals

The first step of any publishing project, of course, is to define the publication's goals. If an outside client is involved, the job of establishing the publisher's goals usually involves discussions between the client and the account manager. For an in-house project, it might be the job of the producer, in conversation with any of the managers whose departments will be served by the Web site. There is no single way of getting the needed information, and each design group will look for different kinds of information. Most of the information you need to obtain is the same as for any publishing project: an understanding of the audience you're trying to reach and the message you want that audience to understand. With Web design, though, you will need to ascertain some special information. Since Web design often requires a trade-off between download speed and flashy effects, it's important to reach an understanding of which end of that spectrum the client is aiming for. And since certain effects can be viewed only by visitors using certain browsers (→**21**), you will need to define the target software as well.

This step should end with a document describing the goals of the project—a **creative brief**—which should be signed off on by any managers who will need to approve the design. Such a document will ensure that everyone involved shares the same expectations and will help inform decisions as the site develops.

Phase 1: Conceptual Development

GOALS AND MESSAGES

Determine the Following
1 Primary and secondary goals of the product
2 Primary and secondary goals of the client/publisher
3 Primary and secondary audience description (interests, needs, skills, capabilities, assumptions)
4 Audience capabilities (platform, browser/app, connection speed, degree of Net savvy and Net experience)
5 Platform descriptions (make, models, RAM, hard drives, CD-ROM, data load for each)
6 Top three messages the product needs to convey
7 After you've thought through these issues, rethink the goals.
8 Are they the true goals or merely the obvious ones?

Content
1 Does this product use primarily existing content?
2 If yes, how is it to be repurposed? In what ways will it be made appropriate to the interactive medium?
3 If new, how will it be captured and created? How much will there need to be?
4 Does this product use data entered by users? If so, how much and in what forms?
5 What can be done with it once entered?

Structure and Interpretations
1 What is the primary organization of the content?
2 What are other organizations that can be made available for other modes of searching, viewing, browsing, learning, exploring, and understanding?
3 What are the main presentation ideas of the structure of the title/project?
4 What are the most important and compelling features?
5 Are there any novel interactions? If so, what are they?
6 Will any new or emerging technologies be employed?
7 Will the audience be able to use them (or will the audience be given the necessary means and support to use them)?
8 What is the level of interactivity?
9 Are there any adaptive technologies employed?
10 Which ones and how?
11 Are there any cocreative features?

Sensorial Design
1 Describe the overall visual elements and styles of this product (use adjectives if necessary).
2 Describe the overall auditory elements and styles of this title.
3 Describe the text elements and written portions of this title.
4 Describe any ideas about animation style and use.
5 Describe any ideas about video style and use.
6 Describe the sophistication of programming needed.
7 Describe any current authoring systems that are intended for use or modification.

Market Testing
1 What are the environmental issues that concern the user of this product?
2 Which of these are most important to them?
3 Who are the competitors for this product?
4 How do these competitors rate on the environmental issues?
5 What are their strengths and weaknesses?
6 How can these strengths and weaknesses be addressed?
7 What are the best opportunities, and how can these be used to an advantage?
8 What are the most critical weaknesses, and how can these be eliminated?
9 Where are the best positions within the field of competitors?

Team
1 Who are the primary members of the production team? What are their roles and responsibilities?
2 What is their experience?
3 Are there technical, programming, marketing, and media professionals represented on the team?

WEB DESIGN USUALLY STARTS with a formal fact-finding procedure, during which the design team determines the client's requirements for content, look and feel, and function. This illustration shows the document Vivid Studios uses to gather this information.

creative brief
A statement of the goals of a design process.

Site architecture requires very tight right-brain/left-brain integration. You have to be able to organize the information and then also realize how that's going to work on the screen.

STEFAN FIELDING-ISAACS, ART & SCIENCE

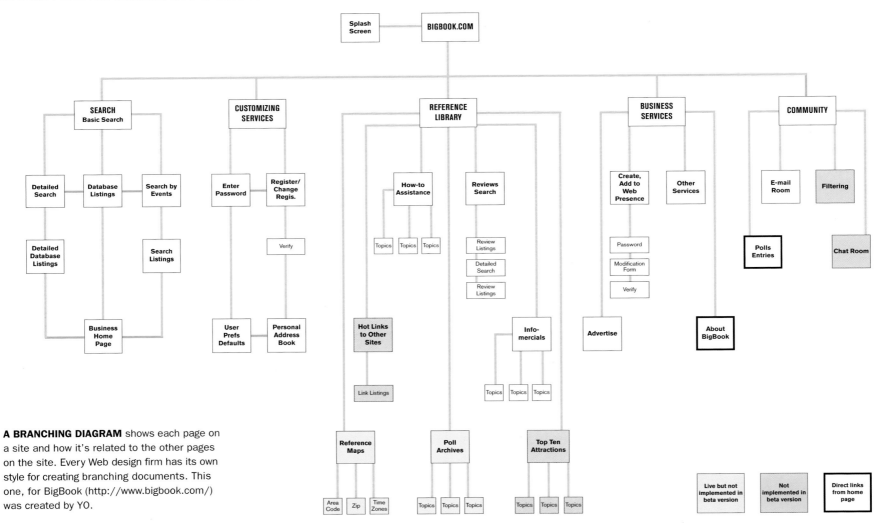

A BRANCHING DIAGRAM shows each page on a site and how it's related to the other pages on the site. Every Web design firm has its own style for creating branching documents. This one, for BigBook (http://www.bigbook.com/) was created by YO.

Information Architecture

Once the site's goals are understood, the planning of content can begin. On a Web site, that might include functions—such as online product sales or community meeting areas—as well as traditional, informational content like product information. This job usually falls to someone called an **information architect**, a term very descriptive of the task at hand, which is building a structure for the site that will hold the information and offer the functionality described in the creative brief.

For sites for which the main goal is the distribution of information, the design team may get most of the content from the client or publisher. For sites in which the purpose is more playful or less well-defined, the team may pull in the services of a copywriter to plan a creative approach to the message.

With the content determined, the next decision is how the content will be organized in the hyperlinked structure of the Web—probably the most challenging and specialized form of Web design. Complex enough when the fairly straightforward interfaces of text, graphics, and hyperlinks defined the Web, it's even more complicated now that the options are enhanced by a variety of technologies for animation and interactivity. For this reason, the planning of a Web site usually depends on the collaboration of a whole team of talents, including production engineers as well as information architects. The engineers can keep an eye on the technical implications of any design directions being discussed: Will a particular type of interaction require too much traffic on the server, and thus cause slowdowns? Can a particular effect be realized using Java or another programming language, or not? How much time would it take to implement? Is an even more elegant solution possible using the newest tools?

The process of "information architecture" should result in a document that defines the structure: usually a **storyboard** or a **branching diagram**, showing what pages the site will include and what kinds of information each page will contain.

The architecture determines what's going to go on the page. Then, once you know what's there, you start to think, "What are we trying to say, what kind of technology are we going to use, and what mood are we trying to set?"

JOHN GROTTING, STUDIO ARCHETYPE

branching diagram
In Web design, a diagram that shows what pages a Web site contains and how they are related to one another.

information architect
For any publishing project, the person responsible for determining how information will be organized for the publication. In Web design, the information architect is responsible for deciding how the information will be arranged on the pages of a Web site and how it will be accessed by the user.

storyboard
A document that shows the planned sequence of frames for video or any other time-based storytelling form.

> # The logic chart is a point of reference throughout the project. It's also a reflection of the directory structure, so the person scanning the photos knows where to put them, the person creating the content knows where to find them, and clients know what they're looking at when we show them layouts.
>
> PETER SEIDLER, AVALANCHE

The branching diagram forms the backbone on which the interface designers and writers, artists, HTML coders, and other team members and can begin building. It also provides the information the project manager will need to predict talent and scheduling needs—whether special skills such as programming or animation will be required, for example.

The branching diagram also provides the information the project manager or production engineers need to define directories and filenames for the final files—an important detail for building a working site, with functioning hyperlinks, later in the process.

For sites that depend on any kind of interactivity, the next stage in the design process should be the creation of a **functional specification**. While the branching diagram describes how the site will be *organized,* the functional spec (sometimes also called a technical spec or engineering spec) describes how the site will *behave.* That document provides the blueprint the engineers will use to make sure the proper code gets written.

YO

functional specification
A document that describes the functions a site will offer and the characteristics of each function. The functional specification codifies the expectations for any programmed interaction on a site and should provide all the information the programmers need to begin their work.

PAGE ARCHITECTURE maps out the kinds of information on each page, or each type of page, in the Web site. It's at this stage—after the site architecture is complete and the content of each page is determined—that the designer can determine such interface issues as which elements of each page will be text and which will be graphics.

Page Architecture and Interface Design

Once the branching diagram is complete and approved by the client, the team knows what information and functions need to be on each page of the site, and a more detailed, page-by-page design phase can begin.

This stage can also be broken into a couple of parts. The first stage might be called **page architecture**, in which the designers decide how the elements of each page will relate to one another on screen and how they will interact with the site as a whole. This will probably include creating a navigation system for the site: a standard set of links that users can quickly learn for navigating through the pages.

Only after the team understands how the site and pages are structured are decisions made about how the pages actually *look*—the stage that might be called graphic design. The interface designer defines a "look and feel" for the information, directing the work of illustrators and HTML coders to create a logical, attractive, and appropriate interface. Many designers think in pictures and develop ideas visually, so sketches for possible looks and graphic elements may begin much earlier in the process, but it's only at this stage, with the structure and function of the pages solved, that the design can be finalized.

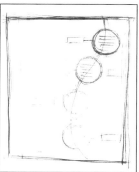
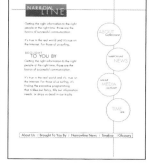

GRAPHICS, TEXT, and the other elements of a Web site may go through several iterations as the site's requirements are refined. The sketches here show the development of the design for the home page of Narrowline, a site that matches Web advertisers with Web sites that reach their chosen audiences.

HOT
http://www.narrowline.com/

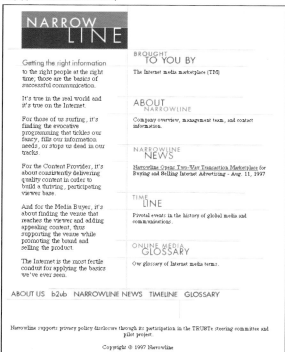

page architecture
A plan for the placement of information on a page.

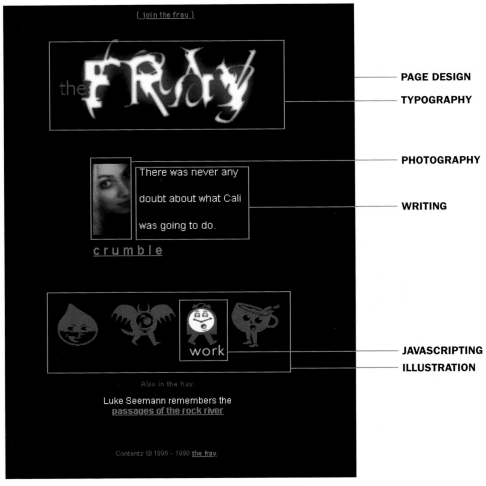

PAGE DESIGN

TYPOGRAPHY

PHOTOGRAPHY

WRITING

JAVASCRIPTING

ILLUSTRATION

DEREK M. POWAZEK
http://www.fray.com/

A WEB PAGE COMBINES the work of a whole team of creative and technical talents. This simple page required the work of a writer, an illustrator, a photographer, a designer, a typographer, a JavaScript programmer, and an HTML expert.

Creating the Content

With the structural plan in hand and the look and feel understood, the content creators can begin the job of fleshing out the site.

An extensive team may be required to create the content for a site. Writers will be responsible for creating concise, effective copy for each page; editors and copyeditors will be required to fine-tune it.

Illustrators, animators, and sound and video specialists may be called in to create the site's visual identity and multimedia sequences, working with the production engineers as necessary to prepare the media in the small file sizes and specialized formats required on the Web.

As the team members whip up their copy and artwork, the producer puts out fires, obtains (or gives) any necessary approvals, and ensures that everyone is working toward the common goal and deadline.

Programming and Scripting

Simple tools for interactivity—the ability to jump from page to page using hyperlinks, the ability to send e-mail to a specified address—are built into HTML. Anything that goes beyond that—collecting data from forms, or returning a response to user input or actions—requires programming.

Programs for some of the simplest, most common actions—counting visitors to the site, responding to a click on a portion of an image—are available free on line. Most others will require a programmer to construct a script (→**182**): a list of instructions for the computer to follow in response to a user's input.

The writing of simple scripts is often one of the jobs assigned to production engineers, whose tasks might include HTML production as well as scripting. As programming possibilities grow, though, so will the need for more specialized programmers, who can create interactive interfaces, hook in back-end databases, and create other custom behavior for Web sites, using programming languages such as Java (→**188**).

As Web pages become more complex, the link between programming and design becomes even tighter, and success relies on the ability of designers and programmers to collaborate to make ideas come to life using all available technology.

Production

In many ways, the world of Web production has a lot in common with the world of print production in the early days of desktop publishing. Before desktop design software automated many production tasks, those tasks were performed by typesetters and paste-up artists.

By late 1996, the first "desktop publishing" programs for the Web had begun to appear, but they were not sophisticated enough to replace specialized HTML experts. WYSIWYG HTML editors (→**80**) can be used to create simple Web pages, but even they require some knowledge of HTML, and at this writing, most production engineers still find it easiest to hack the HTML by hand. Software for laying out Web pages is slowly becoming more sophisticated, but until the technology is in place, the jobs of design and production will be split on most Web teams, with designers creating prototypes and production teams taking care of the mechanical aspects: preparing the graphics, coding the HTML files, and the rest.

Since basic HTML is relatively simple to learn and use, many designers opt to do at least basic coding themselves. It's important to remember, though, that HTML is not simply a layout tool. It works hand-in-hand with HTTP (→**10**), scripting languages, various browsers, and all the other technologies that are part of a working Web system. Using HTML wisely requires

www.narrowline.com			
107 items, 257.5 MB available			

Name	Date Modified	Size	Kind
▽ About	Fri, Sep 12, 1997, 1:46 PM	—	folder
index.html	Fri, Aug 8, 1997, 8:52 PM	61K	SimpleText text document
▽ B2UB	Today, 12:10 PM	—	folder
benefits.html	Fri, Aug 8, 1997, 7:50 PM	61K	BBEdit text file
faq.html	Mon, Aug 11, 1997, 8:07 PM	61K	BBEdit text file
formbuy.html	Sat, Aug 9, 1997, 2:08 PM	31K	Internet Explorer 4.0 document
formpub.html	Sat, Aug 9, 1997, 2:09 PM	31K	Internet Explorer 4.0 document
index.html	Tue, Aug 12, 1997, 3:02 PM	61K	SimpleText text document
▽ infographic	Today, 12:13 PM	—	folder
▷ images	Fri, Sep 12, 1997, 1:46 PM	—	folder
index.html	Tue, Aug 12, 1997, 3:59 PM	31K	Internet Explorer 4.0 document
results.html	Fri, Aug 8, 1997, 7:17 PM	61K	BBEdit text file
buyers.cgi	Sat, Aug 9, 1997, 2:08 PM	31K	BBEdit text file
▽ Glossary	Fri, Sep 12, 1997, 1:46 PM	—	folder
index.html	Fri, Aug 8, 1997, 6:54 PM	61K	SimpleText text document
▽ images	Fri, Sep 12, 1997, 1:46 PM	—	folder
72.gif	Thu, Aug 7, 1997, 3:30 PM	31K	document
About.gif	Mon, Jul 28, 1997, 7:39 PM	31K	document
abouthome.gif	Thu, Aug 7, 1997, 7:14 PM	31K	Photoshop® GIF file
benefits.gif	Fri, Aug 8, 1997, 3:25 PM	31K	Photoshop® GIF file
bottomline.gif	Thu, Aug 7, 1997, 11:30 PM	31K	Photoshop® GIF file
brought.gif	Thu, Aug 7, 1997, 7:31 PM	31K	Photoshop® GIF file
CFP97.jpeg	Mon, Jul 28, 1997, 7:56 PM	61K	document
cleartour.gif	Sat, Aug 9, 1997, 2:05 PM	31K	Photoshop® GIF file
extension1.gif	Thu, Aug 7, 1997, 9:07 PM	31K	Photoshop® GIF file
extension2.gif	Thu, Aug 7, 1997, 9:06 PM	31K	Photoshop® GIF file
extension3.gif	Thu, Aug 7, 1997, 9:06 PM	31K	Photoshop® GIF file
faqsbuyer.gif	Fri, Aug 8, 1997, 3:25 PM	31K	Photoshop® GIF file

THE COMPLETED FILES—HTML files, maps, images, and other media—are all sorted into logical directories (folders) on the server. The location and name of each file should be planned early in the production process, because that information is required to create working hyperlinks to the pages. (This directory is from the Narrowline Web site at http://www.narrowline.com/.)

familiarity with the ins and outs of all those parts. There's no reason, of course, that a designer can't master all that, and every Web designer should at least be knowledgeable about what HTML can and can't do with page layout (→**82**), but because HTML coding is time-consuming and requires skills that don't necessarily overlap with those of a designer, final HTML production is usually handed off to specialized production engineers.

In a nutshell, a production engineer's job is to pull together the disparate files—graphics, text, sound, animation, video, scripts—into pages that work over the Web and with the target browsers. Production engineers' responsibilities include some or all of these tasks:

• Setting up and saving the files in an appropriate directory structure on the server

• HTML coding, or verifying and fine-tuning HTML files supplied by the designers

• Preparing graphics and other media for low-bandwidth transmission

• Writing any necessary scripts

• Creating and testing the hyperlinks

• Making sure the code works in all target browsers

Publishing

The final stage of Web site development, as in any other publication process, is the "publishing" itself: making the final product available to its audience, whether that means the employees inside a company or the world at large. On the Web, this stage is much easier than in any other medium. When the files are deemed ready to go, an engineer just copies the final files into the appropriate directories on an HTTP server. (If the server is off site, the engineer might use an FTP program (→8) to copy the files across the Internet.) Anyone on the network—the Internet or a corporate intranet—who knows the right address can then log on and view the files.

Most Web teams use an internal **staging server** on which they can post the final files and test the links, scripts, and other functions before the site goes "live." To work correctly, this server should be an exact replica of the real server, with the same files, directories, and scripts.

Design companies working for outside clients may or may not offer to host clients' Web sites on their own servers. Setting up a Web server needn't be difficult, but Web site hosting is a challenging job, requiring round-the-clock troubleshooting. Remember, the site is available only as long as your server is working correctly. If the system is down or the bandwidth is insufficient, visitors will be turned away and may never return.

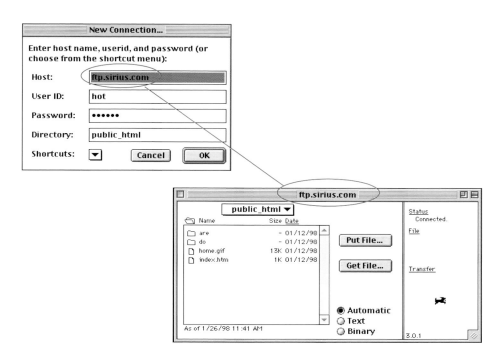

IF YOUR WEB SERVER is off site, you can use an FTP program to copy the files to the server over the Internet. To do it in Fetch, the FTP program for the Macintosh shown here, you simply log onto the server (here, ftp.sirius.com), select the files and folders you want to copy, and click the Put File button.

staging server
A server that has the same setup as the server that will be used to publish Web files, used to test Web pages on line before they are made publicly available.

http://www.internic.net/

domain name
A name by which an Internet server is known (e.g., "peachpit.com"). The first part of the domain name provides a unique, plain-language identifier for the Internet server. The part following the period is usually a three-letter code signifying the type of site: for example, *.com* for commercial, *.edu* for educational institution.

InterNIC
The service that registers domain names for commercial Internet users.

YOU CAN REGISTER your own domain name using InterNIC, the central clearinghouse authorized by the U.S. government for assigning Internet domains. By the time you read this, other services may also be in the same business.

Publicizing Your Site

The ease of publishing on the Web has a flip side. The publisher is saved the trouble and expense of mailing the publication to subscribers or shipping copies to bookstores, but if the work doesn't appear in readers' mailboxes or catch their eye on a bookstore shelf, how will they know it exists? The role of publicity is arguably more important in Web publishing than in any other medium. Luckily, there are several good ways to pull readers to your Web site.

Perhaps the most important step is to register an easy-to-remember **domain name**. If you've registered your company name as your domain name, potential readers can go directly to your site by typing the name in their browser. It's often the first method people try for finding a site. Ask your Internet Service Provider about registering your domain name, or do it yourself. As we wrote this, the U.S. government was in the process of working out new ways to let companies and individuals register domain names, but the current system involves a central service called **InterNIC**, where registering a domain name costs $100 for the first two years ($50/year thereafter).

The standard marketing tools open to any business can also be powerful tools for publicizing your Web site. Everyone has seen television commercials, magazine advertisements, and billboards that list Web addresses for everything from microbreweries to the latest movies. Every magazine that has an online edition lists its Web address on its masthead or table of contents. Marketing materials mailed to clients can also highlight the advent of a new Web site. A company that spends significant amounts on customer support could quickly recoup the cost of advertising its Web address once customers start looking to the Web site, instead of to more costly sources such as 800 numbers and beefy customer support departments, to answer their questions. The payback is also clear, of course, if you sell products from your Web site.

If you don't have an advertising budget, though, you'll be glad to know that effective publicity tools are also available, for free, on the Web itself.

Many people find what they need on the Web through online **search engines**. Although there are lots of these, just a handful of key ones are referred to by the vast majority of Web users. (They include Yahoo, Excite, AltaVista, Lycos, and Infoseek.) Through these services, potential visitors can find your site by simply typing a keyword on the service's search page. In addition to a search facility, Yahoo and other directories list registered sites in subject categories that users can click through to find sites. Most Internet search companies crawl the Web regularly to find and index new pages, but to make sure your site is noticed as quickly as possible, you can register with

http://www.lycos.com/

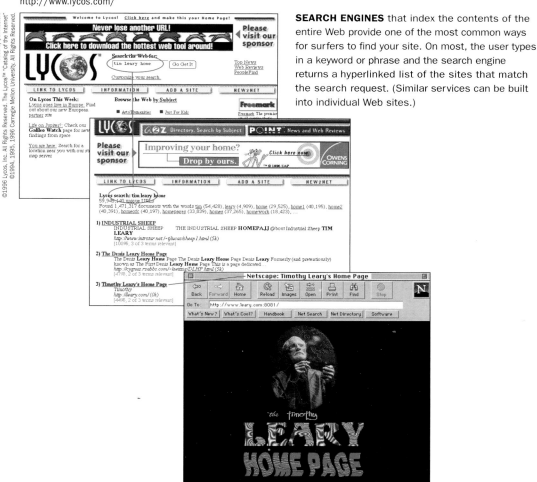

SEARCH ENGINES that index the contents of the entire Web provide one of the most common ways for surfers to find your site. On most, the user types in a keyword or phrase and the search engine returns a hyperlinked list of the sites that match the search request. (Similar services can be built into individual Web sites.)

CHRIS GRAVES/JOEY CAVELLA/RETINA LOGIC
http://www.leary.com/

search engine
A program that searches through electronic information. Web search engines such as Lycos and InfoSeek search through indexes of the entire Internet in response to user queries.

DAVID SIEGEL/PURVI SHAH
http://www.highfive.com/master.html

COOL SITE SERVICES make it their business to point visitors to sites they think are the best on the Web. The popular High Five and Cool Site of the Day sites are shown here.

BEE ANDREWS/RICHARD GRIMES/MIKE BATEMAN
http://cool.infi.net/

these companies directly. You can also use a few tricks in your Web page coding to ensure that your pages are indexed correctly by the automatic indexing engines used by the search services. (You'll find sources for information about that in the Online resources list at the end of this chapter.)

Next, look for other sites on the Web that reach the same people you'd like to reach, and let their publishers know you're there. Many sites have a page of links that point their readers to sites of related interest. It's also a good idea to look for Internet newsgroups that serve your audience and post news of your site there. (You can find relevant sites and newsgroups by doing your own search in the search services we talked about in the preceding paragraph.)

Last but not least, if you think your site is something special, propose it to one of the many "cool site" listing pages. These sites are run by self-appointed taste-makers who scan through the thousands of sites presented for their attention and anoint a select few to be called "cool." Getting on one of these lists can bring a large audience, since they're followed by many thousands of readers with a wide range of interests. Cool Site of the Day is the most famous; we name some more in the Online list on the next page.

What's Your Role?

The term *Web design* is a loose one—it can include one or all of the processes described in this chapter. As you saw from the examples in the last chapter, successful Web design companies come in all shapes and sizes. Many Web design firms limit the services they offer to the "design" parts of the process: information architecture and interface design. Others take on HTML production as well. Some offer a complete set of services, including programming and production, and even host sites on their own servers. To fill gaps in their resources, many Web design firms seek out strategic partnerships with companies that offer skills they don't have in-house, teaming up with independent writers, programmers, and Internet service providers.

Especially in the early days of Web design, firms that offer soup-to-nuts services may have an edge. Since Web publishing is such a new field, few companies that need a Web site have any in-house expertise for managing the process and so will look for consultants who can guide them through the steps and find the necessary talent for bringing a Web site to life.

Online: The Process of Web Design

Coding for Search Engines
http://www.searchenginewatch.com/

"Cool Site" Services
http://www.projectcool.com/sightings/
http://cool.infi.net/
http://www.highfive.com/

InterNIC
http://www.internic.net/

Publicizing Your Site
http://www.2020tech.com/submit.html
http://www.netpost.com/clickview/

Web Search Services
http://altavista.digital.com/
http://www.excite.com/
http://www.infoseek.com/
http://www.lycos.com/
http://www.yahoo.com/

We've found that smaller companies in particular want us to provide a full range of services: the ability to host their site and the ability to publicize it in addition to design and coding. With larger companies, hosting isn't such an issue: They've got their own IS capabilities. Some larger companies come to us just for design, because they have an in-house production staff.

STEFAN FIELDING-ISAACS, ART AND SCIENCE

Structuring the Site

A Web site's pages are linked to one another—and to the rest of the Web—by a series of hyperlinks. Any page can link to any other anywhere in the world. Given that the movement through a site is so unpredictable, with each page linked to any number of others, what do we mean when we talk about a Web site's structure?

Although no designer can control the path a Web user chooses to travel through information on the Web, it is a Web designer's job to make the content of a site available and enticing to every visitor who finds his or her way there. That requires both a careful analysis of the content you're presenting—determining its main messages or components—and skills for helping visitors find and understand those messages. Doing this successfully combines the tasks of information architecture—the creation of a structure for the site's information—and interface design—the crafting of tools that help visitors navigate that structure and find information that will be of interest to them. Those are the tasks we'll discuss in this chapter.

Information Architecture: What Goes Where

The structure of a Web site grows from the way you want visitors to, first, understand and, second, get to the information you post there.

Your initial conversations with your client during the site definition stage we talked about in the last chapter (→**41**) should uncover the basic outlines of the content you'll be presenting. This phase should define what information the client wants to have available, what interactions the client wants to offer, and the client's broader marketing goals: the ideas and impressions visitors to the site should take away with them. For example, an online flower shop might want its customers to have access to a complete catalog of available bouquets (content), to be able to order flowers on line (interaction), and to learn that the company offers bouquets for every occasion and convenient and inexpensive service (marketing message). A bank may want to detail its checking, savings, and investment plans (content), let users make contact by e-mail with "personal bankers" and check their account balances on line (interaction), and create the impression that the bank is trustworthy as well as innovative enough to serve its customers online (message). All three facets are key in planning any site. The site's final content and the way it presents itself to the user must achieve all these goals.

Information architecture should be driven by human behavior. You've got to make the system fit the user, not the other way around. Focus groups, user testing, and past experience with how users have reacted to earlier designs should be your guide.

STEFAN FIELDING-ISAACS, ART & SCIENCE

A Structure That Allows for Change

The contents of a Web site will—or should—change constantly. Visitors should feel that the site will hold something new for them each time they visit, giving them a reason to return to the site again and again. Planning and designing a Web site is therefore a lot like creating a new magazine. Content planners must think in terms of content categories ("departments"), not specific content, when planning the site's sections.

This factor affects the interface as well as the structural design of a site. Designers should think in terms of rules, or templates, for styling the content, thinking ahead to the uses to which each element might be put. That's not to say that new features can't have their own individual design, but as with a magazine, the site's graphic identity should remain constant while the specific content changes.

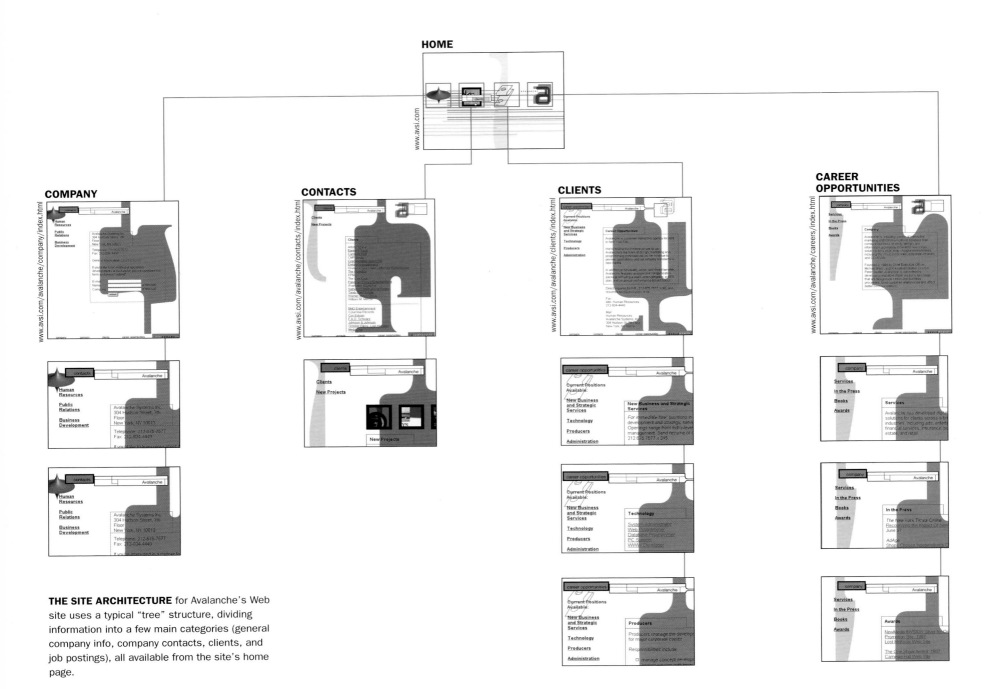

HOME

www.avsi.com

COMPANY

www.avsi.com/avalanche/company/index.html

CONTACTS

www.avsi.com/avalanche/contacts/index.html

CLIENTS

www.avsi.com/avalanche/clients/index.html

CAREER OPPORTUNITIES

www.avsi.com/avalanche/careers/index.html

THE SITE ARCHITECTURE for Avalanche's Web site uses a typical "tree" structure, dividing information into a few main categories (general company info, company contacts, clients, and job postings), all available from the site's home page.

With the goals understood, the challenge becomes how to achieve those goals creatively and effectively using the technology of the Web. Despite everything we've said about the Web's current limitations, it is potentially the most flexible of media. Using basic HTML tools, the Web can work like an encyclopedia (random-access reference information), a book (sequential pages), a magazine (graphically presented "departments"), or a promotional brochure (an unfolding "pitch"). Adding multimedia to the mix, it can mimic more familiar electronic media such as television (an active, animated presentation), a slide show (sequential, bite-size messages), or a computer game (mysterious clues). Interactive technologies, such as Shockwave (→**153**), JavaScript (→**186**), and Java (→**188**), can turn a Web page into online software, providing real-time interaction and access to up-to-date, searchable information based on back-end databases. For instance, an interactive site might allow visitors to use online questionnaires to determine the right personal banking plan or bouquet.

There are countless ways to execute and combine such effects, so it's impossible to lay down rules for right and wrong ways to create a Web site's structure. At the same time, though, a few simple tests (described on the next page) can help you gauge the effectiveness of your site plan.

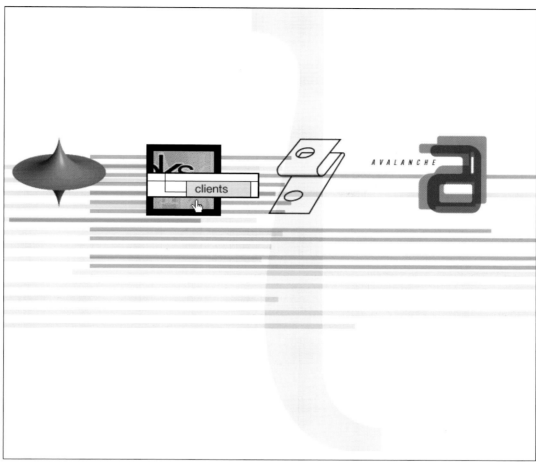

AVALANCHE
http://www.avsi.com/

AVALANCHE'S HOME PAGE provides access to the four sections of the site. Here, JavaScript creates an interactive effect: rolling the mouse over a graphic displays the name of the section the graphic links to.

Ask yourself these questions:

Have you created a logical structure that represents the view of the information you want to convey? In most cases, a visitor to your **home page** should be able to see at a glance what information your site has to offer, a goal best achieved by determining and offering a limited set of content categories. Common wisdom and cognitive psychology experts hold that the set should be limited to no more than about seven basic groups, the number of separate items that most people can grasp at one time.

It's all interrelated. Sometimes working on the architecture provides insight into how the navigation should work, and sometimes the interface provides insight into the architecture.

JOHN GROTTING, STUDIO ARCHETYPE

home page
Sometimes used as a generic name for a Web site, but usually referring to the top page of a site structure, providing access to all other pages on the site.

Does the content of each page represent a logical module of information? The hyperlinked structure of the Web counts on the ability of users to get straight to the information they need, from a variety of different starting points. The best way to achieve that is to limit each page to one topic. Imagine the banking site we talked about earlier. Rather than combining information for all its checking plans, it might put a description of each plan on a separate page. The site might then link to the page on business checking plans from a page about checking plans in general and also from another page on the site that details special services for businesses. Keeping each module of information on its own page also makes updates easy; when the information needs updating, you change it in only one place.

Does the structure pass the three-click test? No important information should be more than three clicks away from the home page and, if possible, no more than three clicks away from any page on the site. On the Web, remember, each click costs the visitor valuable time, so the information you want everyone to see, or the information most likely to be looked for, should be as close as possible to the top of the structure. And as we'll describe in the next section, you can put more information within easy reach by using thoughtful navigation strategies.

Site Navigation: Making Content Accessible

With the basic site structure defined, the next task for the designer is making it easy for visitors to find the information they need on the site. On the Web, that means creating a system of hyperlinks that will allow visitors to move around the site efficiently.

Web designers can count on a built-in set of navigation controls that are standard in Web browsers. These include **bookmarks**, **history lists**, and Forward and Back buttons. Users will learn to depend on the browser's controls for such functions, and designers shouldn't confuse the issue by duplicating them in their site's interface.

Creating site-specific navigation tools requires, first, deciding which pages will be linked to what others. Part of this is ad hoc and logical. (The information about a bank's business services would clearly need a link to the business checking plans, for example.) The other part is more systematic—coming up with a sitewide plan for putting as many pages as possible at the visitors' fingertips, no matter where they are on the site.

The simplest way to do this is to offer a link to the site's home page from every other page on the site; once users return there, they can find their way back down the hierarchy to any other piece of information

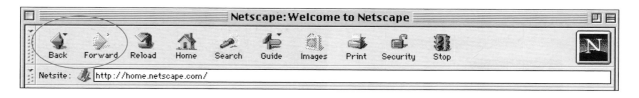

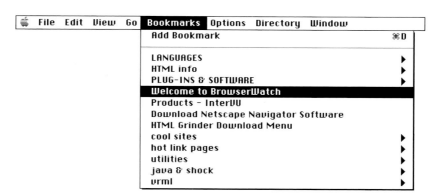

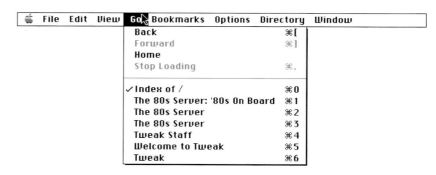

BROWSERS HAVE a set of navigation tools built in. Users can always retrace their steps using the Back button and the history list, follow an earlier path again using the Forward button, and mark often-visited pages with bookmarks.

bookmark
An electronic record of a particular page's URL, stored with a user's browser preferences, allowing the user to return to that page by choosing the page's name from a menu.

history list
A list of pages that the user has visited during that online session, listed in a browser menu so that the user can choose the page's name to return to it.

A SEARCH FEATURE helps visitors find the page they want by entering a word or phrase describing the content they're looking for.

WITH FRAMES, you can set site navigation tools apart in a separate section of the window. The navigation bar at the bottom of this page stays in place no matter what the window size.

A SITE TABLE OF CONTENTS helps visitors find their way to any page on the site from a central location.

on the site. A somewhat more powerful option is a **navigation bar**, a standard element that lists the site's main sections on every page, offering a deeper level of access with a single click. For more complex sites, a site index or table of contents is a popular tool. And particularly large sites often offer a search function that allows the visitor to look for occurrences of particular words or concepts anywhere on the site.

HTML frames (→**94**) let you divide the browser window into separate, independently scrollable regions, each holding a different HTML file. One popular use for frames is to isolate a site's navigation elements into their own frame, which stays constantly on screen while pages requested by hyperlinks appear in other sections. You can even use frames to create an entirely new window to hold your site's navigation tools.

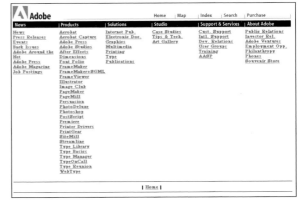

Integrating Look and Feel

After the essential structure of the site is documented and you've decided how to provide access to its different levels, it's time to think about interface: the way your site presents itself to the user. Interface design is responsible for creating a strong subjective impression as well as an easily understood overview of how the site works. Ideally, a strong interface seamlessly melds navigational tools and the graphic identity that gives a Web site its character.

Anyone creating site-specific navigation methods must first be aware of the navigation conventions already built into Web browsers. For example, visitors will work on the assumption that at every site they visit, text hyperlinks will look the same. Preferences for whether or not they are underlined and the color they are displayed in can often be set in each browser, but all Web users know that colored text (and bold text on some nongraphics systems) signals a hyperlink. Web designers need to respect that convention and refrain from coloring any text that's not a link. The flip side of this is that they can take advantage of that convention to identify links in graphics by showing them as colored text.

Another convention of graphical browsers is to have the pointer turn into a pointing hand when it passes over a hyperlink. Designers can count on that interface to tip off users that a graphic is "live." Likewise,

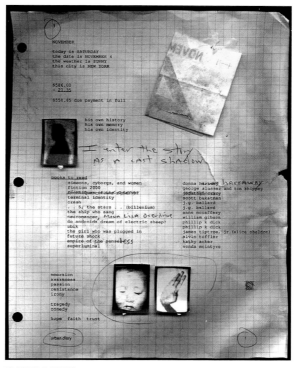

JOSEPH SQUIER
http://gertrude.art.uiuc.edu/ludgate/the/place/urban_diary/page1/diarypage1.html

GRAPHICS AND LAYOUT combine to create a graphic environment that complements the content. At left, a notebook of childhood memories is presented as a type-written scrapbook, and each image acts as a hyperlink.

On every site we try to think about the interface in innovative ways. When we did the FAO Schwarz site, the lead designer and I spent a couple days walking around the store and playing with things to get the vibe.

PETER SEIDLER, AVALANCHE

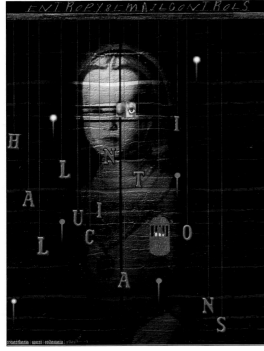
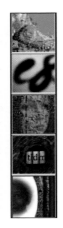

AURIEA HARVEY
http://www.entropy8.com/hallucinations/index.html

A MYSTERIOUS LAYERED LOOK identifies Entropy8, a personal site (and design business calling card) by Auriea Harvey. The navigation bar, in a separate window, lists the site's sections by graphic identity rather than by name.

KLUTZ PRESS, a publisher of children's books, has a site that looks—and acts—like a goofy playhouse. Visitors click on the pictures and furniture to call up games as well as the publisher's catalog.

DAVID SIEGEL
http://www.klutz.com/treefort/chicken.html

they should make sure to replicate that interface when creating non-HTML interfaces for Web sites using tools like Shockwave (→**153**) or Java (→**188**).

These conventions aside, any other clues about how to move around your own Web site—and reasons the visitor might want to—are up to the site's own user interface to convey. The art of interface design is to create an environment that includes the information users need in a quickly assimilated and attractive manner.

As with site architecture, interface design has too many possibilities to be subject to simple rules, yet there are a few guidelines against which you can test your ideas.

Ask yourself these questions:
Does the interface convey a "look and feel" appropriate to your client's message? Illustrations, metaphors, and layout should all combine to convey the image your client has named as a goal—friendly, sophisticated, businesslike, whatever.

Will the use of your site be obvious to first-time visitors? A site's use will be more obvious to visitors if you use familiar metaphors and conventions—a map for navigating a geographic area, a labeled door for entering a new area, a question mark icon indicating a help section, or a beveled interface indicating a clickable button—but that's not to say that there's no room for originality. It's almost impossible, of course, to know whether what seems like a clear interface to you will be equally obvious to others. Providing a set of instructions isn't necessarily a bad idea, but if you're depending on visitors to read them before they use your site, you know you're in trouble. The only way to really find out whether your interface is working is with user testing: Running tests with people who have never used or seen your site can tell you how likely it is that someone who has no history with the site and its development will understand your solutions.

Are cues and feedback consistent? Any interface has to be learned to some extent. Even when an interface uses only the most time-honored conventions, a visitor starts by testing his or her assumptions about how it will work. If a tool works as expected—if clicking an upward-pointing arrow takes you to the top of the page, for instance—the visitor learns a skill (getting to the top of a page), is encouraged to explore more, and learns to trust the interface. If on another page the upward-pointing arrow behaves differently, that trust is broken, the skill is unlearned, and the visitor is discouraged from exploring. A hallmark of a good interface is that it uses metaphor, location on screen, shape, color, sound, and every other cue consistently, reassuring visitors that their efforts will be rewarded.

The navigation graphics are part of the site's identity. They're not purely for getting to information.

JOHN GROTTING, STUDIO ARCHETYPE

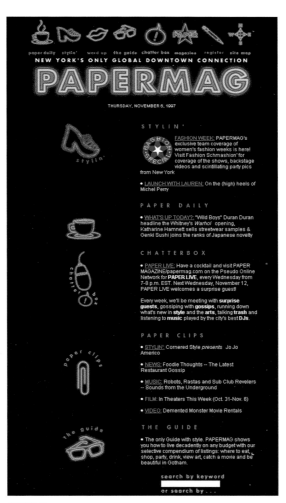

SOCIO X
http://www.papermag.com/

THE NEON-LIGHTED GRAPHICS of PaperMag appropriately evoke the nightlife of New York, which is the site's topic.

User Testing

An interface that seems perfectly clear to its designer may be extremely opaque to someone who hasn't been involved in its development, or to someone to whom the color red—or any other interface cue—simply has a different connotation. Because the success of a Web site depends on the ability of a wide variety of users to understand its clues, it is of prime importance that designers understand just how a broad range of people react to the interface choices they've made.

Anyone developing a very high profile site might find time spent testing designs with broad-based focus groups a worthwhile investment, but most projects, and most schedules, won't be able to afford such formal testing. Most designers can, however, get time with friends, colleagues, and others who won't mind looking over prototypes at different stages of development. While a second, third, or fiftieth opinion may not be more worthwhile than your own, extra feedback is bound to point out some issues you may not have thought of and, perhaps, point the way to more universal solutions.

The interface design and the architecture are inseparable. During the planning stages, I'm going to be changing the structure to accommodate the interface, or vice versa. Otherwise you end up with a pretty interface that's impossible to use.

STEFAN FIELDING-ISAACS, ART & SCIENCE

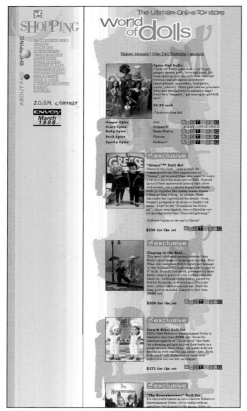

BRIGHT COLORS, lively typography, and, of course, lots of dolls dress up the FAO Schwarz World of Dolls page.

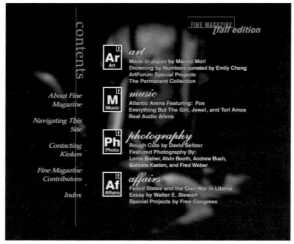

Does the design accommodate lowest-common-denominator systems? Too often, designers depend on graphics to convey important navigation information and content, making the site unusable to visitors who don't have access to graphics. This is not to say that you can't use graphical navigation systems on your site. It only means that you may sometimes need to provide alternate paths for text-only browsers, and you should be careful to take advantage of the methods for accommodating text-only systems that are built into HTML's image tags (→**125**). Similarly, if your target audience includes users on low-bandwidth systems and older browsers, you should be careful to plan interface elements with minimum file sizes and avoid using Shockwave (→**153**) or other specialized media to excute your ideas.

FINE MAGAZINE features fine arts in a suitably elegant interface. The "periodic table" section identifiers carry through all the site's pages as a graphic navigation bar.

AVALANCHE
http://www.faoschwarz.com/shopping/

GENE NA/KIOKEN/KAHNG NA DESIGN
http://www.finemagazine.com/

The Home Page

The term *home page* is used in a couple of different ways. Often, it is used as a synonym for Web site, as in "Bob has just posted his own home page." More often, though, it refers to the "front page" of a site: the one you land on if you type the site's domain name, and the one from which all the other pages on the site can be reached.

As, usually, the first—and sometimes the only—page any visitor to your site will see, the site's home page is arguably its most important feature, and so worth a little special attention in this chapter. Like the cover of a book or magazine, or the opening credits of a TV show, its primary role is to state your message—whatever that may be—loud and clear.

Web designers have struggled to find the right balance of content and style on their home pages. One school of thought argues that the home page should highlight, and provide direct links to, as much of the site's content as possible. Another abhors the crowded and confusing page that such an approach can create and opts for simple home pages with nothing but links to the site's main sections. Some models mimic magazine covers or newspaper layouts. The samples shown here illustrate some possible approaches.

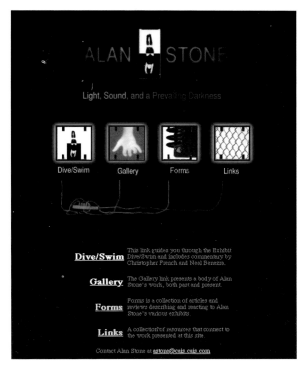

JEFF GATES/ANDY SPANGLER
http://www.ewg.org/pub/home/stone/dive/index.html

A HOME PAGE usually has several standard elements: the company branding, a map of the site's main sections (often offered in both graphic and text views), and a feedback link.

GURL uses cartoonish icons to represent the magazine's irreverent tone.

REBECCA ODES
http://www.gurl.com/

The front page is your first chance. This is where people have to decide whether they want to use your site or not. I like to make home pages that you actually get something out of—you're not required to click on anything to get to the basic information.

MATTHEW BUTTERICK, ATOMIC VISION

THE PLACE, by poet, photographer, and teacher Joseph Squier, lures visitors in with a timed splash screen leading to a mysterious environment labeled with evocative section titles. The idea here is to encourage exploration.

soapbox

artist

reviews

debt

urban diary

life with father

anatomy

outside

? ?

the place

JOSEPH SQUIER
http://gertrude.art.uiuc.edu/ludgate/the/place.html

THE MORE INFORMATION you offer on the home page, the more likely a visitor will see something of interest. The '80s Server shows a colorful, tabloid-style home page.

STEPHAN WILLIS
http://www.80s.com/entrance.html

Accommodating Advertising

More and more, Web designers face a challenge that magazine designers have contended with for decades—advertising. The basic issues are the same in any medium: how to give advertisers prominence without overwhelming the site's own content, how to make clear what is an ad and what isn't, and how to accommodate a hodgepodge of graphics that aren't under the control of the site designer.

As Web advertising has matured, a set of standard ad sizes has been established, saving advertisers the trouble and expense of creating new ads for each site they appear on. The most common ad size is the standard ad "banner," 468 x 60 pixels , but a number of other formats are also appearing.

Web designers are also still experimenting with the challenge of differentiating ads from a site's own content. Different sites use rules, borders, space, frames, and other devices to create the requisite graphic distance.

Where to place ads on a Web page is another question with a variety of answers. Advertisers, of course, prefer that their ads appear as close to the top of the page as possible, to be visible on screen without scrolling. (Borrowing an old term from newspaper publishing such placement is often referred to as "above the fold.") Some sites have begin placing

ads *between* pages; when the user clicks on a link, the ad appears for a timed interval before the new page is displayed.

As advertisers take advantage of attention-grabbing effects such as animation, interactivity, and sound, ads create even more competition on the page—a real threat on the Web, of course, since the advertiser's goal is to entice the viewer to click on the ad and be transported to the advertiser's own site, and away from yours.

Online: Structuring the Site

Microsoft's User Testing Results
http://www.microsoft.com/workshop/author/plan/improvingsiteusa.htm

Site Structure Tips and Guidelines
http://www.useit.com/
http://www.webreview.com/wr/pub/Web_Architect/

Copyright © Macromedia

MACROMEDIA
http://www.macromedia.com/

MAKING ADS STAND OUT from the site's own content is the biggest challenge facing designers of ad-supported Web sites. Macromedia creates a border by building ads into its page banner. Clicking the ad opens the advertiser's site in a new window. The banner is just one type of ad you'll see on the Web.

HTML Basics

We introduced HTML, the Hypertext Markup Language, back in the first two chapters of this book. You already know that it was created along with the Web to provide a hyperlinked interface to the content of the Internet; that it's the basic format for almost all Web pages; that it's developing quickly, as industry coalitions and software companies do their best to keep up with the needs of Web designers. But in order to design for the Web, you're going to have to get to know HTML a lot better than that.

HTML is the backbone on which Web pages are built, and its characteristics determine what you can and can't do on the Web. Even if you'll be working with a production team and you don't code pages yourself, you'll still need to understand HTML's idiosyncrasies in order to design for the Web.

We'll cover specific HTML techniques for controlling page layout, typography, graphics, sound, video, and interactivity in other chapters. In this chapter, our task is to give you some context for understanding just how HTML works and what you'll use it for.

Viewing the Source

Basic HTML isn't really hard to master. Many of the codes it uses are simple descriptive words (e.g., *align="center"*) or abbreviations (*B* for bold, for example) for the effect they create.

The quickest way to become acquainted with HTML is to take advantage of a command you'll find in almost any browser: View Document Source, which lets you see the HTML that makes up any page you read on the Web. When you compare the tags in the HTML file to the results in the browser, you'll begin to understand what can be done and how it's accomplished.

The basic information you'll learn in this chapter— the parts of an HTML file, the anatomy of a tag, the different types of tags, and the different versions of HTML—should be all you need to understand how HTML files work. You'll find more help in the quick reference boxes in this book, which show the syntax of individual tags as we discuss them, and from the HTML reference in the back of this book (→**204**). And if you really want to dig into the code, any bookstore has dozens of HTML primers, describing in detail how the language works.

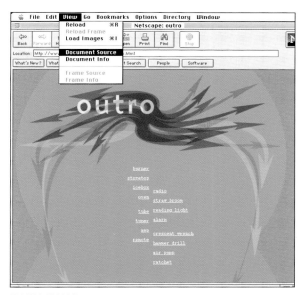

ATOMIC VISION
http://www.atomicvision.com/outro/

```
<HTML>
<HEAD>

<TITLE>outro</TITLE>

</HEAD>

<BODY BACKGROUND="pix/outro_back5.gif" TEXT="#FFFFFF"
VLINK="#CFD65E" LINK="#ffffff" BGCOLOR="#55AC6F"
ALINK="BCD642">

<TABLE BORDER=0 CELLSPACING=0 CELLPADDING=0 WIDTH=598>
<TR>
<TD COLSPAN=5 VALIGN=bottom ALIGN=left>
<IMG  SRC="./pix/arrows_top.gif" ALIGN=TOP WIDTH="593"
HEIGHT="214" BORDER="0"></TD>
</TR>
<TR>
<TD VALIGN=top><IMG SRC="./pix/arrows_left.gif" ALIGN=top
WIDTH="135" HEIGHT="315" BORDER="0"></td>
<!-LINKS->
<TD ALIGN=right VALIGN=top WIDTH=158><FONT SIZE=0>

<TT><A HREF="http://www.eden.com/~hexlux/">burner</A><P>
<A HREF="http://www.panix.com/~nam/firerain/frnming.html">
stovetop</A><P>
<A HREF="http://www.contrib.andrew.cmu.edu/~woferry/Temple.html/">
icebox</A><P>
<A HREF="http://www.nothingness.org/SI/journaleng/
formularyubanism.html">oven</A><P>
<BR>
<P>
<A HREF="http://www.wt.com.au/safetyline/smartmov/noise_sm.htm">
tube</A><P>
<A HREF="http://www.travelnow.com/tinnitus"/>tuner</A><P>
<A HREF="http://www.eecs.harvard.edu/collider.html/">amp</A><P>
<A HREF="http://emanate.com/comtrad/noise/friendly.htm">remote
</A></TT><P></FONT></TD>

<TD><IMG SRC="./pix/space.gif" ALIGN=top WIDTH="7"
HEIGHT="1" BORDER="0"></TD>

<TD ALIGN=left VALIGN=top WIDTH=158><FONT SIZE=0>
```

VIEWING THE SOURCE CODE of HTML documents is the quickest way to learn HTML. The Netscape Navigator interface is shown in the screen at left, but most browsers have a similar command.

HTML is the fastest way to get information onto a Web page. You can embed lots of plug-ins and applets in it, but we hardly ever do, because the download overhead is rarely worth it. Usually, pure HTML works best.

MATTHEW BUTTERICK, ATOMIC VISION

SGML: The Parent of HTML

HTML springs from an international standard for electronic document exchange known as SGML (Standard Generalized Markup Language), a system widely used in government and educational organizations. Familiarity with the ideas behind SGML can help Web designers understand why HTML is like it is.

SGML was designed to allow publishers to reuse the same documents in several different media, with several different applications, or in several different layouts without re-creating the file each time. SGML accomplishes this in two ways (which are also key to HTML). First, SGML files are pure text, a format readable by pretty much any software. (Saving files as text also means that organizations need never fear the danger that otherwise threatens electronic files: that the software or system for which the document was created will become obsolete, and the files will thus become unreadable.) Second, the codes in SGML don't describe the layout of the file; they describe its structure. The tags label types of information—title, heading, quote, and so on—and leave it to the software that processes it to assign a layout to each element. (That's the secret of the document's reusability.)

The SGML standard doesn't specify any particular set of tags. Instead, different communities or industries can create sets of tags that make sense for the documents they use. The banking industry might use one set of tags, for instance, while chemical engineers use another. HTML is the set of SGML tags created to enable Web publishing.

What Is HTML?

HTML is not a file format in the sense that QuarkXPress or Microsoft Word have file formats. As we explained earlier, HTML documents are pure ASCII—text only—and can be read by practically any application. HTML is actually a set of codes, or "tags," that are embedded in these text files, between angle brackets.

Most people think of HTML as a language that describes the layout of text in an HTML file, but that's not exactly right. HTML tags can affect the layout of the file (in ways we'll describe in the next chapter), but HTML is actually a *structural* markup language. It was designed to name the different elements of a document so that they can be dealt with appropriately by the browser; used as it was meant to be used, HTML doesn't specify layout.

There are lots of different types of elements in an HTML page—not just the ones that actually appear as text in the browser window. In addition to paragraphs, headings, and other text, HTML tags label elements like scripts (the <SCRIPT> tag) (→**187**), multimedia objects and embedded programs (the <OBJECT> tag) (→**190**), hypertext anchors (the </A> tag) (→**78**), and other special elements. The browser's programming tells it how to interpret and handle each tag, whether that means to display it in the page or take another action, like loading a script or image file.

Types of Tags

Although it's clear that there are several different types of HTML tags, it's hard to define just what those types are. New HTML tags spring up whenever a new feature or behavior is needed in Web pages. HTML started out as an extremely simple application of SGML, with just a handful of tags—enough to tag the key parts of very basic documents, plus an extra feature that identified text anchors for hyperlinks. The first additions were to support graphics (→**124**) and interactive forms (→**168**). When Netscape, the first commercial Internet browser maker, entered the picture, HTML's growth went into hyperdrive. Tags appeared for features like tables (→**90**), frames (→**94**), background colors (→**130**), and interactive scripts (→**187**). You can split these tags up in any number of ways, and every HTML reference you look at will probably split them up differently.

In one sense, there are two types of tags: those that belong in the head of an HTML document, supplying general information about the file, and those that belong in the body, tagging the content that is shown in the browser window.

For designers, though, perhaps the most useful breakdown is to think of the tags as falling into two main groups:

Structural tags, which label the parts of a document: headings, paragraphs, lists, tables, images, and so on.

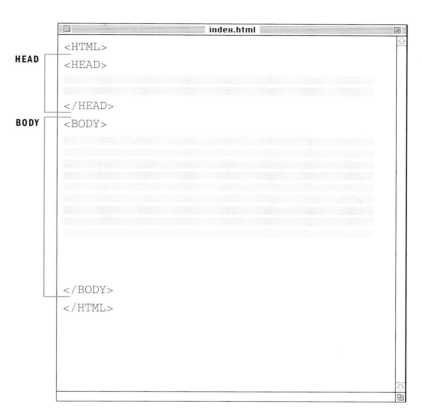

EACH HTML DOCUMENT has two main sections: the head, which gives the browser general information about the file, and the body, which includes the information that will be displayed in the browser window. The head of the file is delineated by <HEAD> and </HEAD> tags, and the body is delineated by <BODY> and </BODY> tags. Some browsers also require an <HTML> tag at the top of the file and a </HTML> tag at the end, which tell the browser to interpret the file as HTML and not plain text. All other HTML tags fall within these delimiters.

HTML Tags by Group

STRUCTURAL TAGS

Tags that label different types of content. The browser acts on each tag appropriately, whether that means displaying the element it marks in an appropriate way or initiating an appropriate action.

File level	<HTML> <HEAD> <BODY> <META> <TITLE>
Section level	<DIV> <DIR> <DL> <MENU> <OL> <UL>
Paragraph level	<BLOCKQUOTE> <P> <DD><DT><LI>
Phrase level	<ABBR> <ACRONYM> <CITE> <CODE> <DEL> <DFN> <EM> <INS> <KBD> <PRE> <Q> <SAMP> <SPAN> <STRONG> <VAR>
Headings	<H1> <H2> <H3> <H4> <H5> <H6>
Rules	<HR>
Form elements	<FORM> <BUTTON> <FIELDSET> <INPUT> <LABEL> <LEGEND> <OPTGROUP> <OPTION> <SELECT> <TEXTAREA>
Table elements	<TABLE> <CAPTION> <COL> <COLGROUP> <TBODY> <TD> <TFOOT> <TH> <THEAD> <TR>
Frameset elements	<FRAMESET> <FRAME> <IFRAME> <NOFRAMES>
Interactive elements	<A> <AREA> <MAP> <SCRIPT> <NOSCRIPT> <PARAM>
Additional code and media	<APPLET> <EMBED> <IMG> <LINK> <OBJECT>

STYLE TAGS

Tags that give specific instructions about the look of the element

Line breaks	 <NOBR> <WBR>
Font	<FONT face=>
Font size	<BIG> <SMALL> <FONT size=>
Font color	<BODY alink=> <BODY link=> <BODY text=> <BODY vlink=> <FONT color=>
Font style	<B> <I> <S> <STRIKE> <SUB> <SUP> <TT> <U>
Placement	<CENTER> <IMG align=>
General style information	<STYLE>

Style tags, which tell the browser exactly how to present the labeled text.

For the most part, "official" HTML, defined by the W3C HTML specifications (→**74**), sticks pretty tightly to structural tags. This is in keeping with the basic tenets of SGML (→**70**)—to use the markup language to specify only the structure of a document and leave it to the piece of software that reads the file to format it according to that system's capabilities and the user's preferences.

Many of the tags in the second group—style tags—were added by browser manufacturers eager to fulfill designers' demands for more control over the look of documents. In the Web's early days, the modicum of control offered by such tags were just about the only way to exert any influence at all over Web page layout. As you'll see as we go along, however, most of those tags have served their purpose and should fade away over time, replaced by the more orderly, complete control offered by style sheets (→**98**).

The Anatomy of a Tag

An HTML tag usually has several parts. The "start tag" tells the browser that a particular element is about to begin: Text following the tag should be treated according to the rules for that element. Most HTML codes also use an "end tag," which signifies the end of the element. The end tag is usually a repeat of the start tag, preceded by a slash (/) character. (The beginning of an ordered list is marked by the <OL> tag, for example, and the end by the </OL> tag.)

In addition, many tags have optional or required "attributes," which give the browser additional information about how the tag should be interpreted. The "attributes" follow the start tag, inside the start tag's bracket delimiters. Attribute names are often followed by an equal sign (=) and then the attribute's "value."

In the chapters that follow, we'll talk about how to use different tags and different attributes to achieve particular effects.

<FONT size=3>applicable text</FONT>

THE START TAG defines the beginning of an element.

ATTRIBUTES add additional information about how the tag should be interpreted. Attributes are added inside the start tag delimiters. Many attribute names are followed by an equal sign and then by the value of the attribute.

THE TEXT that the tag applies to goes between the start and end tags.

THE END TAG defines the end of an element. The end tag is a repetition of the start tag, but beginning with a slash (/) character.

Managing the Different Versions of HTML

As we explained earlier, HTML tags describe the elements of a Web page, and browsers interpret those tags appropriately. It sounds simple enough, but the situation is thornier than it seems. Surprisingly—and unfortunately—not all browsers support all HTML tags. And browsers that support the same tags might treat them in different ways.

One reason for this situation rests with the variety of hardware that browsers run on. The Web and HTML are designed to work on viewer hardware ranging from teletype terminals to high-powered graphics workstations to Braille readers. Appropriately coded HTML documents can be interpreted by each of these systems, but the teletype software won't, of course, support elements like splashy graphics.

The second problem has its roots in the history of HTML. As we've already described, HTML is a growing language, with new tags added in each version of the HTML specification. One complication, then, is that older browser versions won't support tags that were introduced after those browsers were released. (The chart on the next page shows roughly which browser versions support which versions of HTML.)

Another complication is that browser manufacturers haven't always stuck to tags described in the official

---

HTML

2.0

The first official HTML specification, documenting the language as it was used when the Web started to gain popularity. This set of tags is universally supported across different browsers. As HTML 2.0 was being documented, work was simultaneously undertaken on proposed additions to it.

Netscape Extensions

Tags created by Netscape and supported in its own browser software.

3.0

The first set of proposed extensions to HTML 2.0 never made it past the draft stage. In the meantime, so many new extensions had been added by Netscape and Microsoft that it became clear that a truce had to be called.

Microsoft Extensions

Tags created by Microsoft and supported in its own browser software.

3.2

HTML 3.2 once again essentially documented the de facto standard—features, including text wrap around images, table layouts, and other layout controls that were supported by the current browsers and already in wide use. Then work began again on trying to return HTML to its SGML roots.

4.0

Currently a proposal from the IETF, HTML 4.0 accommodates both SGML purists and designers with its adoption of style sheets, which, once again, separate structural markup from layout controls. HTML 4.0 acknowledges the layout controls documented by HTML 3.2 but "deprecates" them in favor of the newly documented style sheet controls.

THE OFFICIAL HTML SPEC, managed by the W3C, has gone through three versions so far: HTML 2.0, HTML 3.2, and HTML 4.0. The process hasn't always been smooth, however. In the Web's early days, Netscape and Microsoft muddied the waters by supporting their own home-grown tags, called Netscape and Microsoft extensions, which fragmented the language.

HTML specs. While a central standards group—the W3C (→**22**)—set out to document and develop the language, Microsoft and Netscape—the publishers of the most popular browsers—started supporting their own home-grown tags, developed to give designers more layout options. The home-grown tags became known as the Netscape and Microsoft "extensions." Many (but not all) of those extensions were included in HTML 3.2 and have since been added to most browsers, but this history means that support for many tags is spotty. Also, because the tags were implemented in browsers before rules for their use were hammered out through the W3C, some tags may be implemented in different ways in different browsers. The table tags, for instance (→**90**) were implemented first by Netscape with certain attributes and possible values and implemented by Microsoft a little differently before their official specification in HTML 3.2 ironed out the differences and new browsers from both companies began implementing the standard.

By 1997, Web publishers were getting fed up with the complications caused by conflicting tags, and the browser companies began to see the error of their ways. Version 4.0 of Microsoft Interent Explorer sticks pretty closely to HTML 4.0. Version 5.0 of Netscape's browser should also be well-behaved.

Meanwhile, though, lots of Web pages had been built, and lots of browsers had been distributed supporting only the earlier tag sets. Most browsers currently in

It's always expensive and complex to attempt to maintain different versions of content for specific browsers. We used to do it quite a bit, but now we feel that with 90 percent of the world using 3.0 browsers, we can stick to the 3.0 base very effectively.

BRIAN BEHLENDORFF, ORGANIC

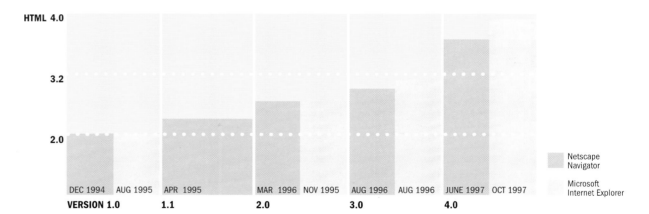

THE HTML SPECIFICATIONS and browser technology develop simultaneously. As a rule, each new browser release supports the current HTML spec, plus a few more experimental tags. This chart gives a rough idea of the relationship between different browser releases and the level of HTML they support.

Multiple versions of a site are a lot of extra work to maintain, unless the site is being served out of a database. We usually recommend that our clients NOT support multiple versions of their site, and when they see the cost savings spelled out, they always agree.

NATHAN SHEDROFF, VIVID STUDIOS

Dynamic HTML: What Is It?

In this chapter, we have talked about HTML 2.0, 3.2, and 4.0: the different versions of standard HTML. Another term you'll hear a lot, though, is "dynamic HTML" (often abbreviated as DHTML).

Dynamic HTML is pretty loosely defined; it's actually more a marketing term than a real version of HTML. Dynamic HTML is, in the simplest sense, HTML that moves—pages that can change their display in the browser window in response to user actions or according to a scripted plan. More technically, the term is used to refer to a set of technologies supported by the 4.0 browsers—style sheets, CSS positioning, JavaScript—that allow this to happen. We'll be describing all of these technologies later in the book. And in our chapters on multimedia and interactivity, we'll talk about how you can use dynamic HTML to achieve those effects.

use support the HTML 3.2 tag set, but some older browsers can't even do that. Coding pages with the tag set described by HTML 2.0 is the only way to be sure that every visitor will be able to read them, but those tags don't offer much in the way of layout control.

One answer to the problem is in crafty coding. Sometimes you can use two sets of code in a single page to do the same thing. This works because browsers are designed to ignore any tags they don't understand, so each browser will interpret only the code it's designed to handle and act as if the other code isn't there. For example, say you want the first-level headings in your page to use the typeface Arial, be light blue and indented a quarter inch, and have 12 picas space above and 6 picas below. In the 4.0 browsers, that kind of control is possible with style sheets (→**98**), so you tag your heading with <H1> (for a first-level head) and use the style sheet to set the indentation, color, typeface, space above and below, and just about anything else you want.

Now, since only the latest browsers will see those effects, you begin building your fall-back positions. (In Web design, this is sometimes referred to as "graceful degradation"—really.)

HTML 3.2's <FONT> tag (→**112**) lets you specify a system font and the font color, but none of the other settings, so you take what you can get. Inserting the <FONT> tag means that visitors with mid-range browsers at least get those effects.

The oldest browsers won't understand either the <STYLE> tag or the <FONT> tag, so they will simply display the heading with the default settings for a level 1 head: about 16-point Times (or the user's default font), black, flush left, with a space above and below.

As you can see, coding for a range of browsers can get fairly complex—and the example we described here is just one way to go about it. (For instance, if you wanted *everyone* to see your blue, indented, sans-serif heads with the right space above and below, you could set the type in a graphics program and insert a graphic for each heading.) The upshot is that designing a Web page is always a balancing act. You need to make a set of assumptions about your audience and a set of decisions about how you'll use HTML to meet that audience's needs. You'll need to decide how much work you want to invest in optimizing pages for different browsers: the path of least resistance is to use only the most widely supported codes, but if part of your site's goal is to wow visitors with your cutting-edge design, it may be worthwhile to make your code more complex, or even create entirely different pages for users with different browsers. Your decision about what tactics to use might even be different for different pages on the same site.

The last thing to remember is that, even keeping these rules in mind, HTML coding is a bit of a crap-shoot. There are now dozens of different browser versions in use, taking into account the different releases of each browser and the differences that occur even between the same browser versions on different platforms. This points out one of the most important rules of Web design: The only way to make sure your visitors will see what you want them to see is to test your pages in every browser you want them to work with.

If it's any consolation, things are probably as bad now as they'll ever get. Over time, an ever-higher percentage of Web users will have browsers that support HTML 4.0, and tagging may get easier. In the meantime, though, you've got to make careful judgments about what types of browsers you want to address and how much effort it makes sense to spend on each one—and just keep testing.

Content Negotiation: Delivering Just What the Browser Orders

Each time a browser requests a page from a Web server, the browser sends information about itself along with the request. You can create scripts that use this information to send different pages to different browsers. For example, you could send a page that used HTML 4.0 tags only to 4.0 browsers and send a simpler, HTML 2.0 page to everyone else. This process is called "content negotiation." You can also use scripts to determine whether or not a user has a required plug-in installed, a process called "object detection."

Content negotiation and object detection get around the problem of trying to code one-version-fits-all documents, but it also creates lots of extra work because it means you need to keep multiple versions of every page.

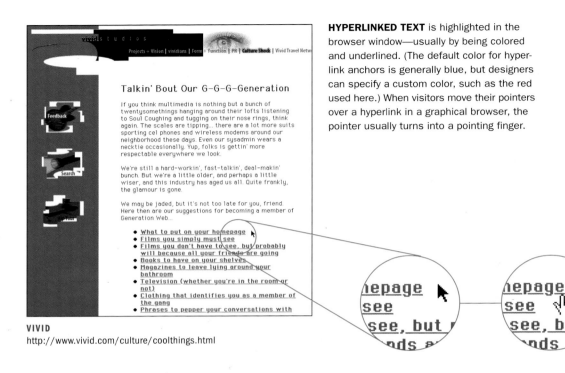

HYPERLINKED TEXT is highlighted in the browser window—usually by being colored and underlined. (The default color for hyperlink anchors is generally blue, but designers can specify a custom color, such as the red used here.) When visitors move their pointers over a hyperlink in a graphical browser, the pointer usually turns into a pointing finger.

VIVID
http://www.vivid.com/culture/coolthings.html

Navigating the Web With HTML

We'll talk about a wide variety of HTML tags in other chapters of this book. For this "basics" chapter, though, we'll introduce just one: the tag that gave the Hypertext Markup Language its name and makes the Web the Web.

The secret of HTML's hyperlinking abilities is a single tag: <A> (it stands for "anchor"). The <A> tag and its companion </A> tag surround the text you want to use as an anchor for your hyperlink. (You can also use an image as an anchor.) The *href=* attribute of the tag names the Internet location the anchor will link to.

In a browser window, the <A> tag has several effects. The most obvious to the user is that the anchor is highlighted. (In most graphical browsers, anchor text is blue and underlined.) When the user passes the mouse over the anchor, the cursor turns into a pointing hand. And when the user clicks on the anchor, the browser fetches the file named in the *href=* attribute. It's an amazingly simple—and amazingly powerful—system.

Other attributes of the <A> tag let you create live areas in image maps (→**126**) and send the retrieved file to particular windows or frames (→**94**), actions we'll discuss in other chapters.

If the file named by the *href=* attribute is an HTML file or is in another format supported directly by the

START TAG	ATTRIBUTES	END TAG	EXPLANATION
<A>		</A>	Creates a hyperlink anchor
	coords="*coordinates*"		For an image map, the coordinates of the graphic's live area
	href="*URL*"		The file to be called by the hyperlink
	name="*name*"		Names a section of an HTML document. That name can then be used in the *href=* attribute of another <A> tag.
	shape="default" OR "rect" OR "circle" OR "poly"		For an image map, the shape of the live area created by the <A> tag
	target="*frame*" OR "_blank" OR "new" OR "_parent" OR "_self" OR "_top"		Used with frames, names a frame in which the file should be displayed.

browser, the file opens in the browser window. If not, the browser calls on a helper application (→**11**) that can open the file.

The <A> (anchor) tag, like every other tag that names a file on the Web, depends on a standard way of finding files, wherever they exist in the world. This naming convention is referred to (usually) as a **URL** (pronounced either "U-R-L" or "earl"), which stands for Uniform Resource Locator. (Sometimes you'll see it referred to as URI, for Uniform Resource Identifier, or URN, for Uniform Resource Name.)

If you have used a DOS system, you'll be familiar with the form of a URL: it's similar to a DOS pathname. Instead of a disk drive, though, the URL begins with a protocol name (http, ftp, and so on), followed by a colon and two slashes (forward slashes, instead of the backward slashes used in DOS). Then comes the name of the server and the directories and subdirectories that hold the file, separated by slashes. Last is the filename. (If no filename is given, some Web servers assume a default filename such as index.html or default.html.)

PROTOCOL NAME   **DIRECTORY**   **FILENAME**

http://www.domain.com/dir/subdir/file.html

SERVER NAME   **SUBDIRECTORY**

A URL (Uniform Resource Locator) is built like a DOS or Unix pathname. Instead of a disk drive name, a URL begins with a protocol name (such as *http* for a Web server), followed by a colon and two slashes. Next comes the name of the Internet server that the file is stored on (usually known by a unique domain name), followed by the directories on that server that hold the file, separated by slashes. Last comes the filename.

URL
Uniform Resource Locator, a standard method of naming and finding files on the World Wide Web. Also sometimes referred to as URI (Uniform Resource Identifier) or URN (Uniform Resource Name).

WYSIWYG HTML EDITORS like Dreamweaver (right), text editors like BBEdit (for the Macintosh, opposite left) and HTML filters like BeyondPress, an XTension for QuarkXPress (opposite right), offer three different ways to create HTML files. WYSIWYG editors are designed to hide HTML from page authors, letting them work in a graphical user interface that displays the page very much as it will appear in a browser window. Text editors are for HTML coders who want to hack the code themselves. BBEdit's special HTML extensions add dialog boxes and palettes to help with the coding, but you can do the job in any word processor, including Microsoft Windows' Notepad and the Macintosh's SimpleText. HTML filter programs let you work in a familiar program like QuarkXPress and then translate the file to HTML.

DREAMWEAVER

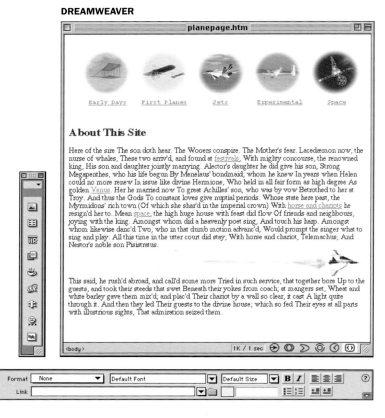

Creating HTML Files

There are lots of ways to create HTML documents. Many popular word processing and page layout programs have the ability to save files as HTML documents. **HTML filters**, which convert files from popular applications such as QuarkXPress and Microsoft Word to HTML, can also do the job. You can also get word processing programs specially designed for HTML formatting, ranging from text editors that let you pick HTML tags from menus and palettes to **WYSIWYG** (what-you-see-is-what-you-get) programs that let you drag images into place and add styles to text with menu commands without ever seeing the HTML code.

Many industry insiders compare learning HTML to learning PostScript: You had to do it when the language was new, but now the code is completely hidden behind page layout and graphics program interfaces. Someday that may come to pass, but most designers agree that it's not true yet. Today's WYSIWYG tools let you create basic HTML pages without ever typing a tag, but most accomplished Web designers still prefer to code their HTML pages directly. As we've described in this chapter, and as you'll see when you start looking at the HTML source for Web pages, there are lots of ways to achieve a given effect on screen, and many designers are reluctant to let programs make their tagging choices for them.

BBEDIT WITH HTML TOOLS

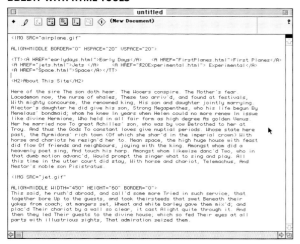

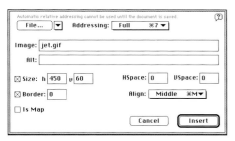

BEYONDPRESS

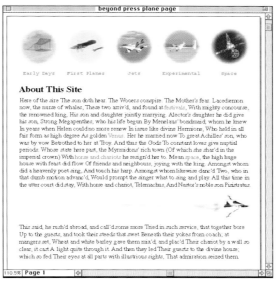

About This Site

Here of the sire The son doth hear. The Wooers conspire. The Mother's fear. Lacedæmon now, the nurse of whales, These two arriv'd, and found at festivals, With mighty concourse, the renowned king, His son and daughter jointly marrying. Alector's daughter he did give his son, Strong Megapenthes, who his life begun By Menelaus' bondmaid; whom he knew In years when Helen could no more renew In issue like divine Hermione, Who held in all fair form as high degree As golden Venus. Her he married now To great Achilles' son, who was by vow Betrothed to her at Troy. And thus the Gods To constant loves give nuptial periods. Whose state here past, the Myrmidons' rich town (Of which she shar'd in the imperial crown) With horse and chariots he resign'd her to. Mean space, the high huge house with feast did flow Of friends and neighbours, joying with the king. Amongst whom did a heavenly poet sing, And touch his harp. Amongst whom likewise danc'd Two, who in that dumb motion advanc'd, Would prompt the singer what to sing and play. All this time in the utter court did stay, With horse and chariot, Telemachus, And Nestor's noble son Pisistratus.

This said, he rush'd abroad, and call'd some more Tried in such service, that together bore Up to the guests, and took their steeds that swet Beneath their yokes from coach; at mangers set, Wheat and white barley gave them mix'd, and plac'd Their chariot by a wall so clear, it cast A light quite through it. And then they led Their guests to the divine house; which so fed Their eyes at all parts with illustrious sights, That admiration seized them.

Online: HTML Basics

Browser Support for HTML

http://www.blooberry.com/html/supportkey/a.html

HTML Editors and Filters

http://www.astobyte.com/products/BeyondPress/

http://www.barebones.com/

http://www.macromedia.com/software/dreamweaver/

HTML Specifications

http://www.w3.org/MarkUp/

Learning HTML

http://www.cnet.com/Content/Builder/Authoring/Basics/

http://www.excite.com/computers_and_internet/internet/web_page_design/html/

http://www.hotwired.com/webmonkey/html/

http://www.ncsa.uiuc.edu/General/Internet/WWW/HTMLPrimer.html

http://www.projectcool.com/developer/html.html

http://www.webdeveloper.com/categories/html/

http://www.webreference.com/

http://www.webreview.com/wr/pub/HTML/

http://www.zdnet.com/products/htmluser/

Microsoft Internet Explorer HTML Support

http://www.microsoft.com/workshop/author/default.asp

Netscape Navigator HTML Support

http://developer.netscape.com/docs/manuals/htmlguid/

SGML

http://www.w3.org/MarkUp/SGML/

Page Layout With HTML

HTML's design capabilities have come a long way from the earliest days, when browsers simply stacked each element, one after another, in the browser window, flush left. First, Netscape extensions and table layout tags added tools for creating grids and white space. And now, full control over layout and typography are at hand with HTML style sheets, which designers can use to specify typeface, leading, indents, and even exact placement for each page element.

In the last chapter we described how HTML developed, beginning with the most basic structural tags, then adding design features willy-nilly with each new browser release until, at last, a truce was reached around HTML 4.0, which established a standard layout method: applying style sheets to structural elements, just as designers are used to doing in other media. Style sheets, with their ability to control position on the page as well as typographic settings, should finally provide a working solution to Web page layout. Until the world is using browsers that support the new standard, though, designers need to design pages with the entire history of HTML in mind. In this chapter, we'll show how layout effects can be achieved with a variety of methods and describe the benefits of each approach.

Structural Tags: The Building Blocks of HTML Layout

As we explained at the beginning of this book (→**21**), HTML has a lot in common with the typesetting systems used in the days before desktop publishing. Codes embedded in the file tag each element. Then the layout of each element is determined by specifications programmed into the typesetting software.

On the Web, the typesetting software is in each browser, which interprets the HTML code according to its own particular layout instructions. The tricky part is that, for older browsers, designers have no control over the typesetting specs that determine the look of the page; they're preprogrammed into the browser, and nothing can affect them. Browsers that support HTML 3.2 give designers control over a few different effects—typefaces and the placement of graphics, for instance—but rely on the built-in defaults for most specs. With style sheets, designers at last gain that control. Style sheets provide type specifications for each element that override the built-in defaults—returning to a traditional method of page layout.

Until most Web users have upgraded to browsers that support style sheets, the trick to HTML layout is to work with all these methods at once. Web designers need to code pages so that they work in early browsers—the ones that make up their own minds about the layout of each element. Then, designers can add HTML 3.2 style tags and style sheets for those browsers that understand them.

The key to both approaches is structural tags. In early browsers, the structural tags you use will control layout. In browsers that support style sheets, the structural tags provide the backbone on which you hang the layout instructions that will determine the page's look.

We tend to do pages that support a variety of browsers, which is much easier than supporting different pages for different browsers. But the level of differentiation between the two sets of code is really dependent on how much money the client is willing to invest.

STEFAN FIELDING-ISAACS, ART & SCIENCE

START TAG	DEFINITION	END TAG	SPECIFICATION
<BLOCKQUOTE>	Block (indented)	</BLOCKQUOTE>	12-pt. Times, indented 48 pixels from the left and right quotation margins
<P>	Paragraph		12-pt. Times, 16 pixels space above and below
<HR>	Horizontal rule		2 pixel line, flush left
<H1>	Level-1 head	</H1>	24-pt. Times bold, flush left
<H2>	Level-2 head	</H2>	18-pt. Times bold, flush left
<H3>	Level-3 head	</H3>	14-pt. Times bold, flush left
<H4>	Level-4 head	</H4>	12-pt. Times bold, flush left
<H5>	Level-5 head	</H5>	10-pt. Times bold, flush left
<H6>	Level-6 head	</H6>	8-pt. Times bold, flush left
<DIR>	Directory list	</DIR>	12-pt. Times indented 48 pixels, preceded by a bullet, indented 36 pixels. <LI> starts a new item.
<DL> **<DT>** **<DD>**	Definition list	</DL> </DT> </DD>	<DT> (definition term) 12-pt. Times, flush left <DD> (definition) 12-pt. Times, indented 48 pixels
<MENU>	Menu list	</MENU>	12-pt. Times indented 48 pixels, preceded by a bullet, indented 36 pixels. <LI> starts a new item.
<OL> **<LI>**	Ordered (numbered) list	</OL>	12-pt. Times, indented 48 pixels, first line preceded by Arabic numeral and indented 33 pixels. (The *type=* attribute can be used to change the numbering style to upper- or lowercase letters or Roman numerals.) <LI> starts a new item.
<UL> **<LI>**	Unordered (bulleted) list	</UL>	12-pt. Times, indented 48 pixels, first line preceded by a bullet and indented 36 pixels. (The *type=* attribute can be used to change the bullet style.) <LI> starts a new item.

HTML'S STRUCTURAL TAGS name a document element, not a particular design, but most browsers use similar specifications for each tag. The specifications shown here are those used on a PC in Netscape Navigator. Other browsers may use slightly different specs.

Using Structural Tags for Layout

Used as they were meant to be, structural tags create the kind of layout you might have last used typing up a college term paper: a couple levels of heads, double spaces between flush-left paragraphs, and one basic typeface, Times. In short, the preset styles create a lowest-common-denominator layout—readable but boring.

The default settings are usually the same from browser to browser. Text tagged <BLOCKQUOTE> will usually be 12-point Times, indented about half an inch on each side, for example.

Structural tags aren't really meant for design. Using HTML as it was meant to be used means simply tagging each element appropriately: <H1> for a top-level head, for instance, and <BLOCKQUOTE> used only for indented quotations. (This ensures that HTML files can be used, according to the tenets of SGML, in other applications as well.) Of course, that leads to a very boring page, and HTML doesn't have enough structural tags to label any except the most basic elements, anyway, so very few page authors actually use HTML that way.

Instead, designers quickly figured out that they could use HTML tags for their design attributes, rather than their structural purpose. If they wanted their text in 14-point Times rather than the default 12-point, they could simply tag all their text <H3>. A half-inch margin around text could be achieved by tagging all the text with <BLOCKQUOTE>. Two <BLOCKQUOTE> tags result in a deeper margin. Because the basic tags are so few, and because the available typefaces are, usually, limited to two, the variety is limited. In the early days of the Web, though, this was the only available method of exerting any control at all over the look of pages.

Designers should remember that this approach isn't foolproof. The defaults you count on may change from browser to browser and even from one release of a particular browser to another. And all your assumptions are blown as soon as independent-minded readers decide to set their own preferences. Text you thought safe at 12-point Times might actually be seen as 16-point Chancery Script.

About The World Wide Web Consortium

The World Wide Web Consortium exists to realize the full potential of the Web.

W3C is an industry consortium which develops common standards for the evolution of the Web by producing specifications and reference software. Although W3C is funded by industrial members, its products are freely available to all.

The Consortium is run in the United States by the MIT Laboratory for Computer Science and in Europe by INRIA, in collaboration with CERN where the web originated. For details on the joint initiative and the contributions of CERN, INRIA, and MIT, please see the statement on the joint World Wide Web Initiative.

Membership Information

W3C Membership is open to any organization which signs a membership agreement, further detailed in the Prospectus.

To learn about individual members and visit their World Wide Web sites, see the Members of the W3 Consortium.

Services

The W3C provides a number of public services:

- A repository of information about the World Wide Web for developers and users, especially specifications about the Web;
- A reference code implementation to embody and promote standards
- Various prototype and sample applications to demonstrate use of new technology

Any products of the consortium are available during development and on initial release to members. However, one month after a formal internal release, all software produced by or officially contributed to the W3C is available for general public use, commercial or otherwise.

Further information

- Frequently Asked Questions about W3C
- Help wanted: come and work with the W3C Team at MIT or INRIA
- Overview slides about W3C
- People of the W3C
- How to contact W3C
- Press Information

W3C is hosted by the MIT Laboratory for Computer Science and in Europe by INRIA with support from DARPA and the European Commission.

http://www.w3.org/consortium/

USING HTML 2.0 as it was intended results in a lowest-common-denominator layout reminiscent of a college term paper—or word processing circa 1983.

ad319

In February of 1993, ad319 was born from the simultaneous efforts of three artists and designers trained in traditional mediums, all of whom were attempting to embrace new digital technologies. The founding members of ad319 were Kathleen Chmelewski, Nan Goggin, and Joseph Squier. The idea of working as a collective seemed an effective way to pool our knowledge, and an efficient means of addressing the issues we face as contemporary artists, designers and educators. One outgrowth of this collaborative approach has been the @art gallery.

Feedback is welcomed.

ad319 members also collaborate on the creation of electronic artwork. Their most recent piece is Body,Space,Memory, which exists as a separate Web site. It was very favorably reviewed by HotWired in April of 1995. A CD-ROM version of Body,Space,Memory was exhibited at the Centre George Pompidou in Paris from November 1994 to January 1995.

Additionally, Joseph Squier maintains his own site for Web-based artwork, which is called the place.

ad319 also curated an exhibition of electronic art for the Krannert Art Museum. Art as Signal: Inside the Loop was a survey of the best contemporary electronic art from around the world. It ran from November 1995 to January 1996. An accompanying CD-ROM catalog will be produced during the summer of 1996.

These projects were made possible through the substantial support of several groups at the University of Illinois; including the Center for Graphic Technology, the Advanced Information Technologies Group; and the Women, Information Technology, and Scholarship group.

AD319

http://www.art.uiuc.edu/@art/ad319/ad319.html

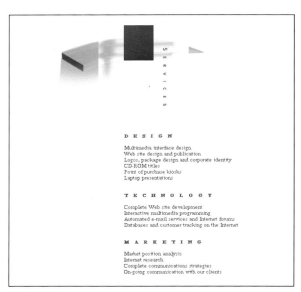

```
                            S
                            E
                            R
                            V
                            I
                            C
                            E
                            S

D E S I G N

Multimedia interface design
Web site design and publication
Logos, package design and corporate identity
CD-ROM titles
Point of purchase kiosks
Laptop presentations

T E C H N O L O G Y

Complete Web site development
Interactive multimedia programming
Automated e-mail services and Internet forums
Databases and customer tracking on the Internet

M A R K E T I N G

Market position analysis
Internet research
Complete communications strategies
On-going communication with our clients
```

AVALANCHE

http://www.avsi.com/

USING STRUCTURAL TAGS as they were never meant to be used adds new layout options. Using five <BLOCKQUOTE> tags (as in the ad319 page, left) creates a deep indent. Multiple <LI> tags (as used in the page from Avalanche's old site, above) creates a similar white space. (The headings in Avalanche's page were created using <PRE>.) The Sito site uses straightforward list layout, but adds space around its intro text with <BLOCKQUOTE>. Using HTML 2.0 codes, like these, rather than the HTML 3.2 table tags or the HTML 4.0 style sheets that would create the same effect, ensures that the intended effect will be seen in even the oldest browsers.

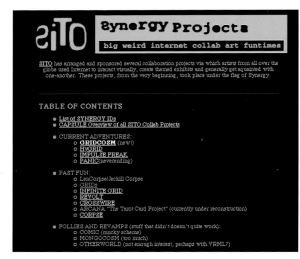

ED STASNY

http://www.sito.org/synergy/

Controlling Layout With <PRE>

An HTML 2.0 trick that deserves special mention is the <PRE> (preformatted text) tag, which was created to let page authors specify an exact layout for text. Any text between <PRE> and </PRE> tags is displayed exactly as it is typed, including extra spaces and any returns (which are usually ignored inside other tags). Using <PRE>, designers can arrange text painstakingly with the space bar—an effect especially useful for poetry or for other layouts in which the placement of sparse text is key. By default, most browsers display <PRE> text as 10-point Courier.

TEXT TAGGED AS <PRE> is laid out exactly as it is typed in the HTML file (right), allowing designers to lay out text precisely. By default, <PRE> text is displayed in the Courier typeface.

JULIET MARTIN
http://www.bway.net/~juliet/oooxxxooo/Parenthesis.html

START TAG	ATTRIBUTES	END TAG	EXPLANATION
<PRE>		</PRE>	Marks text that should be laid out exactly as typed

THE ALIGN= ATTRIBUTE for the <IMG> tag lets designers wrap text around graphics. The *hspace=* and *vspace=* attributes create space between the image and the surrounding text.

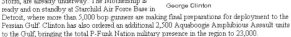

Clinton Threatens To Drop Da Bomb On Iraq

CHOCOLATE CITY--In an address before an emergency session of Parliament Monday, George Clinton said he is prepared to drop Da Bomb on Iraq if Saddam Hussein does not loosen up and comply with U.N. weapons inspectors by the Clinton-imposed deadline of March 1.

"For Saddam Hussein to refuse to let U.N. officials inspect Iraqi weapons facilities as per the terms of Iraq's 1991 Gulf War surrender is decidedly unfunky of him," Clinton said. "While the decision to drop Da Bomb is never an easy one, unless Saddam gets down with this whole U.N.-inspection thang and seriously refunkatizes his stance by March 1, we will have no choice but to tear the roof off Baghdad."

Preparations for the military strike, dubbed Operation Supergroovalisticprosifunkstication Storm, are already underway. The Mothership is ready and on standby at Starchild Air Force Base in

George Clinton

Detroit, where more than 5,000 bop gunners are making final preparations for deployment to the Persian Gulf. Clinton has also ordered an additional 2,500 Aquaboogie Amphibious Assault units to the Gulf, bringing the total P-Funk Nation military presence in the region to 23,000.

According to General William "Bootsy" Collins, the primary goal of the ground assault is to breach Hussein's presidential palace, capture the Iraqi leader, and "put some serious funk in his trunk."

Collins acknowledged that the mission would not be easy.

JACK SZWERGOLD/ANDREW WELYCZKO
http://www.theonion.com/onion3307/clintondropsdabomb.html

Orphaned Tags

Most of the extensions introduced by Netscape and Microsoft were deemed useful and were later incorporated into official HTML. But not all of them. The history of HTML is littered with tags that failed to enter the language because they were considered too annoying or too antithetical to HTML principles or because they were replaced by standard HTML methods for achieving the same effects.

<BLINK> (blinking text), introduced by Netscape in Navigator 1.1, fell into the first category. Other orphaned tags include Microsoft's <MARQUEE> (a scrolling message across the browser window, introduced in Internet Explorer 2.0), and Netscape's <MULTICOL>, <SPACER>, and <LAYER> tags, which were introduced with Navigator 3.0 and 4.0, after the Web community clearly saw that such specific style tags were the wrong way to go about extending HTML.

These tags live on the browsers of the companies that introduced them, largely so that any pages created with them in the past will display correctly. But few Web designers still use them.

HTML Extensions and HTML 3.2

The layout tags described in HTML 3.2 actually crept onto the Web bit by bit, introduced piecemeal by early versions of Netscape's and Microsoft's browsers, as Netscape or Microsoft extensions (→**74**). These extensions included new structural tags, like those for tables (→**90**). Here, we'll talk about what we called style tags in the last chapter (→**72**): tags that were designed to control the way elements look on screen.

For layout purposes, perhaps the most important of the extensions was the *align=* attribute for the <IMG> tag (→**124**), which allowed designers to wrap text around graphics. Used straightforwardly, the new attributes allowed designers to place graphics at the right or left margin, with text wrapping around them as in a magazine layout. The accompanying *vspace=* and *hspace=* attributes were used to create space between the graphic and the surrounding text. Even more cleverly, though, designers used it to wrap text around graphics with transparent backgrounds (→**122**), opening up expanses of white space on HTML pages for the first time.

Other tags that gave designers a bit of control were the <CENTER> tag, allowing designers to center text and graphics on the page, and Microsoft's *leftmargin=* and *topmargin=* attributes for the <BODY> tag, creating a way to add space around the edges of a page without resorting to <BLOCKQUOTE>.

As you can see, the controls were far from rich, but Web designers got some great mileage out of them, creating some surprisingly elegant pages.

The next step forward, introduced in Navigator 2.0 and adopted by Internet Explorer 3.0 (and then canonized by HTML 3.2) were the table and frame tags, structural tags that allowed designers to create a real grid for Web pages.

START TAG	ATTRIBUTES	END TAG	EXPLANATION
<BODY>		</BODY>	Marks the text to be displayed in the browser window
	leftmargin=*n*		Sets a left margin, described as a number of pixels
	topmargin=*n*		Sets a top margin, described as a number of pixels
<CENTER>		</CENTER>	Marks text that should be centered in the window
<HR>			Inserts a horizontal rule
	align="right" OR "left" OR "center"		Specifiies the rule's placement
	color="#*RRGGBB*" OR "*name*"		A color for the rule, specified in hexadecimal or as a color name
	noshade		Removes the rule's default drop shadow
	size=*n*		The width (height) of the rule, in pixels
	width=*n* OR "*n%*"		The length of the rule, in pixels or as a percentage of the window width
<MULTICOL>		</MULTICOL>	Marks text that should be set in multiple columns
	cols=*n*		The number of columns
	gutter=*n*		The amount of space between columns, in pixels
	width=*n*		The width of the column set, in pixels
<SPACER>		</SPACER>	Creates a blank space in the page layout
	align="left" OR "right" OR "top" OR "texttop" OR "middle" OR "absmiddle" OR "baseline" OR "bottom" OR "absbottom"		For *type=block*, tells the browser how to wrap the adjoining text around the space
	height=*n*, width=*n*		For *type=block*, the width and height of the empty space
	size=*n*		For *type=horizontal* or *type=vertical*, the size of the empty space, in pixels
	type="horizontal" OR "vertical" OR "block"		Tells the browser to create a space in the current line (*horizontal*), to create a vertical space above the next item (*vertical*), or to create a rectangular space (*block*)

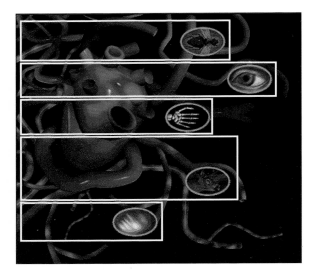

```
<HTML><HEAD><TITLE>B Domonkos Home</TITLE></HEAD>
<BODY BGCOLOR="#000000"
BACKGROUND="../images/backhome.gif">

<TABLE CELLPADDING="0">
<TR>
<TD WIDTH="349" HEIGHT="68" ALIGN=RIGHT VALIGN=BOTTOM>
<A HREF="illustration.html"><IMG SRC="../images/fly.gif" HEIGHT="61"
WIDTH="84" BORDER="0"></A></TD>
</TR>
</TABLE>

<TABLE CELLPADDING="0">
<TR>
<TD WIDTH="428" HEIGHT="52" ALIGN=RIGHT VALIGN=TOP>
<A HREF="movies.html"><IMG SRC="../images/eye.gif" HEIGHT="57"
WIDTH="82" BORDER="0"></A></TD>
</TR>
</TABLE>

<TABLE CELLPADDING="0">
<TR>
<TD WIDTH="320" HEIGHT="61" ALIGN=RIGHT VALIGN=BOTTOM>
<A HREF="3d.html"><IMG SRC="../images/hand.gif" HEIGHT="60"
WIDTH="81" BORDER="0"></A></TD>
</TR>
</TABLE>

<TABLE CELLPADDING="0">
<TR>
<TD WIDTH="361" HEIGHT="110" ALIGN=RIGHT VALIGN=BOTTOM>
<A HREF="blueroom.html"><IMG SRC="../images/blue.gif"
HEIGHT="66" WIDTH="92" BORDER="0"></A></TD>
</TR>
</TABLE>
```

Page Layout With Tables

HTML's table layout tools were designed with traditional tables in mind—the kind that hold statistics within a page—but designers quickly adopted them for structuring whole pages. With tables, designers can specify different-width columns to break up a page horizontally and discrete rows to control vertical space. Table cells can include text, graphics, and even other tables.

HTML tables don't provide the same kind of flexibility you can get from page layout programs such as QuarkXPress or PageMaker. The grids they create can't accommodate overlapping columns or some other niceties that add the sophisticated asymmetry possible with print layouts. In the environment of the Web, tables can also be problematic for other reasons. Complex tables can choke some browsers, and the fact that visitors' font and screen sizes are unpredictable means that fixed-size rows and columns may cut off parts of the table's content from view. (Table cells can also be flexible, expanding with the cells' contents and reflowing as viewers change their window sizes.) On the other hand, tables do allow designers to specify, to the pixel, exactly where text or images will be placed on a page—a control they never had before.

BILL DOMONKOS
http://www.bdom.com/documents/homepage.html

HTML TABLES let you position items at particular pixel locations on screen. In this example, the designer uses table cells of different widths and heights to stagger the graphic buttons (aligned at the bottom right of each cell) on top of a background graphic.

Patrolling Despair
by Olivier Laude

These photographs were taken along the U.S.-Mexican border between San Diego and Tijuana, where a large number of undocumented immigrants cross into the United States in search of seasonal work - and hope for more. Some commute daily between the two very dissimilar countries, while others seek more permanence in their lives. Some cross into the States to visit, like tourists, for a week or a day, knowing they would never be admitted by U.S. authorities. Others sell sweaters or food within a few feet of the border to those wishing to cross with bare necessities.

Then there are the human smugglers, some good, some bad; apprentice smugglers (usually small children and teenagers); drug pushers as well as thieves of all ages; families with small children, grandmothers, single mothers on their way to meet a distant husband; and a lot of young healthy men looking for work, adventure, relatives - or simply because it's there. The border is a strange mixture of humor, fear, exploitation, everyday life, fortitude, resignation, strength and courage, not necessarily in that order. Every day this narrow stretch of land sees thousands treck across its marshes and dried river beds, and every day it's the same story but with different characters, except for those who were caught and try again. Any permanance or familiarity is bred in those who remain, those servicing this continous migration: border patrol officers, thieves, smugglers and - although they are the minority - a few unfortunate souls lost to drugs, mental illness or to the world.

The photographs in this series attempt to capture the ongoing trials, hardships and good spirits of this continous flow of people immediately before and after crossing the border. I focused solely on the area where a wall, erected by the U.S. Army Corps of Engineers in 1992, serves as a reminder of the difficulty - futility - of trying to stop undocumented immigration into the States. This story concentrates, not on the interception efforts of the U.S. Border Patrol, but rather on the border as a strip of land where the lives of undocumented immigrants are at their most vulnerable and volatile.

Here their lives become entirely shaped by only one goal: the actual flight across an international border dotted on both sides with obstacles both natural and manmade. This story is about routine events which have taken place and continue to take place every day of every year, an epic struggle that has become almost mundane and habitual and for which no real solution is in sight.

I spent about 10 days living on the border, but daytime on the border is generally dull and uneventful; instead I photographed between sunset and dawn. Those nights might have been typical or extraordinary to anyone on the border at that time. They might have been life threatening, terrifying or just plain fun depending on whom you talked to. Some might have been homesick or glad to be away from home, while others prayed, cursed their fate or laughed at it and moved on. I came away from the border thinking that there is probably no better way to characterize it than as a microcosm of both Mexican and U.S. culture, both equally ignorant of the other and bent on remaining that way. The human traffic have better things to think about, and Americans have relegated decisions to their elected representatives, border patrol officers and a handful of activists on both sides of the political and geographical fence.

AMY FRANCESCHINI/DAVID KARAM/MICHAEL MACRONE/OLIVIER LAUDE
http://atlasmagazine.com/photo/laude_despair/index.html

AVALANCHE
http://www.ear1.com/

HTML TABLES can create strict grids or more freeform shapes.

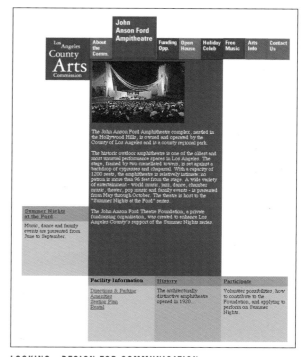

LOOKING - DESIGN FOR COMMUNICATION
http://www.lacountyarts.org/ford.html

START TAG	ATTRIBUTES	END TAG	EXPLANATION
\<TABLE\>		\</TABLE\>	Surround all the tags that make up the table
	align="left" OR "right" OR "center"		The table's alignment in the window
	background="*URL*"		An image file to be used as the table's background
	bgcolor="*#RRGGBB*" OR "*name*"		The color of the table's background, using RGB values (expressed in hexadecimal) or a color name
	border=*n*		A width for the table's border, in pixels. *border=0* means no border.
	cellpadding=n		The space between each cell's border and its contents, specified in pixels
	cellspacing=n		The space between each cell's contents, specified in pixels
	cols=n		The number of columns in the table
	height=*n*, width=*n* or *n*%		The table's total height and width, specified in pixels or (for width) as a percentage of the window size
	rules="none" OR "groups" OR "rows" OR "cols" OR "all"		Specifies which rules will appear in the table
\<CAPTION\>		\</CAPTION\>	Creates a caption for the table
\<COL\> **\<COLGROUP\>**		\</COLGROUP\>	Create column groupings. \<COL\> allows authors to set attributes for several columns at once; \<COLGROUP\> groups the columns structurally, so that they will be laid out together in a browser window.
	align="left" OR "right" OR "center" OR "justify" OR "char"		The alignment of the cells' contents
	span=n		The number of columns in the group
	valign="top" OR "middle" OR "bottom" OR "baseline"		The vertical alignment of the cell's contents relative to its borders
	width=*n* OR "0*"		A default width for each column in the group. "0*" means each column should be just wide enough to hold its contents.
\<TD\> **\<TH\>**		\</TD\> \</TH\>	Mark the data (\<TD\>) or heading (\<TH\>) that goes in each table cell
	align="left" OR "right" OR "center"		The data's alignment in the cell
	background="*URL*"		An image file to be used as the cell's background
	bgcolor="*#RRGGBB*" OR "*name*"		A color for the cell's background
	colspan=n		The number of columns the cell spans
	height=*n*, width=*n* OR *n*%		The height and width of the table cell, in pixels or (for width) as a percentage of the table size
	rowspan=*n*		The number of rows the cell spans
	valign="top" OR "middle" OR "bottom" OR "baseline"		The vertical alignment of the cell's contents relative to its borders
\<THEAD\> **\<TFOOT\>** **\<TBODY\>**		\</THEAD\> \</TFOOT\> \</TBODY\>	Group cells into a table heading, table footer, and table body, respectively. Browsers may scroll table bodies while leaving the header and footer in place.
\<TR\>		\</TR\>	Creates a new table row. \<TR\> and \</TR\> contain a set of table cells defined by \<TD\> and \<TH\>.
	align="left" OR "right" OR "center" OR "justify" OR "char"		The alignment of the contents of the row's cells
	bgcolor="#RRGGBB" OR "name"		A color for the table row's background
	valign="top" OR "middle" OR "bottom" OR "baseline"		The vertical alignment of the row's contents relative to the cell's borders

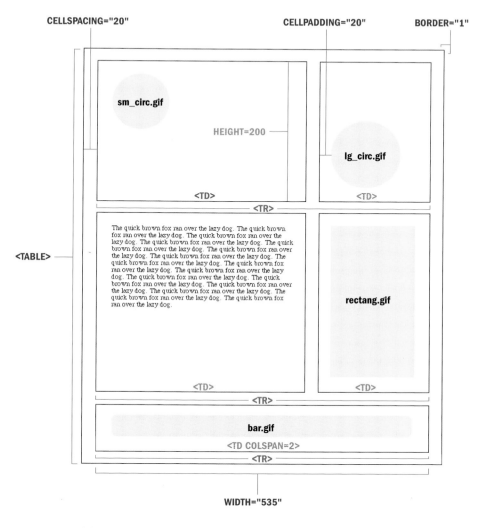

CELLSPACING="20"

CELLPADDING="20"

BORDER="1"

sm_circ.gif

HEIGHT=200

lg_circ.gif

<TD>

<TD>

<TR>

<TABLE>

The quick brown fox ran over the lazy dog. The quick brown fox ran over the lazy dog. The quick brown fox ran over the lazy dog. The quick brown fox ran over the lazy dog. The quick brown fox ran over the lazy dog. The quick brown fox ran over the lazy dog. The quick brown fox ran over the lazy dog. The quick brown fox ran over the lazy dog. The quick brown fox ran over the lazy dog. The quick brown fox ran over the lazy dog. The quick brown fox ran over the lazy dog. The quick brown fox ran over the lazy dog. The quick brown fox ran over the lazy dog.

rectang.gif

<TD>

<TD>

<TR>

bar.gif

<TD COLSPAN=2>

<TR>

WIDTH="535"

AN HTML TABLE is set up from a series of rows and columns. The <TABLE> tag's *width=*, *height=*, and other attributes define the overall dimensions of the table. Then the table is constructed row by row. A <TR> (table row) tag, creates each row; <TH> (table head) and <TD> (table data) tags mark the content of each cell. Cells can hold any kind of data, including graphics or other media.

```
<HTML>
<HEAD><TITLE>TABLE</TITLE></HEAD>
<BODY BGCOLOR="WHITE">

<TABLE WIDTH="535" BORDER="1" CELLSPACING="20"CELLPADDING="20">

    <TR ALIGN=LEFT>

        <TD VALIGN="TOP" HEIGHT="200">
        <IMG SRC="sm_circ.gif">
        </TD>

        <TD VALIGN="bottom">
        <IMG SRC="lg_circ.gif">
        </TD>

    </TR>

    <TR ALIGN=LEFT>

        <TD VALIGN="TOP">
        The contents of each cell is embedded  between &lt;TD&gt; (table
        data) tags. It can include graphics, plug-ins, or even other tables. You
        can align cell contents horizontally and vertically in a number of ways
        within the cell. The text (or other content) is inset by the number of
        pixels set in the cellpadding= attribute. You can set a specific height
        and width for a cell using the &lt;TD&gt; or &lt;TH&gt; tag's height=
        and width= tags. If you don't use those attributes, the cell will be as
        wide and tall as it needs to be to fit the cells' contents.
        <IMG SRC= "pixel.gif" WIDTH=300 HEIGHT="1">
        </TD >

        <TD>
        <IMG SRC="rectang.gif" WIDTH="140" HEIGHT="260">
        </TD>

    </TR>

    <TR ALIGN=CENTER>

        <TD COLSPAN=2>
        <IMG SRC="bar.gif">
        </TD>

    </TR>

</TABLE>

</BODY>
</HTML>
```

EACH PAGE OF THIS STORY (a feminist's musings on the significance of wearing sexy clothes) creates a different outfit out of frames. Readers literally undress the text. When they drag a frame border to resize the frame, text flows into the new window.

frames
An HTML feature that lets designers split the browser window into separate units, each of which can hold a separate HTML file and can scroll and be updated separately from the rest of the window.

inline frame
A frame that is not part of a frameset but is defined individually.

JASON HUANG/YOSHI SODEOKA
http://www.word.com/desire/garterbelt/

Dividing the Window With Frames

Similar in some ways to tables, but offering some different advantages (and disadvantages) are **frames**. Like tables, frames let designers divide a window into any number of horizontal and vertical rows and columns. But unlike table cells, each frame can hold a separate HTML file, and each frame can scroll separately.

Frames can be individually named. That name can then be used as the target for a hyperlink (→**78**) so that a click in one frame can change the contents of another. This makes frames a natural solution for setting off the navigation controls for a site; the navigation controls always remain on screen while new pages are loaded into a separate frame.

Like table rows and columns, frames can be fixed in size or scale to fit the content. They can also be designed with or without borders and scrollbars.

HTML 4.0 includes a new feature called **inline frames**, free-floating frames that can be placed at any pixel coordinate within a window.

In the opinion of many Web users, frames have been a mixed blessing. You can't print or bookmark a page that's inside a frameset, and some users find navigating within frames confusing. Even given these caveats, though, frames can sometimes provide a practical solution to Web design problems.

AVALANCHE

http://www.oneclub.com/

WINNERS OF THE ONE SHOW are listed in the right-hand frame of this site. Clicking on a link there displays the selected work in the large center frame.

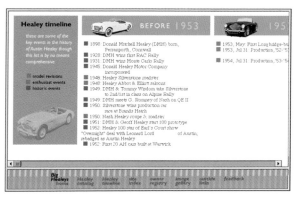

ROGER LOS

http://www.austinhealey.com/big.html

SITE NAVIGATION is set off in a frame across the bottom of the Austin-Healey site. On this page, a timeline fills the upper frame; users scroll horizontally to move through the years.

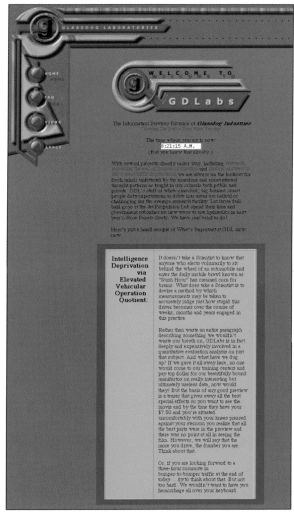

LANCE ARTHUR

http://www.glassdog.com/the_lab/toppage.html

A CONTROL PANEL and the site's branding are set off in frames across the top and left side of this site for GlassDog Labs.

Frames are a great concept, but the way they're implemented doesn't work that well. We no longer use them.

FRED SOTHERLAND, CNET

START TAG	ATTRIBUTES	END TAG	EXPLANATION
\<FRAMESET>		\</FRAMESET>	Encloses all the tags that make up a set of frames
	border=*n*		Sets a border (*1* or "*yes*") or omits a border (*0* or "*no*") around a frame. (Microsoft's browser uses the numbers, Netscape's the words.)
	bordercolor="#*RRGGBB*" OR "*name*"		A color for the border, specified as RGB values (in hexadecimal) or as a color name
	cols="*col1, col2, col3, ...*"		Sets up a frameset as a set of "columns." The set of columns is specifed by giving a width for each one. Widths can be specified in pixels, as a percentage of the window size, or as an asterisk (*), meaning that the column should take up the remaining space. If more than one column is specified with an asterisk, the space is divided evenly among them.
	frameborder=0 OR 1 OR "yes" OR "no"		Sets a border (*1* or "*yes*") or omits a border (*0* or "*no*") around a frameset. (Microsoft's browser uses the numbers, Netscape's the words.)
	rows="*row1, row2, row3,...*"		Sets up a frameset as a set of "rows." The set of rows is specifed by giving a width for each one. Widths can be specified in pixels, as a percentage of the window size, or as an asterisk (*), meaning that the row should take up the remaining space. If more than one row is specified with an asterisk, the space is divided evenly among them.
\<FRAME>			Specifes the attributes of one frame within a frameset
	bordercolor="#*RRGGBB*" OR "*name*"		A color for the border, specified as RGB values (in hexadecimal) or as a color name
	frameborder=0 OR 1 OR "yes" OR "no"		Sets a border (*1* or "*yes*") or omits a border (*0* or "*no*") around a frame.
	marginheight=*n*		Creates a margin at the top and bottom of the frame (specified in pixels)
	marginwidth=*n*		Creates a margin at the left and right sides of the frame (specified in pixels)
	name="*name*"		A target name for the frame (used by \<A> tags to send linked files to that particular frame)
	noresize		Prevents users from resizing the frame (by omitting the resize box)
	scrolling="yes" OR "no" OR "auto"		Includes or omits a scroll bar for the frame. By default (or using "*auto*") a scroll bar appears if the frame's contents go beyond its borders.
	src="*URL*"		The URL of the file to be placed in the frame
\<NOFRAMES>		\</NOFRAMES>	Marks content that should be displayed in browsers that don't support frames. Browsers that support frames ignore any code marked with \<NOFRAMES>.

FRAMESETS ARE SET UP either as a set of rows or as a set of columns. Multiple framesets can be nested to create columns within rows, or vice versa. Once the frameset is defined, individual \<FRAME> tags are used to name the content and set the style of each frame; a separate file is loaded into each frame. The \<NOFRAMES> tag sets off copy that will be shown on browsers (prior to Navigator 2.0 and Internet Explorer 3.0) that don't support frames. The \<IFRAME> tag, new in HTML 4.0, creates an inline frame.

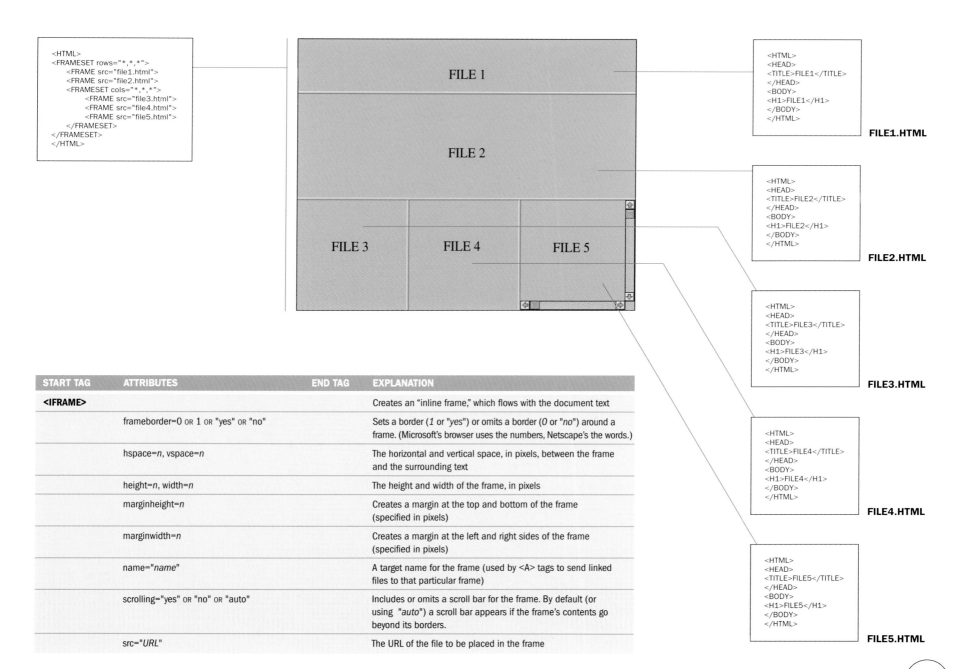

```
<HTML>
<FRAMESET rows="*,*,*">
    <FRAME src="file1.html">
    <FRAME src="file2.html">
    <FRAMESET cols="*,*,*">
        <FRAME src="file3.html">
        <FRAME src="file4.html">
        <FRAME src="file5.html">
    </FRAMESET>
</FRAMESET>
</HTML>
```

FILE 1

FILE 2

FILE 3   **FILE 4**   **FILE 5**

```
<HTML>
<HEAD>
<TITLE>FILE1</TITLE>
</HEAD>
<BODY>
<H1>FILE1</H1>
</BODY>
</HTML>
```
FILE1.HTML

```
<HTML>
<HEAD>
<TITLE>FILE2</TITLE>
</HEAD>
<BODY>
<H1>FILE2</H1>
</BODY>
</HTML>
```
FILE2.HTML

```
<HTML>
<HEAD>
<TITLE>FILE3</TITLE>
</HEAD>
<BODY>
<H1>FILE3</H1>
</BODY>
</HTML>
```
FILE3.HTML

```
<HTML>
<HEAD>
<TITLE>FILE4</TITLE>
</HEAD>
<BODY>
<H1>FILE4</H1>
</BODY>
</HTML>
```
FILE4.HTML

```
<HTML>
<HEAD>
<TITLE>FILE5</TITLE>
</HEAD>
<BODY>
<H1>FILE5</H1>
</BODY>
</HTML>
```
FILE5.HTML

START TAG	ATTRIBUTES	END TAG	EXPLANATION
<IFRAME>			Creates an "inline frame," which flows with the document text
	frameborder=0 OR 1 OR "yes" OR "no"		Sets a border (*1* or "*yes*") or omits a border (*0* or "*no*") around a frame. (Microsoft's browser uses the numbers, Netscape's the words.)
	hspace=*n*, vspace=*n*		The horizontal and vertical space, in pixels, between the frame and the surrounding text
	height=*n*, width=*n*		The height and width of the frame, in pixels
	marginheight=*n*		Creates a margin at the top and bottom of the frame (specified in pixels)
	marginwidth=*n*		Creates a margin at the left and right sides of the frame (specified in pixels)
	name="*name*"		A target name for the frame (used by <A> tags to send linked files to that particular frame)
	scrolling="yes" OR "no" OR "auto"		Includes or omits a scroll bar for the frame. By default (or using "*auto*") a scroll bar appears if the frame's contents go beyond its borders.
	src="*URL*"		The URL of the file to be placed in the frame

```
<STYLE>
   H1 { font-family : Helvetica ; font-size : 14 pt ; color : red }
   H2 { font-family : Helvetica ; font-size : 12 pt ; color : black }
</STYLE>
```

SELECTOR   PROPERTY   VALUE

STYLE SHEETS ARE simply lists of layout specifications for different HTML elements. In CSS, each specification consists of a selector, which names the element the styles apply to, and a list of style properties and their values, enclosed in brackets. (The CSS specification defines the possible properties and values.) A colon separates the property from its value. Multiple property settings can be provided for a single element; in such a list, the property and value pairs are separated by semicolons.

cascading style sheets (CSS)
The most widely supported style sheet language for Web publishing.

CSS1
The first version of the cascading style sheet language.

DSSSL
Document semantics and style specification language, a popular style language for SGML publishing.

style sheet
Layout specifications added to an HTML file.

XSL
Extensible style language, a style language under development as a companion to XML.

Specifying Layout With Style Sheets

Beginning with HTML 3.2, HTML includes support for a layout solution that, at last, strikes a balance between designers' need to control the layout of Web pages and HTML's premise of specifying structure, not layout, to ensure a document's usefulness across applications. That solution, which promises to revolutionize Web design, is **style sheets**.

Web style sheets work much like the style sheets used in popular word processing and page layout programs. Standard HTML structural tags (<H1>, <P>, and so on) mark each element. Instead of using default layouts for each element, though, browsers will look for specifications—style sheets—defined by the designer. (Browsers will fall back on the default if no style sheets are provided or if they don't support style sheets.)

Just as with style sheets in word processing and page layout programs, a single style definition can be used to style every instance of a certain element with a single command, and designs for entire documents—even entire sites—can be easily changed by simply changing the centrally defined style attributes.

Exactly what style sheets can do is controlled by the specific style sheet language you use. Right now, the standard style sheet language for the Web is called **cascading style sheets** (**CSS** for short). Other style sheet languages, such as **DSSSL** (document semantics and style specification language), were developed for use with other applications of SGML. And **XSL** (→**145**), the extensible style language, is being developed as a companion for XML (→**142**). For now, though, CSS is center of attention: **CSS1** (the first version of CSS) is supported by Microsoft's and Netscape's current browsers.

A style sheet is simply a list of layout specifications for each HTML element in a document. CSS gives a lot more control over HTML layout than has any solution that has come before, letting designers specify such attributes as point size, line spacing (leading), and indents for text. And CSS layout specs can use standard design and typographic measurements like points, picas, and ems, as well as pixels and percentages, to describe a page.

You can add stylesheets to your Web pages in a few different ways, depending on how widely you want the styles to be used. You can import external style sheets (describing, say, standard styles used by your company or publication) using the <LINK> tag in a document's heading. You can use the HTML <STYLE> tag in the document's heading to add document-wide styles. Or you can use a *style=* attribute with just about any HTML tag, to describe styles that pertain only to that element. (For instance, you could add a style property to a <DIV> tag to set styles for the elements within that division or to a <P> tag to affect a

START TAG	ATTRIBUTES	END TAG	EXPLANATION
<STYLE>		</STYLE>	Enclose the style sheets for an HTML document
	type="*MIME-type*"		The style sheet language, defined as a MIME type (e.g., css/text)
	media="screen" OR "print" OR "projection" OR "braille" OR "aural" OR "all"		The media types the style sheet should be used for
<LINK>		</LINK>	Links an external document to the current file
	href="*URL*"		The location of the linked document
	rel="*description*"		The relationship of the linked file to the current document. For style sheets, the setting would be *rel="stylesheet"*
	type="*MIME-type*"		The MIME type of the linked content; for style sheets, usually "text/css"

SEVERAL STYLE SHEETS can be combined in a single document. CSS's cascading order defines which style definitions take precedence when more than one is defined.

Specific to element instance

Specific to element class

Defined by author as important

Defined by user as important

Included with page

User default

Browser default

What Cascading Means

The name "cascading style sheets" comes from the way style sheets are applied to a document's elements. A certain element may have several styles associated with it. The browser uses a default style sheet for everything it displays. Site visitors may also specify a particular style sheet they like as their own default. The page author may import a companywide style sheet using the <LINK> tag, apply additional document-specific styles using the <STYLE> tag in the page heading, and then add special treatments to particular paragraphs or phrases in the document's body. The CSS specification spells out exactly which styles get priority in such cases.

As a rule, each style definition listed in the chart at left takes precedence over the one under it: The user's preference overrides the browser's default, and as a rule, the author's styles override the user's. (Users can override author styles by not accepting external style sheets or by naming some of their preferences as "important.") And more specific specifications override less specific sets.

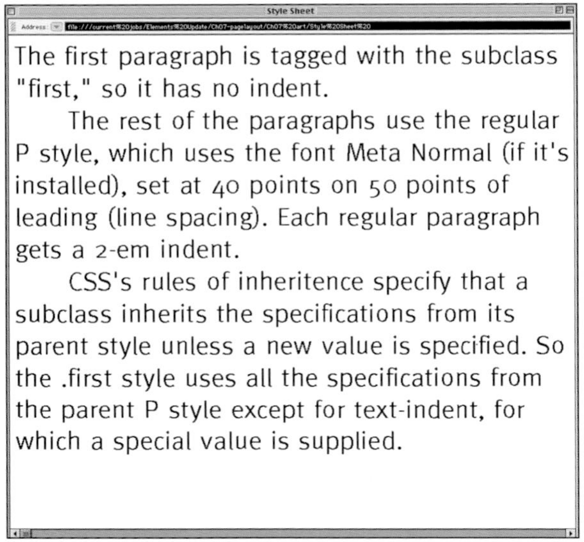

```
<HEAD>
<TITLE>Style Sheet</TITLE>
<STYLE TYPE="text/css">
P       {
            font-family: Meta-Normal, Syntax, Helvetica, Arial;
            font-size: 40pt;
            text-indent: 2 em;
            text-align: justify;
            line-height: 50 pt;
            }
.first    {
            text-indent: 0 em;
            }

</STYLE>
</HEAD>

<BODY BGCOLOR="white">

<P CLASS="first">The first paragraph is tagged with the subclass "first," so it
has no indent. . </P>

<P> The rest of the paragraphs use the regular P style, which uses the font Meta
Normal (if it's installed), set at 40 points on 50 points of leading (line spacing).
Each regular paragraph gets a 2-em indent.</P>

<P> CSS's rules of inheritence specify that a subclass inherits the specifications
from its parent style unless a new value is specified. So the .first style uses all
the specifications from the parent P style except for text-indent, for which a spe-
cial value is supplied. </P>

</BODY>
```

THE STYLE SHEET SHOWN HERE creates a standard style for paragraphs and another for a special class of the P element (P.first) used for first paragraphs under headings. Notice the use of the *font* property, a shorthand notation you can use to combine several font specifications. Also notice CSS's inheritance rules at work here. The subclass (P.first) inherits all the specifications from the parent element (P), so only the differences need to be specified in the subclass's style definition.

class
In HTML 4.0, a group of elements defined by the author. You add an element to a class using the *class=* attribute. With cascading style sheets, designers can assign layout attributes to all the members of a class.

inheritance
In CSS, the principle that elements use the same style properties as any element that contains them, unless those properties are specifically overridden.

single paragraph.) For style sheets to work, browsers must support those tags (introduced with HTML 3.2) as well as the style sheet language itself.

CSS coding is made somewhat simpler by the idea of **inheritance**. In CSS, an element inherits the style attributes of its parent element: for example, text tagged as <EM> would inherit the settings from the <P> (or other) element that contains it. A <P> element could inherit styles given to a <DIV> element above it, or even to the <HTML> tag itself. That way, a page author can define general page attributes (such as a standard typeface or page margin, for instance) just once, then add to or override those styles as needed for particular elements.

An especially powerful use of style sheets is the ability to go beyond the basic HTML tag set by creating element **classes**. Say you had a document for which you wanted to specify two types of paragraph styles: one for standard paragraphs, with an indent on the first line, and another, with no indent, for the first paragraph under a heading. You could tag each standard paragraph with the standard <P> style and create a special class of the <P> tag for the first paragraphs under heads, using the HTML 3.2 *class=* attribute (*<P class="first">*, for instance). Your style sheet could then provide styles for each type (as shown on the example on this page). In that way, you can essentially extend the HTML tag set indefinitely.

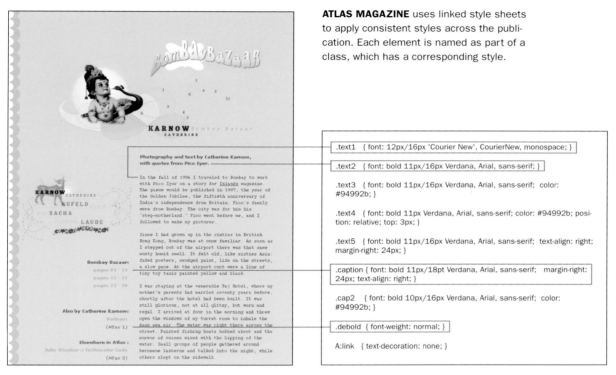

ATLAS MAGAZINE uses linked style sheets to apply consistent styles across the publication. Each element is named as part of a class, which has a corresponding style.

.text1 { font: 12px/16px 'Courier New', CourierNew, monospace; }

.text2 { font: bold 11px/16px Verdana, Arial, sans-serif; }

.text3 { font: bold 11px/16px Verdana, Arial, sans-serif; color: #94992b; }

.text4 { font: bold 11px Verdana, Arial, sans-serif; color: #94992b; position: relative; top: 3px; }

.text5 { font: bold 11px/16px Verdana, Arial, sans-serif; text-align: right; margin-right: 24px; }

.caption { font: bold 11px/18pt Verdana, Arial, sans-serif; margin-right: 24px; text-align: right; }

.cap2 { font: bold 10px/16px Verdana, Arial, sans-serif; color: #94992b; }

.debold { font-weight: normal; }

A:link { text-decoration: none; }

BOTH NETSCAPE AND MICROSOFT support cascading style sheets in their browsers, beginning with Microsoft Internet Explorer 3.0 and Netscape Navigator 4.0. Current versions of both browsers support most of CSS1 and the parts of CSS2 having to do with CSS positioning.

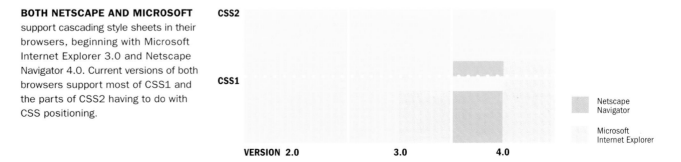

Netscape Navigator

Microsoft Internet Explorer

```
<HTML>
<HEAD>
<TITLE>cssbox</TITLE>
<STYLE>

#square{

        background-color: green;
        padding: 15 px;
        border-width: 3 px;
        border-color: red;
        border-style: solid;
        margin-top: .5 in;
        margin-bottom: 40 px;
        margin-left: 40 px;
        margin-right: 2 in;
        width: auto;
        height: auto;
        clear: both


        }


</STYLE>

<BODY BGCOLOR="white">

<DIV ID="square">

Come back, the Caterpillar called after her. I've something important to
say!

</DIV>


<BLOCKQUOTE>This sounded promising, certainly. Alice turned and
came back again.</BLOCKQUOTE>


</BODY>
<HTML>
```

IN CSS, EVERY ELEMENT is treated as if it were in a box. CSS properties can be used to control things like the box's size and the use of padding, borders, and margins. Other properties can be used to add background colors, scroll bars, and other features to the box, as if the box were its own frame.

Boxes: The Layout Model of CSS

To begin to understand the layout capabilities of CSS, you must first understand that CSS treats each HTML element as if it were in a box. That means you can add things like background colors, borders, and other details to any element, just as if it were in its own table cell. CSS's box properties can be applied to any HTML element, allowing you to adjust the margin and "padding" around it as well as adding a border of any style or color. In addition, you can use CSS's color properties to not only color the type but also to add a background image or background color behind the element, filling the element's box.

By default, an element's box will grow to fit the content inside it, but you can also use the *width* and *height* properties to specify a certain size for the box. (If the size is too small for the box's content, a scroll bar can be made to appear, as if the element were in its own frame) (→**94**).

Understanding CSS boxes and the CSS properties that control them will let you fine-tune a page's measurements to an unprecedented degree. It will also help you understand CSS positioning, a way of using CSS to create complex, layered layouts, as we'll describe in the next section.

CSS Positioning

CSS positioning is not actually part of CSS1 but was introduced to the W3C as a separate proposal and was adopted by both Netscape and Microsoft in version 4.0 of their browsers. (The principles of CSS are built into CSS2.) With CSS positioning, you simply add CSS properties to tell the browser just how and where you want each element's box placed on screen.

The first decision to make is *how* you want the box positioned: with "absolute" or "relative" positioning. Absolute positioning places the element at a named coordinate in the browser window. Relative positioning positions it relative to its default position or to another element that contains it. Another positioning property, *float,* floats the element right or left, to the parent element's boundary, and lets text flow around it.

The position on the page is set with the *top* and *left* properties, measured from the top left of the browser window (or parent element) and described in terms of an x-y grid. (You can specify placement in just about any unit you wish: pixels, ems, points, picas, or percentages of window size.) You can also specify a **z-index**, or layering order, for the element, giving the item a position above or below other elements on the page. By default, the element is positioned wherever it falls in the flow of the document, with a box size large enough to contain the element's content, and a

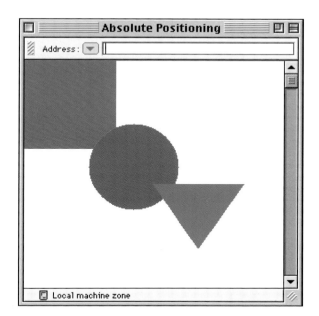

CSS POSITIONING lets you name the exact window coordinates for each element. The *top* and *left* properties name the window coordinates for each iitem. The *z-index=* property defines its layering position. The <DIV> tag separates the document into its component units, and its *id=* attribute provides a name by which each document section can be called from the style sheet.

```
<HEAD>
<TITLE>Absolute Positioning</TITLE>
<STYLE>
#square{ position: absolute; top: 0px; left: 0 px; z-index: 0; }

#circle{ position: absolute; top: 80px; left: 80 px; z-index: 1; }

#triangle{ position: absolute; top: 160px; left: 160 px; z-index: 2; }
</STYLE>
</HEAD>

<BODY BGCOLOR="white">

<DIV ID="square">
<IMG SRC= "square.gif" width="100" height="100"></DIV>

<DIV ID="circle">
<IMG SRC= "circle.gif" width="100" height="100"></DIV>

<DIV ID="triangle">
<IMG SRC= "triangle.gif" width="100" height="100"></DIV>

</BODY>
```

z-index
In CSS positioning, the layering order of an element. The term refers to the element's position in an x-y-z Cartesian coordinate system.

START TAG	ATTRIBUTES	END TAG	EXPLANATION
\<DIV\>		\</DIV\>	Groups the enclosed elements so that the attributes of the \<DIV\> tag apply to those elements
	align="left" OR "center" OR "right" OR "justify"		The alignment of the grouped elements
	id="*name*"		A name for the group. In CSS positioning, this name is used by the style sheet.
\<SPAN\>		\</SPAN\>	Groups a set of words inside a block-level element
	align="left" OR "center" OR "right" OR "justify"		The alignment of the grouped words
	id="*name*"		A name for the group. In CSS positioning, the name is used to identify the group in the style sheet.

FABRIC8
http://www.fabric8.com/

CSS POSITIONING and JavaScript are used to move the mannequin into position and place her speech balloons on Fabric8, a site that spotlights San Francisco's independent clothing designers.

```
<BODY BGCOLOR="#99CC66" TEXT="#000000" LINK="#663300"
VLINK="#669900" ALINK="#000000">

<DIV ID="lyrFeature" STYLE="position:absolute; left:10px; top:8px;
width:119px; height:30px; z-index:501" CLASS="nav">

<A HREF="feature.html" ONMOUSEOVER="rollover(1,'just one
of the many<BR>great products we offer',event); return true;"
onmouseout="rollover(0,'',event)">feature</A>

</DIV>

<DIV ID="lyrList" STYLE="position:absolute; left:130px; top:8px;
width:150px; height:30px; z-index:502" CLASS="nav">

<A HREF="list.html" ONMOUSEOVER="rollover(1,'join our<BR>
international scene',event)" ONMOUSEOUT="rollover(0,'',event)">
<NOBR>mailing list</NOBR></A>

</DIV>

<DIV ID="lyrLinks" STYLE="position:absolute; left:275px; top:8px;
width:150px; height:30px; z-index:503" CLASS="nav">

<A HREF="links.html" ONMOUSEOVER="rollover(1,'web styles we
dig',event)" ONMOUSEOUT="rollover(0,'',event)"><NOBR>linky
dinks</NOBR></A>

</DIV>
```

z-index depending on the order in which the elements are named in the file.

The next question is how you break up your document into the various layers that you'll place on the page. You'll need to group elements that you want to place together and give a name to each group so that you can identify it in your style sheet. Currently, the way you do this is with HTML's <DIV> or <SPAN> tags.

<DIV> and <SPAN> are useful whenever you want to assign an attribute to more than one item. The difference between them is that <DIV> (division) is used to group a set of elements (such as a group of paragraphs), while <SPAN> is used inside an element (to group a set of words). With CSS positioning, you use <DIV> and <SPAN> to define each group you want to position separately in your document. The tags' *id=* attribute lets you give each group a name by which you can address it from the style sheet.

CSS positioning is a cornerstone of dynamic HTML (→**76**), a group of technologies that lets Web designers control HTML elements in all sorts of new ways within the newest browsers. (In fact, CSS positioning is sometimes referred to as DHTML positioning.) In later chapters, we'll talk about how CSS positioning can be used with JavaScript to animate pages and make them interactive. Here, we'll just point out that CSS positioning can give you all the page layout controls of QuarkXPress or PageMaker. In the long run, it should

also lead to dramatically simplified HTML coding, creating a clean and logical way to describe a page's layout, with no ambiguity and without using complex embedded tables and other kinds of troublesome, nonstandard HTML. Once it's better supported by browsers, CSS positioning should finally be the key to powerful, WYSIWYG page layout for the Web.

Now that you understand how a page's architecture can be constructed with CSS positioning, we'll talk about how CSS relates to other technologies for controlling a page's finer points: its typographic layout.

Online: Page Layout With HTML

Cascading Style Sheets and CSS Positioning
http://www.hotwired.com/webmonkey/stylesheets/
http://www.microsoft.com/workshop/author/default.asp#css
http://www.useit.com/alertbox/9707a.html
http://www.w3.org/Style/css/
http://www.webreview.com/guides/style/

Dynamic HTML
http://www.dhtmlzone.com/
http://www.hotwired.com/webmonkey/dynamic_html/
http://www.insidedhtml.com/
http://www.microsoft.com/workshop/author/dhtml
http://www.projectcool.com/developer/dynamic/
http://www.webdeveloper.com/categories/advhtml/
http://www.webreview.com/wr/pub/Dynamic_HTML/

Frames
http://www.cnet.com/Content/Builder/Authoriing/Frames/
http://www.projectcool.com/developer/alchemy/04-frames.html
http://www.webreference.com/dev/frames/

Tables
http://www.projectcool.com/developer/alchemy/03-tables.html

Dynamic HTML is the answer to a designer's prayers. Finally we can control placement to the pixel. We can create compelling and dynamic sites that aren't nightmarish to download. The ability to layer things has made me the happiest webgeek on earth. The fun has just begun.

ANNETTE LOUDON, CONSTRUCT

Web Typography

Many designers think of type as the primary building block of a page's design, and those designers have viewed the Web with dismay. The options for handling type on Web pages have been severely limited, but with the introduction of style sheets, all that is changing: Web designers may finally have power over typeface, type size, leading, and the other traditional specifications of a typographer's art. As with all other aspects of Web design, though, what actually appears on a visitor's screen depends more on what the browser can do than on what's specified.

Mastering Web typography is a matter of understanding the history of HTML, the capabilities of different browsers, and the technologies that drive it all. Understanding Web typography also means understanding something about how computer applications get access to fonts—the process that defines what typefaces you can and can't use on the Web.

In this chapter, we'll talk about how designers can control typography in both old and new browsers, using basic HTML, graphics, and HTML 3.2's <FONT> tag, as well as style sheets. Last, we'll describe how downloadable fonts may—or may not—solve the biggest problem of Web typography once and for all.

Basic System Fonts: Why Most Web Pages Are in Times

As anyone who has ever shared a layout with a colleague or shipped a file to a service bureau knows, most file formats don't actually save fonts in the file itself. Instead, most files simply include information about what fonts are used in the document. In order to be displayed, those fonts must be installed in the system of the computer displaying the file. If the right font isn't there, the system uses a default typeface—usually Courier on Macs, Arial on PCs.

You can see what a problem that would cause on the Web. Since there's no way of knowing which fonts each visitor to your site will have installed, it does little good to specify a font in the file. Accordingly, early HTML didn't include any commands at all for specifying fonts. HTML 2.0 did, however, assume the reader had at least two fonts installed: a regular text font and an alternate, **monospaced**, font, used for special purposes.

In order to display text at all, though, a browser needs to select some typeface to display it in. Since Times and Courier ship with just about every operating system, most browser manufacturers assign those two typefaces as the default text and monospaced typefaces, respectively, and then allow individual users to assign new defaults in their own browsers.

As we'll describe in the next sections of this chapter, browsers have begun to support methods that designers can use to influence which fonts a document will be displayed in—including ways to download fonts along with the HTML file to make sure they're available to the browser. Until those technologies are ironed out, though, Web designers' font choices are, realistically, limited to the small set of fonts that ship with the major operating systems.

MACINTOSH	WINDOWS 95/98	FREE WEB FONTS/ INTERNET EXPLORER
Courier	Arial	Arial Black
Times	Courier New	Comic Sans
Charcoal	Times New Roman	Georgia
Chicago	Wingdings	Impact
Geneva	Symbol	Monotype.com
Helvetica		Trebuchet MS
Monaco		Verdana
New York		Webdings
Palatino		
Symbol		

THE MACINTOSH AND WINDOWS COMPUTERS
ship with different sets of fonts, and the only faces they have in common are Times (called Times New Roman in Windows), Courier (Courier New in Windows), and Symbol. Additional fonts are distributed with Internet Explorer (which is on most Windows machines) and are available free from Microsoft's Web site for both platforms.

monospaced
A term used to describe a typeface in which every character has the same width. Such typefaces are useful for tables, program documentation, or other text in which vertical alignment is crucial.

Phrase Markup Structural Tags

START TAG	DEFINITION	DESCRIPTION
<CITE>	Citation	Italic
<CODE>	Computer code	Courier
<DEL>	Deleted text	Strikethrough
<DFN>	Definition	Normal
<EM>	Emphasized	Italics
<INS>	Inserted text	Underlined
<KBD>	Keyboard	Courier
<SAMP>	Sample text	Courier
<STRONG>	Emphasized	Bold
<VAR>	Variable	Italic

Phrase Markup Style Tags

START TAG	DEFINITION
<B>	Bold
<BIG>	Big size
<I>	Italic
<S>, <STRIKE>	Strikethrough
<SMALL>	Small size
<SUB>	Subscript
<SUP>	Superscript
<TT>	Teletype (typewriter) type
<U>	Underscored

HTML'S PHRASE MARKUP TAGS are used to mark specific words or phrases for special treatment. Like other HTML tags, they can be thought of in two groups: structural tags, which define a *type* of information, and style tags, which specify a particular layout style.

phrase markup tags
In HTML, tags that mark particular words or phrases within a larger element.

Using Phrase Markup Tags

As we described in the last chapter, browsers assign a default layout to every element of an HTML document. We described a set of specifications commonly used for paragraph-level elements like <P>, <H1>, and <BLOCKQUOTE> (→**84**) and described how labeling elements with those tags determines their typography.

HTML also includes a set of tags, referred to as **phrase markup tags**, that allow you to mark phrases within larger elements for special treatment. And once again, knowing how browsers usually set those tags enables you to use them to, de facto, specify a certain type treatment for them.

Like HTML in general, HTML's phrase markup tags can be sorted into two types: structural tags, which label text as a certain kind of information (<DFN> for definition, for example, or <VARIABLE> for a variable in a computer listing), and style tags, which describe a particular layout for the text (such as <I> for italic or <SUP> for superscript). And as with the rest of HTML, the style tags are pretty much on their way out, to be replaced by style sheet layout instructions once browser support for style sheets is in place.

SYMBOL	CODE	DESCRIPTION
	OR	Nonbreaking space
¢	¢ OR ¢	Cent sign
£	£ OR £	Pound sign
¥	¥ OR ¥	Yen sign
|	¦ OR ¦	Broken vertical bar
§	§ OR §	Section sign
©	© OR ©	Copyright sign
«	« OR «	Left angle quotation mark
®	® OR ®	Circled R registration sign
°	° OR °	Degree sign
±	± OR ±	Plus-or-minus sign
²	² OR ²	Superscript 2
³	³ OR ³	Superscript 3
¶	¶ OR ¶	Paragraph sign
¹	¹ OR ¹	Superscript 1
»	» OR »	Right angle quotation mark
¼	¼ OR ¼	Fraction $\frac{1}{4}$
½	½ OR ½	Fraction $\frac{1}{2}$
¾	¾ OR ¾	Fraction $\frac{3}{4}$
ç	ç OR ç	Small c, cedilla
é	é OR é	Small e, acute accent
è	è OR è	Small e, grave accent

CHARACTERS THAT DON'T EXIST in the basic ASCII set can be specified using special "escape" codes. Some of the more commonly used special characters, along with the codes you use to create them, are shown here.

> # Predicting which fonts are likely to be on a user's computer means basing your design on guesswork and probabilities. Luckily, though, some of the old standby fonts actually work pretty well on screen. Verdana and Georgia are excellent. Arial, Geneva, and Helvetica are also good on screen.
>
> ERIC EATON, HOTWIRED

Back to "Dumb Quotes" and Double Hyphens: HTML's Basic Character Set

The reliance on Times and Courier isn't the only reason Web pages often look as if they were created on an IBM Selectric. Another is that the ASCII code set used for HTML documents includes only the most basic characters of the roman alphabet: the 26 letters in uppercase and lowercase, plus basic punctuation—essentially the same characters you'll find on a typewriter keyboard, but a smaller set than we've gotten used to with typesetting systems and personal computers. And standard typographic symbols such as "curly" ("smart") quotation marks and apostrophes and em dashes aren't part of it.

Although such typographic niceties are still missing, HTML does offer a way to use many characters that aren't included in the basic ASCII set. The accented vowels used in non-English languages and commonly used special characters, such as the © and ® symbols, are available in a set of special codes called "escape" codes. Codes are also required to use characters, such as the < and > symbols, that have special meaning in HTML documents. At left is a list of some common special characters that are supported in most browsers.

DEREK POWAZEK
http://www.powazek.com/

NONSTANDARD TYPEFACES
can be included in Web pages
as bitmap graphics. All of these
pages are created entirely from
graphics.

JOHN J. HILL/MARILYN DEVEDJIEV/RON CROUDY/52MM
http://www.52mm.com/

Setting Type in Graphics

Back when use of structural tags was the only way
to influence HTML layout, Web designers found one
simple trick for introducing new typefaces into Web
pages: embedding the type in graphics. By setting
type in an image-editing program like Photoshop and
then saving it as a graphic, designers can use any of
the fonts from their own libraries, and then freeze
them into an image file for display on the Web.

Web purists frown on this practice for several reasons.
First, text in graphics isn't searchable or editable, a
fact that has repercussions that might not be obvious.
It could mean, for example that a page title or other
text set in a graphic can't be read by a search engine
(→**51**), so prospective visitors are less likely to find
your site. Image files also load much more slowly
than HTML text, and they won't be seen by anyone
whose browser doesn't display graphics. Yet using
graphics for text is a popular trick for designers whose
plans call for interesting type treatments.

If you do set type in graphics, you need to take the
same precautions you would always use to minimize
the size of a graphics file (→**136**). You should also be
sure to anti-alias type used in graphics (→**139**) to reduce
the jagginess of its edges and make it easier to read.

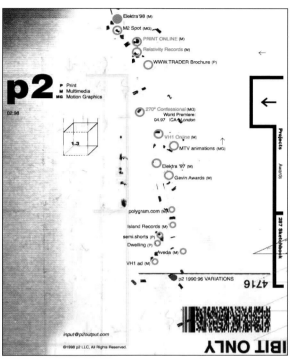

Web site design is software design; you're designing an interactive interface. When you think about how to use graphics on your site, think of them in that context: Do they help the user's interaction?

PETER MERHOLZ, STUDIO ARCHETYPE

START TAG	ATTRIBUTES	END TAG	EXPLANATION
<BASEFONT>			Names default font settings (used in the head of an HTML document)
	color="#*RRGGBB*" OR "*name*"		A color for the text, using an RGB value expressed in hexadecimal or a color name
	face="*name*"		The name of a typeface
	size="*size*"		A type size, from 1 to 7; 3 is the default. The number can be an absolute size from 1 to 7 or relative size from –1 to +3.
<FONT>		</FONT>	Marks text to be set with special font attributes
	color="#*RRGGBB*" OR "*name*"		A color for the text, using an RGB value expressed in hexadecimal or a color name
	face="*name*"		The name of a typeface
	size=*n*		A type size, from 1 to 7; 3 is the default. The number can be an absolute size from 1 to 7 or relative size from –1 to +3.

We've actually found that some users get upset when we specify a particular font on a page; they want to determine what size and typeface the pages are displayed in.

FRED SOTHERLAND, CNET

<FONT> and <BASEFONT>

Netscape Navigator 1.1 introduced the <FONT> tag, along with its *size=* and *color=* attributes, as a way to control the size and color of type for sections of a document. A second tag, <BASEFONT>, with the same attributes, could be placed in the head of an HTML file to set new default font attributes for an entire page. Microsoft added the *face=* attribute to both tags in version 2.0 of Internet Explorer. All these controls became part of HTML 3.2 and are now supported by both browser makers.

Setting type color is pretty straightforward, once you get used to the hexadecimal codes with which most colors are named on the Web (→**132**). (A basic set of color names for common colors like blue and red can also be used.)

Specifying size with <FONT> and <BASEFONT> also requires learning a special system—based on relative type sizes rather than the point sizes designers usually use. The default font size is 3. New type sizes can be set either as an integer from 1 to 7, or using + or – signs to signify an increase or decrease in size; +1 increases the font one size (say from the default 12-point to 14-point, the next standard size for most typefaces). Relative sizes are always computed in relation to the current default size, whether that's the browser default, a default set by the user, or a default set with the <BASEFONT> tag in the document's head.

Setting the typeface is, for reasons we've already discussed (→**89**), more problematic. Using the tag *<FONT face="MetaPlusBook">*, for instance, would have an effect only if the user has that font installed. To increase their chances of success, designers can name more than one typeface with the *face=* attribute, listing them in order of preference. You can also use the generic names "serif" and "sans-serif" as choices of last resort. For example, the tag *<FONT face= "MetaPlusBook, Arial, Helvetica, sans-serif">* would tell the browser to use Meta if it's installed, but if it's not, to try Arial, then Helvetica. And if none of these named faces is installed, the browser should use whatever sans-serif font it has access to.

While gratefully accepted by designers and universally supported by Web browsers, the <BASEFONT> and <FONT> tags are reaching the end of their usefulness, supplanted by the type controls offered for the same features in style sheets, which we'll describe next.

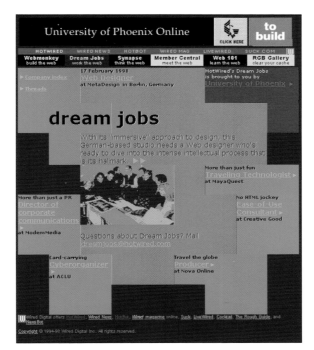

HOTWIRED
http://www.hotwired.com/dreamjobs/

HOTWIRED (above left) uses font controls to set its page in Verdana, with a variety of type sizes and colors. Circumstance (top right) uses graphics for its display type, then uses the font colors attribute to create a palette of yellows for the HTML.

TIM BARBER/DAVID BLISS
http://www.circumstance.com/html2/workframes.html

PROPERTY	POSSIBLE VALUES
SPECIFYING FONTS	
font-family	*family name* OR serif OR sans-serif OR cursive OR fantasy OR monospace
font-style	normal OR italic OR oblique
font-variant	normal OR small-caps
font-weight	normal OR bold OR bolder OR lighter OR *100-900*
font-size	size OR larger OR smaller OR *percentage*
FONT COLOR	
color	*color*
TYPE CONTROLS	
word-spacing	normal OR *length*
letter-spacing	normal OR *length*
text-decoration	none OR underline OR overline OR line-through OR blink
vertical-align	baseline OR sub OR super OR top OR text-top OR middle OR bottom OR text-bottom OR *percentage*
text-transform	capitalize OR uppercase OR lowercase OR none
text-align	left OR right OR center OR justify
text-indent	*length* OR *percentage*
line-height	normal OR number OR *length* OR *percentage*

CSS1 INCLUDES CONTROLS for all the type settings designers are used to using in page layout programs like QuarkXPress.

Type Controls in Style Sheets

We talked about the basic premise of style sheets in the last chapter (→**98**). With Internet Explorer 3.0 and Navigator 4.0, Microsoft and Netscape began supporting cascading style sheets and the HTML tags (such as <STYLE>) that allowed designers to provide layout specifications for each HTML element.

You've already learned how style sheets are added to documents (→**99**) and how they can be used to position elements on a page. Style sheets also offer some pretty advanced type control features as well. (The list at left shows CSS1's typographic properties.)

For typographers, one obvious benefit of style sheets over previous methods of controlling type in HTML is its range of controls. Finally, designers can specify leading and indents for running text and even create drop caps with standard HTML. Another advantage is that you can do all this in the language designers are accustomed to. Instead of specifying that type size should be +1 or 4, as you would with the <FONT> and <BASEFONT> tags, you can simply ask for 14-point. Indents and other features can also be specified in points, picas, ems, or other typographic measurements, as well as percentages or inches.

CSS CENTRALIZES design controls, making it simple to make site-wide design changes with a few keystrokes. This page shows the code and results for two very different typographic looks.

FABRIC8 USES STYLE SHEETS, along with downloadable fonts and JavaScript, to offer up the wildest error message on the Internet, featuring animated type.

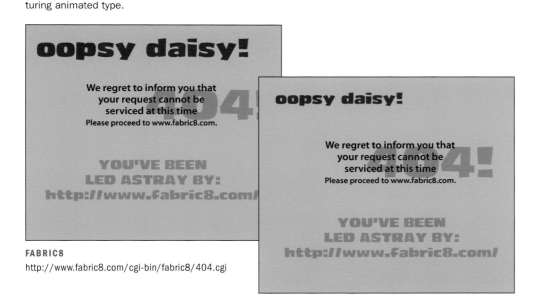

FABRIC8
http://www.fabric8.com/cgi-bin/fabric8/404.cgi

```
A slight change in the style
specifications results in a
completely different look;

<style type="text/css">
<!-- .bodytext2
        {font-family:Verdana, Arial,
        Helvetica, sans-serif;
font-size:12px;
font-style: normal;
line-height:200%;
text-align: left;
color: #FFCCFF}
--></style>
```

```
But, just like HTML and all
cross-browser issues, CSS
at the moment. It is 'suppo
partly in Explorer 3.x but th
As with any other web pag
to test-fly your pages on a
possibly can. MsIE 3.x, wit
important.
```

```
<style type="text/css">
<!-- .bodytext
{font-family: "Times New Roman",
      Times, serif;
font-size: 12px;
font-style: normal;
line-height: 150%;
text-align: left}
--> </style>

It is the line-height:150%,
that provides the leading but
I have cheated with the
paragraph indents and used
a run of   tags
for backward compatibility
with older browsers.
```

```
technologies available now, but the
      The idea behind CSS is that
you can have control over type tha
      Apart from the ability to m
possible to deliver the same conten
browser being used.
      Whether the user has a whi
small, black and white organiser, it
styles that give the optimal user ex
have CSS capabilities, the layout w
satisfactory display.
      This particular block of text
```

JOE GILLESPIE
http://www.wpdfd.com/wpdtypo2.htm

Drop Caps and First Lines: Style Sheet Pseudo-Classes

The creators of cascading style sheets recognized two typographic styles that designers like to use but weren't addressed by HTML: namely, drop caps and special treatments of the first line of copy in a paragraph. To address these, they created a couple of pseudo-elements called *first-letter* and *first-line*.

These pseudo-elements let designers create special treatment for first lines and first letters without resorting to the use of style tags like <FONT size=> or <B>. You treat these psuedo-elements much as you would treat any other structural tag, defining styles for them via style sheets.

```
<STYLE TYPE="text/css" MEDIA=screen>
<!–
@font-face { font-family: Spring98; font-style: normal; font-weight: normal; src: url(/fonts/Spring98.eot); }
@font-face { font-family: Myriad; font-style: normal; font-weight: normal; src: url(/fonts/Myriad.eot); }
.oops5 { font-family: Spring98, Verdana, Arial, Helvetica, sans-serif; font-size:5pt; color: #669900; background-color:#99CC66}
.oops30b { font-family: Spring98, Verdana, Arial, Helvetica, sans-serif; font-size:30pt; color: #669900; background-color:#99CC66}
.oops36 { font-family: Spring98, Verdana, Arial, Helvetica, sans-serif; font-size:36pt; color: #663300; background-color:#99CC66}
.oops48 { font-family: Spring98, Verdana, Arial, Helvetica, sans-serif; font-size:48pt; color: #663300; background-color:#99CC66}
.oops60 { font-family: Spring98, Verdana, Arial, Helvetica, sans-serif; font-size:60pt; color: #663300; background-color:#99CC66}
.oops72 { font-family: Spring98, Verdana, Arial, Helvetica, sans-serif; font-size:72pt; color: #663300; background-color:#99CC66}
.oops96b { font-family: Spring98, Verdana, Arial, Helvetica, sans-serif; font-size:96pt; color: #669900; background-color:#99CC66}
.text24 { font-family: Myriad, Verdana, Arial, Helvetica, sans-serif; font-size: 24pt; color: #000000;}
–>
</STYLE>
```

CSS POSITIONING and downloadable fonts can be combined to create complex typographic effects, as in this demo on Microsoft's site. The combined file sizes for these five subsetted OpenType fonts come to just under 30K.

Reprinted by permission from Microsoft Corporation

SI DANIELS / CALUM BROWN
http://www.microsoft.com/typography/web/embedding/demos/4/demo4.htm

downloadable fonts
Font files that can be downloaded along with an HTML file and read directly by a browser.

OpenType
A font technology, developed by Microsoft and Adobe, that combines the features of TrueType and PostScript Type1 fonts. OpenType is used for Microsoft's downloadable font files.

subsetting
A method of including only some characters of a font in a downloadable font file.

TrueDoc
A font technology, developed by Bitstream, used to compress fonts for download and display.

Downloadable Fonts

While style sheets provide control over just about every aspect of type layout, they can't affect the linchpin of typography—the ability to choose the typeface the text will be set in. Like the <BASEFONT> and <FONT> tags, the *font-family* property has no effect if the font it calls for isn't installed.

The latest browsers have provided an answer to that problem. With Navigator and Internet Explorer 4.0, Netscape and Microsoft have incorporated support for **downloadable fonts**—a way to send font files to the browser along with the HTML page that uses them.

The technologies used by each browser are different in some respects, but the basic idea is the same: a special command in the document's style sheet, *@font-face*, tells the browser to download the named font file. The font file is in a format that the browser can use directly, without requiring users to stop their interaction with the page in order to properly install the font. (The *@font-face* command is part of CSS2; Navigator 4.0 doesn't support it yet; instead it uses the <LINK> tag (→**99**) and lets you name fonts for different elements using the <FONT face=> tag as well as with style sheets.)

The catch is that Netscape and Microsoft—at least when we wrote this—required font files in different formats. Netscape uses a font format called **TrueDoc**, created by Bitstream. Microsoft uses a format called **OpenType**, which it created jointly with Adobe. Bitstream offers an ActiveX control that gives Windows versions of Internet Explorer the ability to read the TrueDoc format, but when we wrote this, that still left out Macintosh and Unix versions of Internet Explorer. What this means is that Web publishers who want to use downloadable fonts will need to either choose to support just one browser or the other, or supply font files in both formats and use content negotiation (→**77**) to deliver one file or the other, depending on which browser requests it. Until Netscape supports *@font-face*, you can also just use both <LINK> and *@font-face* to call the font files; each browser will recognize one method.

Another issue for publishers is the same one that haunts every aspect of Web publishing: download time. The font files are comparatively compact, thanks to file compression and a technique, called **subsetting**, that allows publishers to include only the characters from the font that are actually used in the HTML file. Still, a font file might run 10K–50K at the low end (for a single weight of a subsetted display font) to over 100K (for all weights of a text font)—a significant load over a modem connection. The fact that current browsers don't wait for the font file to be downloaded before displaying the page is a mixed blessing. The result is that the visitor sees the page with default fonts until the downloaded font file is in place, and then is disturbed by a disorienting redraw of the page once the font is loaded.

Fonts for Free? Font Licensing and Downloadable Fonts

Downloading font files to everyone who comes to your Web site sounds like a great deal for your visitors, but what about the font's designer? Aren't there laws against distributing fonts you've bought for your own use?

Yes, there are. Almost every font you buy comes with a license, which usually stipulates that you refrain from just that kind of behavior. Font licenses usually grant use of a font for just one computer or just one output device. The idea of downloadable fonts has caused a lot of consternation among font designers and a lot of head-scratching on the part of Bitstream, Adobe, and other developers of downloadable font technology.

Bitstream's TrueDoc technology gets around the issue by technical means. The font file authoring system doesn't actually embed the original font outlines into the downloadable file. Instead, it re-creates the font in a new technology. Since the font copyright protects the original font code, this transformation essentially transcends the copyright protection.

Downloadable OpenType files go through no such transformation; the original font information is embedded in the downloadable file. The OpenType font format, though, includes a place for font designers to encode their permission—or lack of it—for use of the font in downloadable files. Authoring tools like Microsoft's WEFT won't embed fonts that don't include the designer's permission. (The TrueType format also includes a place for designers' permissions, but PostScript fonts don't, a problem Microsoft hadn't yet solved when we wrote this.)

Once downloaded, the fonts have extra protection to ensure that they can be used only with the HTML file they're created for. Encryption and subsetting also help protect the font information from being extracted and used for other applications.

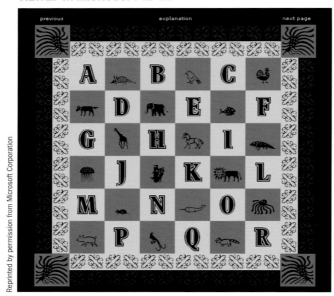

Reprinted by permission from Microsoft Corporation

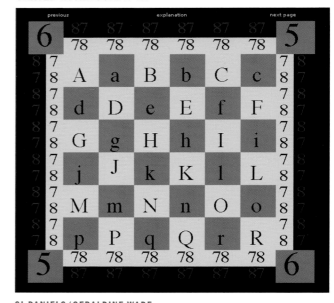

SI DANIELS/GERALDINE WADE
http://www.microsoft.com/typography/web/embedding/demos/3/demo3.htm

A SYMBOL FONT, an ornamental border font, and typographic fonts are combined in a table layout to create this online poster. Because the page uses OpenType fonts and the *@font* command to download them, the fonts can't be seen in Navigator 4.0.

The success and growth of the Web doesn't depend on the ability to render typefaces: Most users just aren't going to be able to distinguish the 14-point bitmap of Times from the 14-point bitmap of any other serif font. Good site design can be done without downloadable fonts, and until bandwidth ceases to be an issue, it will have to be.

MATTHEW BUTTERICK, ATOMIC VISION

Another factor holding up adoption of downloadable fonts is the scarcity of tools for creating the downloadable font files. When we wrote this, only two products included the ability to author TrueDoc files: HexMac's HexWeb Typograph (available as a stand-alone tool or as a plug-in for BareBones' BBEdit or Microsoft's FrontPage HTML editors) and the Quark-to-HTML filter, Extensis BeyondPress (which only includes TrueDoc embedding for the Mac). Microsoft offers a tool for creating OpenType files called WEFT (Web Embedded Font Tool) free from its Web site, but it's available only for Windows computers.

It's too early to know which of these technologies will be adopted by the Web community. What is clear is that it will be some time before either really solves the problem of typeface availability. But if one technology wins out, if authoring tools become more available, and if download times become less of an issue (either because the font files can be more tightly compressed or because faster connections become commonplace) the problem of limited typefaces on the Web will finally be solved.

Online: Web Typography

Downloadable Fonts
http://www.hotwired.com/webmonkey/98/01/index3a.html
http://www.microsoft.com/typography/web/embedding/
http://www.truedoc.com/

Extensis BeyondPress
http://www.astrobyte.com/products/BeyondPress/

General Information on Web Typography
http://www.microsoft.com/typography/web/
http://www.webreview.com/wr/pub/Web_Fonts/

HexMac Typograph
http://www.hexmac.com/hexmac/engl/webtools/typograph2/
 typograph2.html

OpenType
http://www.microsoft.com/typography/web/plans/

Special Characters
http://www.uni-passau.de/~ramsch/iso8859-1.html

Style Sheets
http://www.w3.org/Style/css/
http://www.hotwired.com/webmonkey/stylesheets/
http://www.useit.com/alertbox/9707a.html
http://www.webdeveloper.com/categories/advhtml/
http://www.webreview.com/guides/style/

Web Fonts From Microsoft
http://www.microsoft.com/typography/fontpack/

WEFT
http://www.microsoft.com/typography/web/embedding/weft/

Web Graphics

The explosion of the World Wide Web can be traced to one event: the creation of Mosaic, the first browser able to display graphics. Finally, information on the Internet could have color and personality. And suddenly, the Internet became more than a way to exchange useful information and e-mail; it became an entertainment medium.

Graphics, like text, are subject to tight limits on the Web. The first is size: Since files are transmitted at about 1K per second over a slow modem connection, graphics file sizes are realistically limited to 30K or less (about 30 seconds of download time)—and the smaller the better. Second is format: Forget about TIFF and EPS; most browsers are set up to handle GIF and JPEG—compressed formats that have gained popularity mostly through their use on the Web.

Handled creatively, graphics can turn a Web page into a stylized interface matching anything available on CD-ROM. Handled badly, they can make your page unreadable. In this chapter, we'll talk about the considerations and pitfalls of using graphics for decoration and navigation on the Web.

Formats for Online Graphics

Mosaic, the first Web browser that supported graphics, supported just one format for inline images: **GIF**, an 8-bit, compressed format. GIF is still the basic format for online graphics. Most browsers also support **JPEG**, another highly compressed format. A third format, **PNG**, recently joined the group, with support added at the end of 1997 in Netscape Navigator (version 4.04) and Microsoft Internet Explorer (version 4.02). This is the basic triumvirate of Web graphics formats. And due to their popularity of Web design, most popular graphics applications can now save files in any of them.

Before we go on, we should explain that there are actually two versions of GIF and JPEG. For GIF, the versions are called GIF87a and GIF89a. JPEG has a new version referred to as **Progressive JPEG**. The differences are shown in the table to the right, and we'll explain more about them as we go along.

GIF and JPEG each have particular characteristics that make them appropriate for some types of images, and not for others, but between the two of them, they handle most images quite well. As a rule, images that use few, flat colors are usually best saved as GIF. For complex images, such as photographs, that use many shades and gradations between colors, JPEG can provide significantly smaller file sizes than GIF can. JPEG can also support 24-bit color (up to 16.7 million colors), while GIF can support only 8-bit (256 colors).

Graphics Format Considerations

	GIF87a	GIF89a	JPEG	Progressive JPEG	PNG
Native support in most browsers	•	•	•	•	
Lossless compression	•	•			•
Supports transparent backgrounds		•			•
Supports Interlacing	•	•		•	•
Supports animation		•			
Maximum number of colors	256	256	16.7 million	16.7 million	16.7 million

GIF
Graphics Interchange Format, a compressed bitmap format created by CompuServe. The oldest version, called GIF87a or CompuServe GIF, has been replaced by a newer version, called GIF89a, which supports transparency and animation.

JPEG
A compressed bitmap format, developed by the Joint Photographic Experts Group of the International Standards Organization. JPEG is generally used for photographic images.

PNG
A 24-bit, compressed graphics format, created by Thomas Boutell, which can support multiple levels of transparency and two-dimensional interlacing.

Progressive JPEG
A variation on the JPEG format that supports interlacing.

TRANSPARENCY can make a graphic seem to float on its background.

YO
http://www.peachpit.com/

INTERLACING can be used to flow a graphic into a page in alternate columns and/or rows, so that a rough version of the graphic becomes visible quickly.

PAUL SCHRANK
http://www.siactive.com/pgeek/jb.htm

GIF ANIMATION takes advantage of multiple layers stored in a single GIF89a file. In browsers that support it, the layers are played back sequentially.

Lossless vs. Lossy Compression

JPEG compresses images by discarding parts of the image information it considers nonessential. This kind of compression scheme (called "lossy" compression) results in a great degree of compression but also some degradation of the image quality, especially around sharp edges. GIF and PNG use "lossless" compression schemes that may result in larger file sizes but cause no image degradation. This doesn't necessarily mean that JPEG images will be inferior to GIFs. In photographic images with no sharp edges, for example, the effects of lossy compression are invisible.

JPEG and other lossy compression methods usually offer designers the option of several levels of compression, allowing them to balance the degree of compression against the degree of quality required. There's no magic level that works for every image: Designers need to experiment with each image to determine how much compression it can stand without an unacceptable degradation of quality.

The GIF and JPEG formats also differ in their support of three important features: interlacing, transparency, and animation. Interlacing, a feature of GIF89a and Progressive JPEG, allows the browser to download and display the image in alternate lines, so that a rough version of the entire image becomes visible quickly, and visitors can view and interact with it without waiting for the entire file to download. The other two features are available only in GIF89a. Transparency allows you to specify that one of the colors in an image (usually the background color) should be treated as invisible, allowing you to create irregularly shaped images that float in space. We'll discuss GIF animation, which lets you save a series of images in a single GIF file to be played back sequentially by the browser, more in the chapter on multimedia (→**152**), where we'll describe several ways to animate Web pages.

PNG combines some of best features of GIF and JPEG, Like JPEG, PNG supports 16.7 million colors and compresses photographic images to smaller sizes than GIF does. It allows for transparent backgrounds and interlacing, and it even improves on those features by allowing for various degrees of transparency and for two-dimensional interlacing, which, transmits a rough overall view of the image faster than the one-dimensional scheme used by GIF. (A similar scheme is used by Progressive JPEG.) Since direct support for PNG has only recently been added to browsers, though, its use is still risky on the Web.

Recently, a dark horse format called **FlashPix** has begun to gain some attention. FlashPix files hold several versions of an image, saved in discrete parts and at different resolutions. When rendered according to the **Internet Imaging Protocol (IIP)**, the format allows browsers to quickly display the image at several zoom levels. When we wrote this, though, FlashPix and IIP could be used only through a plug-in.

So far, support for **object-based graphics** is scarce on the Web. (All of the formats we've mentioned so far are **bitmap** formats.) Because object graphics (also called **vector graphics**) describe images as a collection of geometric shapes rather than as a collection of individual pixels, such formats can usually save drawings in smaller files than the image would require as a bitmap, and object graphics can also be zoomed, or enlarged, on screen, without losing any detail. As we wrote this, though, no browser supported object graphics directly, though plug-ins were available for common proprietary formats such as FreeHand, Corel's CMX, and Micrografx's QuickVector. In early 1998, Adobe, Netscape, and Sun proposed a vector graphics standard for the Web based on PostScript, called **PGML**—which, after vetting by the W3C, may well become standard in the future.

JODI DOWNING
http://www.woodmagazine.com/cusserv/shockwave/horsehok.html

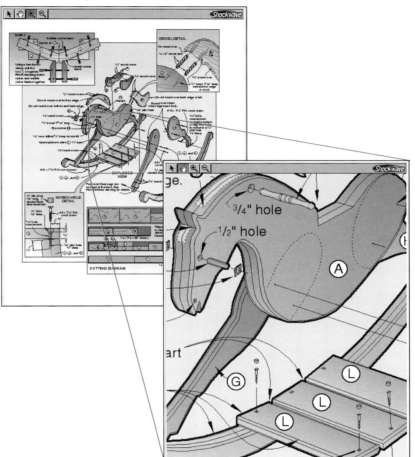

VECTOR GRAPHICS such as FreeHand's Shockwave format (shown here) often have smaller file sizes than do bitmap images. Another advantage over bitmaps is that vector graphics can be zoomed in on to see greater detail. (The Shockwave for FreeHand plug-in includes a zoom tool that changes the size of the graphic on screen.)

bitmap
A graphics format that creates an image using an array of pixels of different colors or shades.

interlacing
A feature of some graphics formats that allows the graphic to be loaded into a Web page in alternate rows and/or columns, allowing visitors to quickly see a rough version of the image.

FlashPix
A graphics format, used by LivePix and Microsoft's PictureIt, that allows for speedy rendering of images at several zoom levels.

Internet Imaging Protocol (IIP)
A method of rendering images that allows the browser or other software to handle an image in discrete sections, allowing for quick rendering.

object-based graphics
Graphics created as an assembly of shapes, or objects. Common object graphics formats are EPS and PICT.

PGML
Precision Graphics Markup Language, a language for describing vector graphics based on PostScript and XML, proposed by Adobe, Netscape, and Sun Microsystems.

transparency
A feature of an image file in which certain colors can be made invisible against a background. GIF and PNG graphics support transparency.

vector graphics
Another name for object graphics, so called because such graphics are created from mathematical splines, or vectors, rather than described as individual pixels.

START TAG	ATTRIBUTES	END TAG	EXPLANATION
\<IMG\>			Inserts an image file into the page
	align="top" OR "texttop" OR "middle" OR "absmiddle" OR "bottom" OR "absbottom" OR "baseline" OR "left" OR "right" OR "center"		The alignment of the image relative to surrounding text
	alt="*text*"		Text that will display in text-only browsers or if the graphic doesn't load correctly
	border=*n*		For hyperlinked graphics, the width of the border, specified in pixels
	controls		Used with *dynsrc=*, displays video controls
	dynsrc="*URL*"		Specifies an AVI file to be inserted
	height=*n*, width=*n*		The height and width of the image, in pixels
	hspace=*n*, vspace=*n*		The space, in pixels, set between the image and surrounding text
	ismap		Specifies that the image is a server-side image map
	loop=*n* OR "infinite"		Used with *dynsrc=*, the number of times the video clip will loop
	lowsrc="*URL*"		Names a low-resolution file to be inserted as a placeholder
	src="*URL*"		The URL of the image to be inserted
	start="fileopen" OR "mouseover"		Used with *dynsrc=*, the event that starts the video clip running
	usemap="*name*"		Names the map to be used for a client-side image map
\<OBJECT\>		**\</OBJECT\>**	Inserts an object (e.g., an image, media file, or program) into the page
	align="top" OR "texttop" OR "middle" OR "absmiddle" OR "bottom" OR "absbottom" OR "baseline" OR "left" OR "right" OR "center"		The alignment of the image relative to surrounding text
	border=*n*		For hyperlinked objects, the width of the border, specified in pixels
	data="*URL*"		The URL of the object to be inserted
	height=*n*, width=*n*		The height and width of the object, in pixels
	hspace=*n*, vspace=*n*		The space, in pixels, set between the object and surrounding text
	standby="*text*"		Text that will be displayed as the object loads
	type="*MIME-type*"		The Internet MIME type of the data, used by the browser to determine whether or not it can display the object
	usemap="*name*"		Names the map to be used for a client-side image map

Inserting Graphics: \<IMG\> and \<OBJECT\>

Since HTML is a text-only format, how can you insert a graphic in an HTML page? The key is the \<IMG\> tag, which tells the browser to insert a specified image file into the text.

The \<IMG\> tag has several possible attributes, but only one is required: *src=* (source), which names the image file that is to be inserted. We talked about the *align=* attribute, used to control the placement of the graphic within the page, earlier (→**88**). We'll discuss the other attributes later in this chapter, as we describe the uses they're put to.

HTML 4.0 introduced a new tag for inserting graphics and lots of other kinds of objects into pages. Appropriately enough, it's called \<OBJECT\>. For images, the tag works much like the \<IMG\> tag, and it uses many of the same attributes (we show the attributes pertinent to images in the box at left). Because it can also be used to embed video, Java applets, plug-ins, and other media, the \<OBJECT\> tag has lots of other attributes as well, which we'll cover later (→**190**). The \<OBJECT\> tag is a fairly new addition to HTML, and because it offers no real advantages over the \<IMG\> tag for images, and because the \<IMG\> tag is supported by even the earliest browsers, \<IMG\> will probably remain the preferred tag for inserting simple inline graphics.

Graphics can also be used as hyperlinks, just like text. To make a graphic "live," you specify the graphic file (with the <IMG> tag), rather than a string of words, with the *href=* attribute of the <A> tag. For example, the code *<A href="nextpage.html"><IMG src="image.gif"></A>* would insert the graphic image.gif on the page as a hyperlink, and clicking it would take you to nextpage.html.

If you use an image as a hyperlink anchor, you'll also need to provide a text-based link for visitors who can't see graphics on their systems. The *alt=* attribute is designed for this purpose, allowing you to supply text that will be displayed in place of the graphic. The *alt=* text also displays in the event that the graphic doesn't load on graphical browsers—if there's a snag in the connection, for instance. If the image is being used as an anchor for a hyperlink, the text specified with *alt=* will act as an alternate hyperlink.

In some cases, you'll probably want to make images available as linked graphics, rather than placing them inline on an HTML page. This gives visitors the option of viewing a large version of a graphic without burdening the main page with the extra download time. Linked images needn't be in HTML pages. You can simply use the graphic's filename as the value for the *href=* attribute in the <A> tag that links to the graphic. The browser will open it in its window, if it's in a format it can read, or with a helper application, if it isn't.

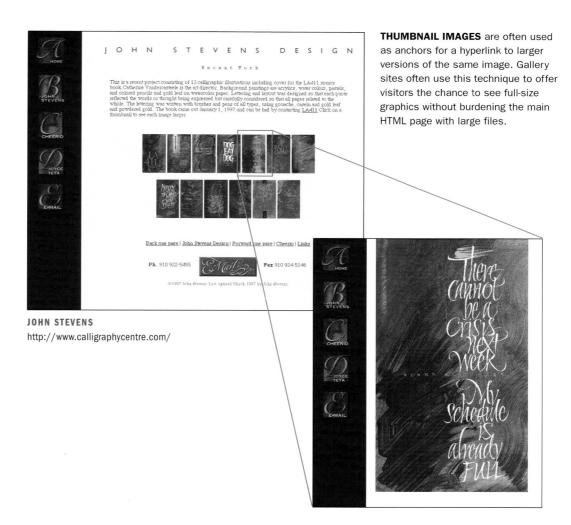

JOHN STEVENS
http://www.calligraphycentre.com/

THUMBNAIL IMAGES are often used as anchors for a hyperlink to larger versions of the same image. Gallery sites often use this technique to offer visitors the chance to see full-size graphics without burdening the main HTML page with large files.

IMAGE MAPS are often used to create a full-page graphic interface for a home page. The Digital Planet image map (shown below) uses a straightforward navigation bar across the top, then adds some fun using JavaScript rollover effects. Pointing to different elements in the image calls up a speech balloon next to the space beauty describing what you'll find behind each planet.

image map
A type of graphic in which different locations in the image (specified by pixel coordinates) are linked to particular destination URLs.

Image Maps

Many designers like to create interfaces in which graphics fill the entire screen, creating a CD-ROM–like effect in which users can interact with different parts of the graphic to jump to different locations. Such an approach is possible using a kind of graphic programming called an **image map**.

Image maps are useful for lots of situations (we show many in this book). They're often used to create iconic navigation bars for a site, for instance, or a metaphoric scene for navigating from a home page.

At last count, there were three different ways to create an image map, each corresponding to a different version of the HTML standard. No matter which you use, though, you can think of an image map in three parts: the image itself, the map information that describes which parts of the image link to what URLs, and the software that, using the image map, translates a click on the image into a request for a particular file. The difference between the three methods is where those parts reside and how they're accessed.

There are no special requirements for the image itself: Any GIF or JPEG image can be used, and you insert it into the page just as you would any other image, using the <IMG> or <OBJECT> tag. You turn it into an image map using one of two optional attributes to those tags: *ismap* or *usemap=*. Simple enough.

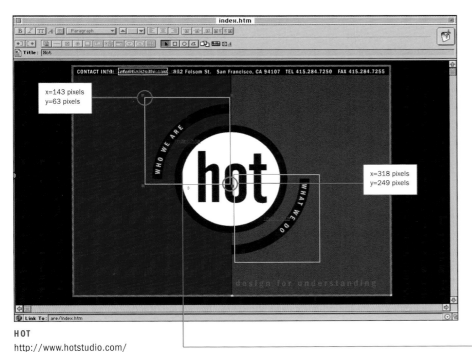

HOT
http://www.hotstudio.com/

IN IMAGE MAPS, different areas of a graphic can link to different URLs. A map file defines the live areas and the URLs they link to, defining each area by its pixel coordinates. The image map shown at left has three live areas: Who We Are, What We Do, and a mailto link. The map file for this client-side image map is included in the HTML file that creates the page (below).

```
<HTML>
<HEAD>

<TITLE>Hot Studio</TITLE>

</HEAD>
<BODY BGCOLOR="black" BACKGROUND="home.gif">
<TABLE WIDTH="100%" CELLPADDING=1 CELLSPACING=1>
<TR>
<TD ALIGN=CENTER VALIGN=CENTER WIDTH="100%">
<MAP NAME="home">
<AREA SHAPE="rect" COORDS="90,1,192,18" HREF="mailto:info@hotstudio.com">
<AREA SHAPE="rect" COORDS="323,227,498,415" HREF="do/index.htm">
<AREA SHAPE="rect" COORDS="143,63,318,249" HREF="are/index.htm">
</MAP>
<IMG SRC="clear.gif" WIDTH="639" HEIGHT="481" BORDER=0
USEMAP="#home" ALIGN="top" ISMAP></TD>
</TR>
</TABLE>

</BODY>
</HTML>
```

Remember that using graphics instead of text always increases download time, so we're careful about using a lot of heavy graphics on the home page. We use heavier media deeper in the site, if we need to, once users are honing in on what they're looking for.

MARK MEADOWS, CONSTRUCT

DAVID YU
http://www.dhky.com/viral.html

DHKY rests navigational graphics on top of a full-bleed background graphic. A client-side image map defines finely tuned polygons that match the oblique shapes of the live graphic areas. The maps' <AREA> tags also include calls to JavaScript commands that create a rollover effect; when the mouse rolls over a live area, text appears naming the section you'll link to.

client-side image map
An image map for which the map information and the map processing program reside on the client (user's) computer. Not all browser software supports client-side image maps.

map file
For server-side image maps, a file stored on the server that holds the map information, linking specific regions of the image to specific target URLs.

server-side image map
An image map for which the map file and the map processing program reside on the server. The coordinates of a user's click are sent to the server for processing.

The first method for creating image maps uses the *ismap* attribute with the <IMG> tag. *Ismap* tells the browser to record the location of any click on the image and send that information back to the server. The <IMG> tag is used as the anchor for an <A> tag, whose *href=* attribute references a **map file** stored on the server. A program on the server uses the map file to match the location of a visitor's click to a particular URL and sends the file at that URL back to the browser. Because the processing of the click and its meaning takes place on the server, an image map created with ismap is referred to as a **server-side image map**,

The *usemap=* attribute can be used with either <IMG> or <OBJECT>. The *usemap=* attribute names a map that is supplied in the HTML file itself. The software that matches the visitor's click to the map file information is in the browser itself. Because the translation of click to URL takes place on the visitor's (client) machine, an image map created with *usemap=* is called a **client-side image map**.

For client-side image maps the map information can be provided in two ways. The most common method (introduced with Netscape Navigator 2.0 and included in HTML 3.2) is to enclose the information with <MAP> tags, using <AREA> tags to define each live area. A new method, introduced with HTML 4.0, uses the <MAP> tag as well, but it lets you define each area using an <A> tag with the *shape=* and *coords=*

attributes to define the live areas. (The *shape=* and *coords=* attributes are used in the same way in the <A> tag as they are in the <AREA> tag.)

So, with three methods available for creating image maps, how do you decide which to use?

Since all the processing is done locally, on the visitor's own computer, client-side image maps are more efficient than server-side image maps, minimizing network traffic and usually returning results faster. With client-side image maps, users also get extra feedback; the pointer turns into a hand when it passes over an image's live areas. Unfortunately, not all browsers support them. Support for client-side maps created with <IMG> and *usemap=* began with version 2.0 of Netscape Navigator and Internet Explorer, and support for the <OBJECT> tag is only beginning to be added (with partial support in Internet Explorer and Navigator 4.0). On the other hand, support for server-side image maps created with <IMG> and *ismap* is pretty universal.

Luckily, you can use a mixture of the server-side and client-side methods in the same file. An <IMG> tag can include both the *ismap* and *usemap=* attributes, and if you supply a map file both in the HTML file and on the server, browsers that support the *usemap=* attribute will use the client-side map, and browsers that don't will go to the server for the map information.

START TAG	ATTRIBUTES	END TAG	EXPLANATION
<MAP>		</MAP>	Marks code that provides image map information for a client-side image map
	name="*text*"		Provides a name for the map (used by the *usemap=* attribute of the <IMG> or <OBJECT> tag
<AREA>			Creates a hyperlink area within a client-side image map created with the <MAP> tag
	alt="*text*"		Text to be displayed in nongraphics browsers
	coords="*coord1, coord2, coord3 . . .*"		The coordinates of the area's boundaries. (Each shape has its own rules for specifying coordinates.)
	href="*URL*"		The URL of the linked file
	nohref		Defines the area as having no hyperlink
	shape="default" OR "rect" OR "circle" OR "poly"		The type of shape being defined; "default" is for the area outside a defined shape
	target="*frame*" OR "_blank" OR "new" OR "_parent" OR "_self" OR "_top"		Used with frames, names a frame or window in which the linked file should be displayed

Image Map Coding Methods

Server-side/HTML 2.0	<A href="mapfile.map"><IMG src="image.gif ismap"></A>
Client-side/HTML 3.2	<IMG src="image.gif" usemap="#map1">
Client-side/HTML 4.0	<OBJECT data="image.gif" type="image/gif" usemap="#map1"></OBJECT>

YOU CREATE AN IMAGE MAP by adding the *ismap* or *usemap=* attribute to the <IMG> or <OBJECT> tag that you use to insert the graphic. The three different types of coding are shown here. All these samples refer to an external map file, which for *ismap* is saved on the server and for *usemap=* is included in the same HTML file.

BACKGROUND COLORS load more quickly than images but still provide a bright look to the page. Text and link colors can be specified to complement the background you choose.

MAGDALENA DONEA
http://www.kia.net/maggy/

Background Graphics and Colors

In the spring of 1995, Netscape Navigator 1.1 began supporting a number of attributes to the <BODY> tag that changed the look of the Web overnight. The *background=* attribute let designers supply a URL for a GIF or JPEG image that would be used as the background of the browser window. The *bgcolor=* attribute let designers specify a color, rather than a graphic, for a simpler yet still eye-catching background. To make the document's text readable against the new colors, designers could now also specify a custom color for the text, and still other colors for links that hadn't been visited, links that had been visited, and "active links"—those that are currently being clicked on.

Suddenly, the sameness that had characterized Web pages was a thing of the past. Designers used background graphics to give pages psychedelic textures— or just something appropriate to the page's theme, like melting clocks for the Surrealism Archive. Some used the new capabilities simply to create a paper-white background for their pages. Others opted for basic black, from which red and yellow text shone like traffic lights. Now surfing from page to page could be more like experiencing a laser light show than turning the pages of a book. The *background=* and *bgcolor=* attributes were quickly picked up by Microsoft and and were included as part of HTML 3.2.

START TAG	ATTRIBUTES	END TAG	EXPLANATION
<BODY>		</BODY>	Marks the text to be displayed in the browser window
	alink="#RRGGBB" OR "name"		Names a color for the active links, using an RGB value expressed in hexadecimal or a color name
	background= "URL"		Names a graphics file to be used as the background
	bgcolor="#RRGGBB" OR "name"		Names a background color
	link="#RRGGBB" OR "name"		Names a color for hyperlink anchors
	text="#RRGGBB" OR "name"		Names a color for nonlinked text
	vlink="#RRGGBB" OR "name"		Names a color for visited links

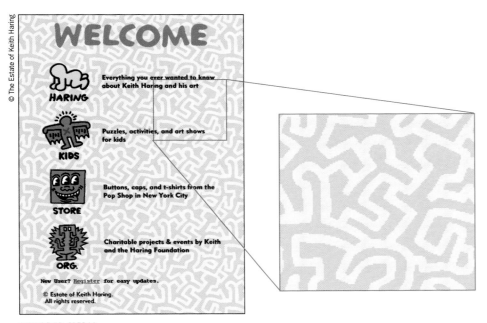

RIVERBED MEDIA
http://www.haring.com/

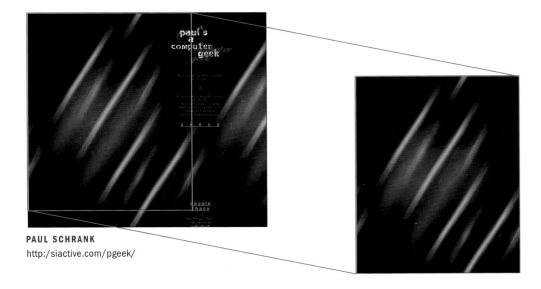

PAUL SCHRANK
http://siactive.com/pgeek/

DAVID SIEGEL/RAY GUILLETTE
http://www.klutz.com/treefort/knots.html

BACKGROUND GRAPHICS can have very small dimensions; they will be tiled to fill the entire window. This tiling can be hidden by careful crafting of the pattern (as in the examples at left). As shown in the Klutz Press example (above), background graphics can even provide important parts of the interface. On that page, a single, narrow tile creates the walls and ladders, a "room" that is then furnished by images that act as hyperlinks to other parts of the site.

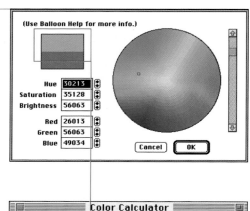

(Use Balloon Help for more info.)

Hue	30213	
Saturation	35128	
Brightness	56063	
Red	26013	
Green	56063	
Blue	49034	

Cancel   OK

Specifying Colors Online

Specifying colors in HTML—for the <BODY> tag's *text=*, *bgcolor=*, *link=*, *vlink=*, and *alink=* attributes, for the <FONT> *color=* attribute, and for style sheets—requires using a code that most designers probably aren't familiar with. The colors are specified as values for the red, green, and blue (RGB) components of the color. That's straightforward enough, given that the Mac or Windows color picker can show the RGB value for any color you choose. The trickier part is that the number that names the value is specified in hexadecimal: base 16, instead of the base 10 system we use for just about everything else.

In hexadecimal, the numbers 1 through 9 are specified just as they are in real life. For the digits 10 through 15, though, hex notation uses the capital letters A through F: A for 10, B for 11, and so on.

If your brain is up to it, you can figure out the hexadecimal equivalent of any decimal number using a regular calculator; some calculators (such as the one that comes with Windows) even have a hexadecimal conversion function. Several color pickers with hexadecimal color value calculators are also available on line. Most WYSIWYG HTML editors let you pick a color from a standard color picker and do the hexadecimal calculating themselves. Browsers also build in a set of basic colors, such as red, blue, yellow, and so on, that can also be specified by name.

Color Calculator

Use this wheel to calculate the color codes for custom background and text colors to display in the Netscape Browser. Click "Pick Color..." and use the dialog box to select a color. The hexadecimal RGB color triplet appears in the field.

More...

RGB Color Triplet:

65DABF

Pick Color...

```
<HTML>
<BODY BGCOLOR=65DABF>
```

ONLINE COLOR PICKERS can help you translate the color you want into the proper hex codes for use in the <BODY> and <FONT> color attributes. In the 6-digit hex code, the first pair of digits gives the red value, the second pair the green, and the last pair the blue. (The interface from Masterform Media's HTML Grinder is shown here.)

Like any other effect, background graphics can be used well or badly. In the worst cases, complex backgrounds with high-contrast patterns make the text on top almost impossible to read. To combat that effect, some page designers then make all the text on the page bold, which only makes matters worse in the low-res environment of a computer screen.

Since background graphics **tile** to fill a window, the actual graphics can be quite small—a necessity since in some browsers the background graphic is downloaded before any of the page's content, and a background graphic that takes too long to download can drive away visitors before they even have a chance to see the rest of your page. Most browsers load the background graphic last, but slow-loading backgrounds can still be annoying. For that reason, background graphics have a realistic size limit of about 10K.

3D Graphics

VRML, the Virtual Reality Modeling Language (→**148**) may one day be the standard method of offering 3D on the Web. But as we wait for the fast 3D processors and better bandwidth that will make VRML more usable, you can turn to simpler methods of creating 3D images on line.

Right now, the only way to make sure every visitor can see your 3D graphics is to save them as GIF or JPEG files after you've rendered them. Done right, the graphics can be stingy with disk space and the effect can be striking, allowing beveled edges, drop shadows, and other dimensional effects.

If you want to rely on plug-ins and ActiveX controls, you can post your graphic in true 3D formats. VRML players ship with the current version of Netscape's and Microsoft's browsers. Another 3D format that may become important on the Web is **QuickTime VR**. Visitors can move left or right, above or below QuickTime VR scenes, but not (so far) through them. Unlike VRML, though, QuickTime VR lets you create 3D scenes from photographs, making it especially useful for applications such as online catalogs.

JPEG

ART & SCIENCE
http://www.socalgas.com/

QUICKTIME VR

VIDEOTRON
http://www.saint-joseph.org/moov/crypte.mov

3D GRAPHICS can be rendered as GIF or JPEG files for posting on the Web. VRML and QuickTime VR, both supported by plug-in players, offer true 3D scenes that visitors can actually navigate through.

VRML

PLANET 9 STUDIOS
http://www.planet9.com/earth/tokyo/

QuickTime VR
A technology created by Apple Computer for creating and viewing 3D scenes.

tile
To arrange an object or graphic across an area by repeating it in contiguous, adjacent areas.

**MACINTOSH
SYSTEM PALETTE**

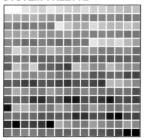

Illustration: John Grimes

BROWSER-SAFE PALETTE

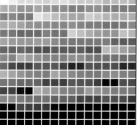

MAPPING YOUR GIF GRAPHICS to the cross-platform browser-safe palette (or a subset of it) ensures that the colors will remain true even on 8-bit systems and on different platforms.

Dealing With Limited Color Palettes

Most designers work in 24-bit color but, unfortunately, most Web surfers don't. As your graphics enter a less-optimal viewing environment—the visitor's own screen—you'll need to remember that, once they're posted, your graphics will be viewed according to the rules of that world, not yours.

For these purposes, we can forget about visitors who aren't viewing graphics at all. Here, we're thinking of those who are viewing graphics at a different bit depth or on platforms other than the one you used to create them. The same graphics look much different on a Mac than on a PC, or in 8-bit rather than 24-bit color.

The first thing to know is that Netscape Navigator, Internet Explorer, and other browsers have their own ideas about what colors to use on 8-bit displays, a 216-color palette, referred to as the "Netscape color cube" or the **browser-safe palette**, which they apply to every graphic displayed on such systems.

This palette begins with the 256 shades that can be displayed on an 8-bit color system, subtracts the 20 colors Windows uses in its own interface and the 13 colors Netscape uses for its logo, and then simplifies the remaining 223 colors into the nearest number achievable using the 3 primary colors of a CRT: 216, based on 6 shades each of red, green, and blue.

Any colors in the original graphic that aren't in the browser palette are **dithered**: two or more colors from the palette are combined to approximate the out-of-range shade. Dithering doesn't create a problem for photographic images, but it does when you want clean, flat colors.

You can avoid dithering by using DeBabelizer, Photoshop, or another image-processing program to map your flat-color images to this browser-safe palette, which is available on line as a Photoshop color lookup table (CLUT) (check the listings at the end of this chapter (→**139**) for resources) and, now, built in to most image-processing software.

The other issue to remember is that the 256-color allowance on an 8-bit monitor has to cover all the images that are shown on screen at one time. Once 256 colors have been used, any remaining colors will simply be mapped to the closest equivalent among the first 256, or approximated by dithering two or more available shades. If you're using a lot of photographic illustrations with different palettes, you can optimize your palettes in your image-processing program. One method is to combine all the images you expect to show on a single page into a single Photoshop document, and then convert it to an 8-bit indexed color image with an **adaptive palette** with no dithering.

It's also important to remember visitors who are using grayscale monitors. Though most grayscale monitors will display at least 256 shades of gray, some may display as few as 4. Accommodating visitors using grayscale means using high-contrast graphics, so that when they're sampled down to, say, 4 shades of gray, the important distinctions (text outlines, for example) are still clear.

And, you guessed it: As with so many aspects of Web design, no matter how many precautions you take, the only way to make sure all your preparations work is to test the results on a variety of systems.

Use the browser-safe palette, but don't limit yourself to it. Make sure all your flat, basic colors are from the palette, but then feel free to vignette them or cast drop shadows, and save out as adaptive color. The thousands of colors crowd will see the gradients in all their glory, and the shadows will dither just as they would anyway.

PETER MERHOLZ, STUDIO ARCHETYPE

adaptive palette
A palette created by choosing the most-used colors in an image.

browser-safe palette
A palette of 216 colors used by browsers on 8-bit systems. Mapping graphics to this palette will ensure that colors remain as expected when displayed on such systems.

dithering
A method of creating a color by combining two or more discrete colors.

STUDIO ARCHETYPE
http://www. studioarchetype.com/

THESE NAVIGATION BARS look like image maps, but they are actually built from individual graphics, most of which are reused on every page. Only the graphics that are "highlighted" to show the current location need to be loaded when the visitor moves to a new page.

bit depth
The number of bits used to record each pixel of information in an image file. Common bit depths are 8-bit (256 colors or shades of gray) and 24-bit (16.7 million colors).

cache
An area of memory or disk space reserved for holding data that is expected to be used again, making it faster to retrieve that data the next time it's used.

indexed color
A photo-editing option that allows you to map an image's original colors to a new, usually reduced, color palette.

Speeding Download Time

The most foolproof way to keep download time short, of course, is to use images sparingly. Fortunately, there are also other ways. Poster-size graphics are possible on the Web if you know how to choose the appropriate image format, wring every extra bit from your images as you prepare them, and use HTML controls that speed downloading.

One trick to minimizing image download time is reusing image files. Browsers generally **cache** images once they are downloaded, saving them on the client machine's disk or in memory so that after the image is downloaded once, it can be displayed again almost instantly. The second use of an icon, navigation bar, or other standard graphic comes nearly for free, in terms of download time.

The next thing to remember is that an image's dimensions are not the most important influence on its file size. Equally important is the number of colors it uses, and how it uses them.

As we mentioned earlier (→**121**), the GIF format is ideal for iconic, flat-color images, while JPEG creates smaller file sizes for photographic images. This is because GIF compresses files by scanning the image *in a horizontal direction* and recording new color data each time the color changes. That means that the fewer times your image's color shifts *from left to* *right*, the smaller your GIF file will be—and, by extension, that gradients and other color shifts that proceed *from top to bottom* have no effect on file size. When creating original art for a Web site, this piece of knowledge could help you create the smallest possible GIF files.

A different measure of the number of colors in a file—its **bit depth**—also has an important impact on the file sizes of GIFs. GIF can save up to 8 bits per pixel (256 colors), but few Web designers would dare to use so many. Flat-color graphics are usually mapped to the 6-bit browser-safe palette (→**134**) or to a subset of that palette. Photographic images usually compress quite well when saved as JPEG, even at 24 bits per pixel, but they need extra help when you want to save them as GIF—if you want to use a transparent background, for instance. In those cases, you'll want to use your image-processing program's **indexed color** tool to apply an adaptive palette to the images. On 24-bit systems, your images can look almost as good as the 24-bit originals. (On 8-bit systems, they will still be dithered to the browser palette.) In many cases, you can choose bit depths as low as 4 or 5 bits per pixel and still have good results.

Another key to keeping graphics from getting in the reader's way is remembering HTML tricks that can help the browser deal intelligently with the art. The most important of these are the *height=* and *width=* attributes of the <IMG> and <OBJECT> tags. These

1 Remap the colors in the original file by loading a "browser-safe" palette.

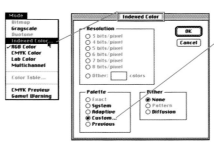
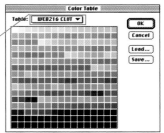

36K

2 Change back to RGB mode.

3 Apply indexed color again, this time using an "exact" palette. Use as few colors as possible without degrading the quality of the image.

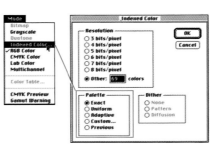
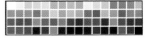

12K

REDUCING GRAPHICS to a minimal color palette can significantly reduce file sizes. Here we show the process (in Photoshop) of mapping a graphic to a subset of the browser-safe palette.

Illustration: Ron Chan, courtesy Agfa

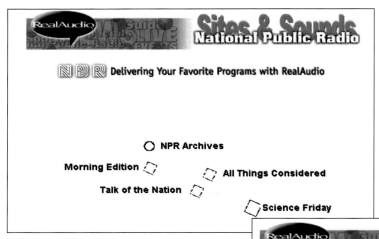

NATIONAL PUBLIC RADIO
http://www.prognet.com/contentp/npr.html

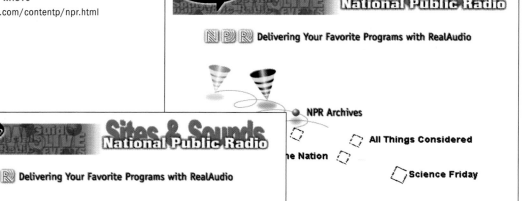

attributes tell the browser how much space the image will take up, allowing it to set that area aside, download the rest of the page contents, and then return to download the slower-loading graphic file. Visitors then have the chance to read—and even move on from—the page without waiting for the images to download completely.

The interlacing possible with GIF, PNG, and Progressive JPEG graphics is another way to save time, quickly building up a rough version of the image that becomes "live" immediately. If it's an image map, readers can click on the graphic and be on their way as soon as they can make out its outline.

A way to make sure a graphic is displayed at once, without waiting for the multiple passes of an interlaced file, is to use *lowsrc=,* another useful attribute for the <IMG> tag. The *lowsrc=* attribute names a low-resolution file that can be displayed while the browser works on loading the higher-resolution version, offering a readable, if fuzzy, version of the graphic on the browser's first pass. The *lowsrc=* attribute isn't supported by every browser, but since it should do no harm in browsers that don't recognize it, you may as well use it. Some crafty designers have used the *lowsrc=* attribute to install an entirely different graphic on the page on the first pass, for a playful, "did I really see that?" effect.

THE LOWSRC= ATTRIBUTE lets designers specify a low-resolution, fast-loading graphic to act as a temporary placeholder for a higher-resolution image. In the example shown here, *lowsrc=* is used to load an image that includes just the text and buttons. On the next pass, a second graphic, which also contains the image of the spinning top, loads, creating a quasi-animated effect.

Anti-Aliasing for Low Resolutions

Last but not least, we introduce another important aspect of the visitor's environment you need to keep in mind as you prepare Web graphics: the low resolution of a computer screen. The average screen resolution—as low as 72 pixels per inch—is much lower than the resolutions—1,200 to 3,600 dots per inch and beyond—used for printed materials. Such low resolutions can cause a stairstep effect (often called "jaggies") on curved and angled edges of graphic shapes. To combat this effect, most graphics programs allow you to "anti-alias" low-resolution graphics. Anti-aliasing blends the edges of graphics with tints of the adjoining color to minimize stairstepping.

The extremely low resolution of screen graphics means that almost all Web graphics should be anti-aliased, but Web designers should be aware of a few effects to watch out for. The first is blurriness. On especially fine shapes, such as small type, the blurred edges of anti-aliasing may well cause more of a problem than jagginess would. The second is that artifacts may occur when an anti-aliased graphic with a transparent background (→**122**) is placed on a new background color. Luckily, the answer to that problem is simple enough: Just make sure to anti-alias the graphic against the color it will finally be placed on.

ANTI-ALIASING BLURS the edges of a graphic to reduce the stairstepping pattern ("jaggies") often seen on low-resolution output devices such as computer screens.

Alternate Web Publishing Formats

Viewing Alternate Formats

XML

Acrobat PDF

VRML

Due to its small file size, its ability to be read across platforms, and its head start in the world of the Web, HTML will likely continue to be the primary format for Web publishing for some time. Meanwhile, though, software companies and online visionaries are looking beyond HTML in an attempt to create more control over the look of pages and explore new types of interactive interfaces.

Perhaps the most important alternate Web publishing format is **XML**, the extensible markup language. Based on SGML (→**70**), it offers Web designers the ability to create their own sets of tags, designed specifically for their own Web publishing needs. Adobe Acrobat's **PDF** allows publishers to create pages in a page layout program and then save the files in an online format that retains all the original fonts and layout. **VRML**—the Virtual Reality Modeling Language—can create 3D interactive environments. In this chapter we'll describe these formats and why and when you may want to use them, instead of HTML, to publish Web pages.

Viewing Alternate Formats

As we've already pointed out (→**11**), publishers can serve up files in any format they want; it won't do much good, however, unless the people they hope to reach have the software they need to read the files. For that reason, the creators of the Web settled on one universal text format—HTML—giving Web publishers a guaranteed base of compatibility. Currently, Netscape and Microsoft are at work building in support for XML (→**142**), which, over time, may become almost as common on the Web as HTML.

To read any other formats, your visitor will need special software, in the form of a plug-in, ActiveX control, or Java player (→**11**). Netscape includes a few plug-ins and Microsoft includes a few ActiveX controls with each browser, so support for the formats they play is almost as good as built-in. The latest browsers can also automatically download players that aren't already available on the user's hard disk. A library of players are available for all sorts of media, ranging from the most common (the CMX Viewer from Corel, for example, displays CorelDraw graphics) to the more specialized (ELT/Net, from Pargon Imaging, is designed to display images in National Imagery Transmission Format, which is used mostly within U.S. government offices).

If you're publishing on an intranet, where your audience is entirely inside a single corporation, you may be able to ensure that everyone has readers already installed for any format you want to use. But if you're publishing more broadly—to a global audience over the Internet—the onus for acquiring the proper software is on the visitor. You can use object detection (→**77**) to determine whether or not the plug-in is present, but asking a visitor to download a player just to read your file is risky. In many cases, the visitor simply won't want to spend the time downloading the player and will just click on by. For that reason, designers need to carefully weigh the risks and benefits of using any alternate format on line.

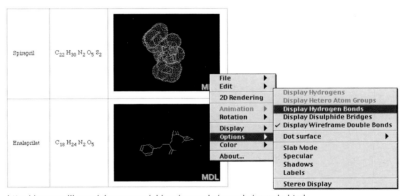

http://www.mdli.com/chemscape/chime/example/sample/sample.html

PLUG-INS can display all sorts of formats that aren't supported directly by browsers. The Chime plug-in from MDL Information Systems, shown here, displays complex molecular models in Chemscape's proprietary format.

PDF
Portable Document Format, an electronic document format created by Adobe Systems and based on PostScript, used by Adobe Acrobat.

VRML
Virtual Reality Modeling Language, a scripting language used to define 3-D shapes for use on the Web. VRML (often pronounced "ver´-mul") supports hyperlinking and programmed behaviors.

XML
Extensible Markup Language, a system, based on SGML, for creating markup languages for the Web. XML support is being built in to both Netscape's and Microsoft's browsers.

WITH XML, page authors can create custom tag sets for special types of documents, such as the play shown here. XML-capable browsers lay out the document according to instructions supplied in attached style sheets.

The Tempest

Dramatis Personae

ALONSO, King of Naples.
SEBASTIAN, his brother.
PROSPERO, the right Duke of Milan.
ANTONIO, his brother, the usurping Duke of Milan.
FERDINAND, son to the King of Naples.
GONZALO, an honest old Counsellor.
ADRIAN
FRANCISCO
    Lords.
CALIBAN, a savage and deformed Slave.
TRINCULO, a Jester.
STEPHANO, a drunken Butler.
Master of a Ship.
Boatswain.
Mariners.
MIRANDA, daughter to Prospero.
ARIEL, an airy Spirit.
IRIS
CERES
JUNO
Nymphs
Reapers
    presented by Spirits.
Other Spirits attending on Prospero.

SCENE A ship at Sea: an island.

THE TEMPEST

ACT I

SCENE I. On a ship at sea: a tempestuous noise of thunder and lightning heard.

[Enter a Master and a Boatswain]

Master	Boatswain!
Boatswain	Here, master: what cheer?
Master	Good, speak to the mariners: fall to 't, yarely, or we run ourselves aground: bestir, bestir.

[Exit]

[Enter Mariners]

Boatswain   Heigh, my hearts! cheerly, cheerly, my hearts! yare, yare ! Take in the topsail. Tend to the master's whistle. Blow, till thou burst thy wind, if room enough!

[Enter ALONSO, SEBASTIAN, ANTONIO, FERDINAND, GONZALO, and others]

ALONSO   Good boatswain, have care. Where's the master? Play the men.

Boatswain   I pray now, keep below.

ANTONIO   Where is the master, boatswain?

Boatswain   Do you not hear him? You mar our labour: keep your cabins: you do assist the storm.

GONZALO   Nay, good, be patient.

Boatswain   When the sea is. Hence! What cares these roarers for the name of king? To cabin: silence! trouble us not.

```
<?XML version="1.0"?>
<!DOCTYPE play PUBLIC "-//Free Text Project//DTD Play//EN">

<PLAY>
<TITLE>The Tempest</TITLE>

<PERSONAE>
<TITLE>Dramatis Personae</TITLE>

<PERSONA>ALONSO, King of Naples.</PERSONA>
<PERSONA>SEBASTIAN, his brother.</PERSONA>
<PERSONA>PROSPERO, the right Duke of Milan.</PERSONA>
<PERSONA>ANTONIO, his brother, the usurping Duke of
Milan.</PERSONA>
<PERSONA>FERDINAND, son to the King of Naples.</PERSONA>
<PERSONA>GONZALO, an honest old Counsellor.</PERSONA>

<PGROUP>
<PERSONA>ADRIAN</PERSONA>
<PERSONA>FRANCISCO</PERSONA>
<GRPDESCR>Lords.</GRPDESCR>
</PGROUP>

<PERSONA>CALIBAN, a savage and deformed Slave.</PERSONA>
<PERSONA>TRINCULO, a Jester.</PERSONA>
<PERSONA>STEPHANO, a drunken Butler.</PERSONA>
<PERSONA>Master of a Ship.</PERSONA>
<PERSONA>Boatswain. </PERSONA>
<PERSONA>Mariners. </PERSONA>
<PERSONA>MIRANDA, daughter to Prospero.</PERSONA>
<PERSONA>ARIEL, an airy Spirit.</PERSONA>

<PGROUP>
<PERSONA>IRIS</PERSONA>
<PERSONA>CERES</PERSONA>
<PERSONA>JUNO</PERSONA>
<PERSONA>Nymphs</PERSONA>
<PERSONA>Reapers</PERSONA>
<GRPDESCR>presented by Spirits.</GRPDESCR>
</PGROUP>

<PERSONA>Other Spirits attending on Prospero.</PERSONA>
</PERSONAE>

<SCNDESCR>SCENE  A ship at Sea: an island.</SCNDESCR>

<PLAYSUBT>THE TEMPEST</PLAYSUBT>

<ACT><TITLE>ACT I</TITLE>

<SCENE><TITLE>SCENE I.  On a ship at sea: a tempestuous noise
of thunder and lightning heard.</TITLE>

<STAGEDIR>Enter a Master and a Boatswain</STAGEDIR>

<SPEECH>
<SPEAKER>Master</SPEAKER>
<LINE>Boatswain!</LINE>
</SPEECH>

<SPEECH>
<SPEAKER>Boatswain</SPEAKER>
<LINE>Here, master: what cheer?</LINE>
</SPEECH>
```

XML

From the Web's first days, Web publishers familiar with SGML (→**70**) have lobbied for browsers that could read any set of SGML tags, not just the subset that is HTML. With SGML, tag sets can be designed for different publishing needs (referred to as "applications" of SGML). Browser support of SGML would mean that control over the set of tags used on the Web would burst beyond the HTML working group, and communities that have specialized formatting and processing needs could create their own markup languages.

It took some time for those hopes to be realized, but it looks like they finally will be, in the form of XML, the Extensible Markup Language. XML was proposed as a specification to the Web standards bodies in late 1997, and Netscape and Microsoft have both announced plans to support it in their browsers.

XML is a variation on SGML streamlined and adapted to make it more practical on the Web. The most important difference is XML's informality. With SGML, every set of tags must be defined and documented in a **DTD** (document type description), a file that describes the tags for that application and the attributes those tags can use. DTDs aren't necessary in XML. Instead, every publisher will be able to create a new tag by simply adding it to a document. Style sheets (→**98**) will tell the browser how to format the element, and scripts (→**186**) can give the browser special instructions for handling it, allowing page authors to create interactive interfaces.

In use, XML is very much like HTML. In fact, with just a couple of minor coding changes, HTML is a legal XML application. The most obvious difference is that in XML each tag must either have an accompanying end tag or include a special end tag character; each <IMG> tag, for example, would need to be followed by a </IMG> tag or have a / character before the tag's closing angle bracket. And since browsers simply ignore tags they don't understand (→**76**), you can make your HTML code XML-compatible without affecting its display in HTML-only browsers.

The value of XML will probably be felt most by industries, such as banking or health care, that need to be able to exchange specialized information in predictable formats. Such communities will be able to deal with elements that, at the current rate, wouldn't make it into the HTML spec until sometime in the next millennium. The health care industry might create a markup language that includes tags like <ALLERGIES> and <DOCTOR>, which could be used to exchange patient records, and then build scripts that find and display just that information. Another advantage of XML is for applications that demand strictly formatted files—files that will be automatically added to a database, for instance. DTDs, though not required in XML, can be used, offering XML software the ability to **validate** XML

Authoring an XML document along with the style sheets you'll need to use it is rather complex, so most people aren't going to pick up XML right away. XML is going to be used first for highly structured content—software documentation, movie review services, and other things that today are stored in relational databases.

BRIAN BEHLENDORFF, ORGANIC

DTD
Document Type Description, a file that defines the tags used in an SGML or XML application. DTDs are required for SGML tag sets. For XML, they are useful for validating documents for applications that require certain elements and certain values for those elements.

validate
For SGML or XML, to verify that a document's content is valid according to the rules specified in the DTD.

CDF, RDF, and PICS: They're All XML

For publishers, XML is interesting as a tool for creating custom tagging languages for different kinds of documents. XML's uses go beyond that, though, creating an easy way for browser manufacturers and others to add new capabilities to their software. Just as browser makers build support for HTML's tag set into their browsers, they can also build in support for other special-purpose XML tag sets.

One application of XML, called CDF (Channel Definition Format) is already built into Internet Explorer starting with version 4.0. CDF tags are inserted into files that define the intervals at which the browser will download channels to which a user subscribes. Users don't even know they're using XML, because the Wizard they use to set their preferences inserts the code automatically.

Other special-purpose uses are planned for the next browser releases. RDF, the Resource Description Framework under development at the W3C, will provide "metadata" (data about data) for a file. An application of RDF spearheaded by Netscape will let you tag a file so that a browser can automatically create an up-to-date table of contents for the file each time it is read. PICS, the Platform for Internet Content Selection, provides a system with which publishers can provide information about their site's contents. It is designed to be used by programs that filter Web content for different audiences.

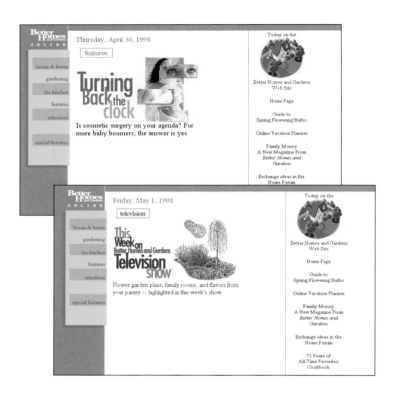

```
<CHANNEL HREF=3D"http://www.bhglive.com/ie4/index.shtml" =
BASE=3D"http://www.bhglive.com/ie4/" =
SELF=3D"http://www.bhglive.com/ie4/cdf/bhg3.cdf">


    <SCHEDULE STARTDATE=3D"1997.09.15T10:46-0800">
    <INTERVALTIME HOUR=3D"12"/>
        <LATESTTIME HOUR=3D"6"/>
    </SCHEDULE>

...

</CHANNEL>
```

ART AND SCIENCE
http://www.bhglive.com/ie4/index.shtml

CDF, the language used to control Microsoft's "channels," is one of the special flavors of XML already being used in browsers.

files (either as they're being authored or as they're being read) to make sure the file adheres to the specified format.

XML offers some advantages to every Web publisher, but nothing so compelling as to make everyone leave HTML behind immediately. With XML, for instance, Web page authors can tag their documents with codes that actually describe the publication's structure: A book like this might use tags like <CHAPTITLE>, <CHAPTOC>, <SUBHEAD>, <CAPTION>, and so on, just as we used in the Quark files to format the original pages for print. On the other hand, this capability isn't much different from what you can already do with style sheets, where you can create classes (→**100**) of structural tags (<.chapterhead>, <H2.subhead>, and so on) to do the same thing.

XML is developing as a language all its own, alongside HTML. The XML working group is developing companion specifications for XML style sheets (described in the sidebar on the opposite page) and a much more advanced (and complex) system for XML hyperlinks.

For the foreseeable future, browsers will probably support both HTML and XML. One day, HTML will probably be understood as a general-purpose application of XML, and WYSIWYG Web authoring applications, which will by then be the standard way of creating Web documents, will create XML-compatible HTML.

XSL STYLESHEET

```
<XSL>
    <RULE>
        <TARGET-ELEMENT TYPE="change-date"/>
        <P COLOR="blue" font-style="italic">
            <CHILDREN/>
        </P>
    </RULE>
</XSL>
```

XML CODE

```
<DOCUMENT>
    <CHANGE-DATE>3 October 1997</CHANGE-DATE>
</DOCUMENT>
```

XSL "CONSTRUCTION RULES" describe the styles to be used for each XML element. An XSL processor applies the XSL rules to the XML code to create the resulting output: in this case, HTML and CSS code suitable for displaying in a Web browser. (Other construction rules could result in other types of output.) As you can see by the familiar angle brackets and tag syntax, XSL is itself an application of XML.

XSL PROCESSOR

RESULTING HTML CODE

```
<P STYLE="color:blue; font-style:italic">3 October 1997</P>
```

XSL: The Extensible Style Language

XSL, the extensible style language created as a companion to XML, offers the same type of formatting and layout controls that CSS, the cascading style sheet language used to control the layout of HTML elements, does. But while CSS contents itself with simply describing the display of tagged elements, XSL goes beyond that to allow authors to describe the behaviors of different elements using scripting languages.

XSL's syntax is quite different from that of CSS. In fact, XSL is another example of XML in action, so instead of the parentheses used by CSS, XSL elements are enclosed in angle brackets and use attributes to define the element's characteristics. And although it takes many of its style controls from CSS, XSL's syntax is actually mostly based on a style language called DSSSL, the Document Symantics and Style Specification Language, created for use with SGML. It's not necessary to use XSL in order to use XML; if all you want to do is describe the layout of XML elements, CSS will do fine. If you want to do things like describe a new order for a document's sections, automatically insert boilerplate text, automatically calculate and insert chapter numbers, or perform other actions that depend on programming logic, you'll turn to XSL.

When we wrote this, XSL was in the very beginnings of its definition process, but Microsoft was supporting it strongly, having already come up with an XSL processor for Windows machines. Chances are that some XSL support will appear in browsers about the same time support for XML does.

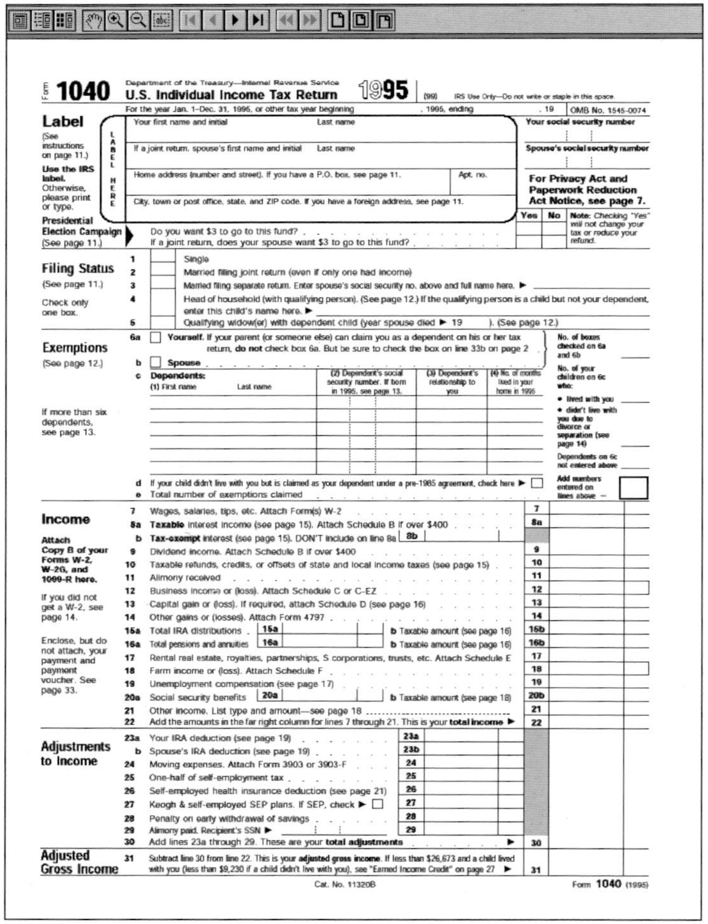

ftp://ftp.fedworld.gov/pub/irs-pdf/f1040.pdf

PDF FILES are useful for pages, such as this IRS form, that require precise formatting. The tool bar at the top of the illustration shows the Acrobat Reader's navigation tools.

PDF can be cumbersome because it requires a plug-in, but if clients already have a huge store of paper documents that they need to make available over the Net, it can be an easy solution.

NATHAN SHEDROFF, VIVID STUDIOS

Acrobat PDF

Before the Web was a household word, Adobe Systems created PDF (Portable Document Format) as a way to store formatted documents on office network systems. Translating a file into PDF solved the problem of how to distribute documents electronically when you're not sure everyone who needs them has the application that created them and you don't want to lose the documents' formatting by reducing them to pure text. When the Web was born, Adobe offered PDF as an alternative to HTML: a way to bypass all of HTML's formatting limitations. Designers could lay out their files in any page layout or word processing program they wanted, then save the files as PDF and publish them on the Web in all their original glory.

To create or read PDF files, authors and readers need Adobe's Acrobat software. The Acrobat Reader, a plug-in or ActiveX component used to display the file, is distributed with some copies of Netscape Navigator and Microsoft Internet Explorer; copies and updates are also available free from Adobe's Web site. The Acrobat authoring system includes software that lets authors create PDF files either by printing to the Acrobat driver or by batch-processing PostScript files or scanned documents. The authoring software also lets you add bookmarks, full text indexes, annotations, and hyperlinks. (The hyperlinks can link to locations both within the file and to any Web URL.)

Although it never emerged as a rival to HTML, PDF has caught on for certain uses on the Web. Many publishers have found PDF useful, for instance, for publishing documents—brochures, product literature, and such—created for other media, without incurring the costs of translating the documents into HTML.

PDF is also useful for publishing documents, such as forms, that rely on small type and precise formatting. The IRS, for instance, distributes its tax forms in PDF format from its Web site. Some publishers also argue that long documents that readers will want to print out are good candidates for PDF.

The Acrobat Reader is one of the Web's most popular plug-ins, so publishers can be pretty confident that most of their audience will have the software installed. Before publishing in PDF rather than HTML, though, authors should consider a couple of drawbacks. One is that PDF files, while compressed from the original page layout files, are still much larger than the same material would be in HTML. Second, visitors reading the PDF files are suddenly thrown into a different interface than the one they're used to in their browsers, with different methods for moving from page to page and other common tasks. Still, for jobs that HTML just isn't up to or for pages that wouldn't make it onto the Web any other way, PDF is a good alternative.

RAYMOND MELVILLE
http://www.adlbooks.com/

FILES MEANT TO BE PRINTED OUT and read off line are good candidates for electronic document formats. This site offers two versions of its newsletter, one for online reading (bottom left) and another that uses Acrobat to retain a newsletterlike format for the armchair (below).

VIRTUAL SOMA, a VRML world created by Planet 9, features the buildings and artists of San Francisco's Multimedia Gulch neighborhood.

PLANET 9 STUDIOS
http://www.planet9.com/vrsoma.htm

VIRTUAL KYOTO offers VRML models of Kyoto's temples, gardens, and other attractions.

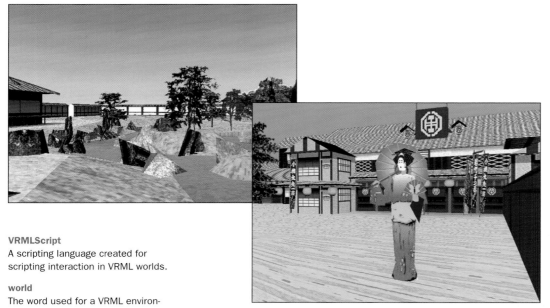

VRMLScript
A scripting language created for scripting interaction in VRML worlds.

world
The word used for a VRML environment, to differentiate it from the "page" interface of 2D formats.

PLANET 9 STUDIOS
www.planet9.com/earth/kyoto/

VRML

VRML (sometimes pronounced "ver´-mul"), stands for Virtual Reality Modeling Language, a scripting language designed to create three-dimensional, interactive interfaces for the Web. VRML leaves the page-oriented interface of the Web behind to launch viewers into a 3D **world**, through which they navigate using special player software.

Links between different 3D scenes are provided via the same URL hyperlinks used in HTML. Interactivity and time-based behaviors can be added using Java (→**188**), JavaScript (→**186**), or **VRMLScript**, a scripting language related to JavaScript but created especially for VRML. Viewing VRML worlds requires special VRML support in a browser, which is currently provided as a plug-in with Netscape's browser and as an ActiveX control with Microsoft's.

VRML, first proposed in 1994, had a later start than HTML, and it has had some serious growing pains. As with HTML, impatient VRML browser vendors first tried to hurry the format's development along by introducing their own add-ons to the language. Unlike HTML, though, browsers can't just ignore nonstandard VRML code; a nonsupported command will make a VRML model unreadable by a competitor's player software. In 1996, however, the VRML industry finalized negotiations on version 2.0 of the VRML spec, which finally consolidated the industry around a single version and opened the door to the delivery of general-purpose VRML viewers. By the end of 1997, Microsoft and Netscape had begun offering VRML 2.0–compliant players from their Web sites. Both companies now automatically distribute the player with some, but not all, browsers.

VRML authoring can be done with special-purpose tools or, more and more frequently, with mainstream 3D modeling packages that include the capability of saving models in VRML format. Intrepid coders can also write VRML by hand.

Although VRML is a compact format as 3D formats go, 3D modeling is notorious for straining the capabilities of personal computers. As the format gains in popularity, VRML software makers will doubtless become more sophisticated about compression, and built-in 3D rendering processors supporting VRML

may become common in personal computers. Meanwhile, though, the art of VRML lies in creating worlds with a minimum number of polygons—the separate shapes that make up a 3D form. Often, realism has to take a back seat to efficiency, as VRML artists focus on creating models that can, above all, be downloaded and rendered quickly.

Online: Alternate Web Publishing Formats

Adobe Acrobat
http://www.adobe.com/Acrobat/main.html

CDF
http://www.microsoft.com/standards/cdf-f.htm

PICS
http://www.w3.org/PICS/

Plug-ins
http://browserwatch.internet.com/plug-in.html
http://home.netscape.com/comprod/products/navigator/version_2.0/plugins/

RDF
http://www.w3.org/RDF/Overview.html

VRML
http://www.construct.net/tools/vrml/
http://cosmosoftware.com/
http://www.microsoft.com/vrml/
http://www.sdsc.edu/vrml/
http://www.vrml.org/

XML
http://www.w3.org/XML/
http://www.microsoft.com/xml/

XSL
http://www.w3.org/Style/XSL/
http://www.microsoft.com/xml/xsl/xslintro.htm

I don't think 3D interfaces like VRML are going to replace HTML. Text is a very old interface and it's not going to go away, but space is another very old interface. You'll use 3D interfaces for what you use space for: to store things, to navigate, to group things.

MARK MEADOWS, CONSTRUCT

Multimedia

The World Wide Web is a true multimedia environment, able to display animation, sound, and video in addition to text and graphics. So far, though, the Web's multimedia possibilities have remained largely untapped. Lack of consensus on standard formats, lack of support in browsers for dynamic media, and, above all, the time it takes to download rich media such as sound and video all discouraged its use. Now, some of those barriers have begun to come down.

Recently, a few sound and video formats have emerged as leaders and are broadly supported via plug-ins. New technologies for animation have significantly reduced the file sizes required for creating dynamic effects on screen. Although file size, especially for sound and video, remains a stumbling block that anyone posting multimedia on the Web will need to contend with, many multimedia effects have become practical options, and even carefully measured multimedia effects can have big payoffs in terms of impact. In this chapter, we'll discuss your options for animation, sound, and video formats on the Web.

Keeping Up With Multimedia

Everyone knows how movies work: Viewers see a sequence of images, each just slightly different from the last, in such quick succession that it seems that only one image is projected and is moving. Digital video and animation work the same way; they require a sequence of digital images to be displayed quickly enough to give the illusion of **real-time motion**. If the sequential images are displayed too slowly (slower than about 24 frames per second), or if one frame is too different from the last, the illusion is lost. Digital sound works in a similar way: discrete sound **samples** must be played quickly to sound natural.

Now think about how that would be accomplished on a computer. As anyone who has worked with digital images knows, even one bitmap graphic can require several megabytes of disk space. Multiply that number by 24 for each second of video or animation, and you're talking about immense files, even for short clips.

These issues are older than the Web. The same challenges have faced digital video and multimedia professionals for years, and the industry has come up with compression schemes, such as MPEG and QuickTime (**→160**), to help squeeze files down to smaller sizes. But compression can do only so much— and never enough to get even the shortest video file small enough to download without an annoying wait over a modem hookup to the Web.

An answer to this problem, called **streaming**, has been created to help avoid the long wait for multimedia download. Streaming technologies let a user begin playing the file while it is being downloaded. The compressed files are sent to the client software, which decompresses them and feeds them, bit by bit, to the player. Later sections are cached in the client computer's memory until it's their turn. This technique removes the tight limits on file size that constrain authors under save-and-play systems; no matter how long the file, the user waits only for the first, short section.

Another way to reduce the wait for multimedia files is to reduce the amount of information the files contain. Animations based on vector graphics (**→123**) can be built right on the viewer's computer; the server can send the relatively small program code that creates the animation sequence, rather than a bandwidth-hogging sequence of graphics files. Some animations can also be created from a single graphic, whose movement is controlled via a script on the user's machine, a technique used by dynamic HTML (**→158**).

Keep these techniques in mind as you read about the different multimedia options described in this chapter. They'll help you understand how one technology measures up to another and how new techniques improve a multimedia experience for a site's visitors.

ANIMATED GRAPHIC

MACROMEDIA FLASH: 1,608 bytes
GIF ANIMATION: 32,126 bytes

VECTOR

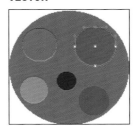

BITMAPPED

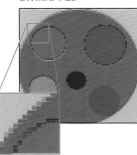

VECTOR GRAPHICS and animations, such as those used by Macromedia Flash, can be created from compact code right on the user's machine. For bitmap graphics, such as GIF graphics, the file contains information about each pixel in the image and each frame of the animation, resulting in much larger file sizes.

real-time motion
In digital animation or video, the effect of natural motion achieved by using a frame rate of 24 to 30 frames per second.

sample
In digital media, a digital recording of sound or visual data, taken and played back at high frequencies to create the illusion of natural sound or motion.

streaming
Describes technologies that feed media files to a player progressively, so that a file can begin playing as it is being downloaded.

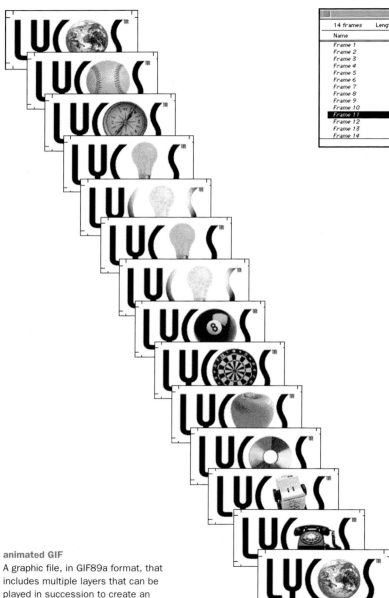

Animated GIF

The ability to include multiple frames of images had always been a feature of the GIF89a format (→**121**), but Navigator 2.0 was the first browser to support **animated GIF**—the ability to play back the layers as animations. Microsoft began supporting animated GIF in Internet Explorer 3.0. (Browsers that don't support the animation feature display only the first frame of the animation.) Tools for creating animated GIFs quickly popped up as shareware and have been built into mainstream graphics and animation programs.

Animated GIFs are downloaded to the browser just like any other GIF graphic; the browser takes care of playing the animation frames in the file. Short sequences can be looped to keep the animation playing until the user moves to a new page (or clicks the Stop button in the browser). Playback can speed along as fast as the client machine can render each frame, or it can be paced by delays specified in the GIF authoring program.

The animated GIF format minimizes file sizes by allowing artists to save only the parts of the image that change with each frame. With careful planning, files can be kept surprisingly small. And animated GIFs are streamed in a sense: The first image will show up as soon as it is downloaded, with the subsequent frames following as fast as the connection allows.

Frames

14 frames Length: 10.70 s Size: 178×71

Name	Size	Position	Disp.	Delay	Transp.
Frame 1	178×71	(0 ; 0)	N	600	–
Frame 2	178×71	(0 ; 0)	N	40	–
Frame 3	178×71	(0 ; 0)	N	40	–
Frame 4	178×71	(0 ; 0)	N	10	–
Frame 5	178×71	(0 ; 0)	N	40	–
Frame 6	178×71	(0 ; 0)	N	20	–
Frame 7	178×71	(0 ; 0)	N	70	–
Frame 8	178×71	(0 ; 0)	N	40	–
Frame 9	178×71	(0 ; 0)	N	40	–
Frame 10	178×71	(0 ; 0)	N	40	–
Frame 11	178×71	(0 ; 0)	N	40	–
Frame 12	178×71	(0 ; 0)	N	40	–
Frame 13	178×71	(0 ; 0)	N	40	–
Frame 14	178×71	(0 ; 0)			

Image Size

○ Minimum Size
◉ Fixed Size:

Width: [100]
Height: [40]

(Cancel) (Ok)

Looping

○ No
◉ Forever
○ [   ] times

(Cancel) (Ok)

ANIMATED GIF FILES hold several frames of graphics, which are played successively in browsers that support them. (Browsers that don't support them display just the first frame.) GIFBuilder, a Macintosh shareware program (shown here), lets designers control features such as the number of times the animation loops, the size of the graphic, and the delay between frames.

DOREN BERGE
http://www.lycos.com/

animated GIF
A graphic file, in GIF89a format, that includes multiple layers that can be played in succession to create an animation.

Animation With Shockwave

A wide variety of animation formats can be supported by plug-ins and ActiveX controls (→**11**). The most important plug-in formats for multimedia are Macromedia's **Shockwave** formats, Shockwave for Director and **Shockwave Flash**.

Macromedia uses the term *Shockwave* to refer to an entire suite of Web formats, players, and authoring tools developed to support its software on the Web. But when people say Shockwave, they're usually referring to Shockwave for Director, the company's first Shockwave product, designed to bring files from Director, the company's popular multimedia authoring program, onto the Web. Shockwave for Director includes a tool, called Afterburner, that translates native Director files into a compressed, streaming format that can be played back in browsers via the company's popular Shockwave plug-in. Shockwave for Director files can include all the sophisticated multimedia features popular on CD-ROM, including animation, sound, and sophisticated interactivity. For people who already know Director, the convenience is wonderful because they can use all the familiar authoring tools to create Web-ready multimedia.

The idea is a great one, but a few drawbacks prevent Shockwave for Director from being the perfect tool for Web animation. One is file size. Although Afterburner compresses Director files to about half their original

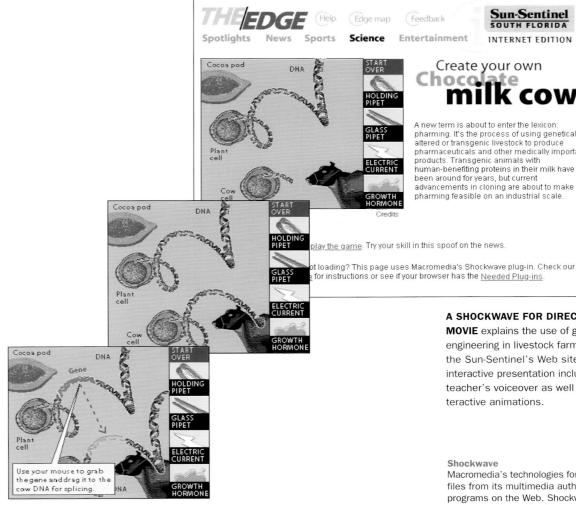

DON WITTEKIND/R. SCOTT HORNER
http://www.sun-sentinel.com/graphics/science/clone.htm

A SHOCKWAVE FOR DIRECTOR MOVIE explains the use of genetic engineering in livestock farming on the Sun-Sentinel's Web site. The interactive presentation includes a teacher's voiceover as well as interactive animations.

Shockwave
Macromedia's technologies for playing files from its multimedia authoring programs on the Web. Shockwave tools, including authoring programs and players, are available for Macromedia's Director, Flash, and FreeHand applications.

Shockwave Flash
An interactive, animated vector graphics format from Macromedia.

SHOCKWAVE FLASH provides dynamic typographic "splash screens" for product design firm IDEO (below) and online clothing emporium HomeWrecker (right). The IDEO site resolves into a JavaScript-based interactive interface. HomeWrecker uses Flash throughout for animated, sound-enhanced interactivity.

JAMES TUCKER/THUNK DESIGN
http://www.homewrecker.com/

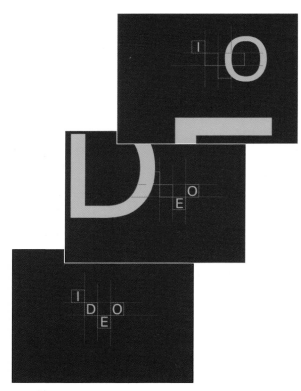

METADESIGN
http://www.ideo.com

size and the files stream over the Web, designers still need to be careful to keep file sizes down. Another drawback is that the kinds of interfaces Director was created for—interfaces you might use for stand-alone CD-ROMs or kiosks, for instance—are foreign in the world of the Web. If you were to take advantage of all of Director's powers, you could end up with an interface that is disconcerting to users who are used to the interface conventions of the Web.

For simple animated and interactive interfaces, a later addition to the Shockwave family, Shockwave Flash, is often a better choice. Flash can't handle some of the complex interfaces you can create in Director; instead, its forte is animation based on vector graphics (→**123**). Flash animations can be interactive as well; you can embed buttons that can link to other Web pages or play other Flash animations and sounds.

As we described earlier, file sizes for vector-based graphics can be much smaller than file sizes for bitmap graphics, and vector-based animations are many times more efficient than bitmap animations such as those used for animated GIFs (→**152**). Instead of downloading a graphic for each frame of the animation, vector formats such as Flash download program code, which the client software (the Shockwave Flash plug-in) uses to create and animate the graphics on the visitor's machine.

The standard Shockwave player plays both Shockwave for Director and Shockwave Flash files; a separate player is also available for Flash only. The formats are so popular that it's fairly likely that visitors to your site will have the software. (Macromedia reports that more than 37 million Shockwave players and plug-ins were downloaded from its Web site in 1997.) Still, as we explained earlier, it is always risky to publish media in a format that requires a plug-in because some of your visitors won't have the player. For that reason, Macromedia and other multimedia companies also offer another way to publish their formats on the Web: using Java, as we describe in the next section.

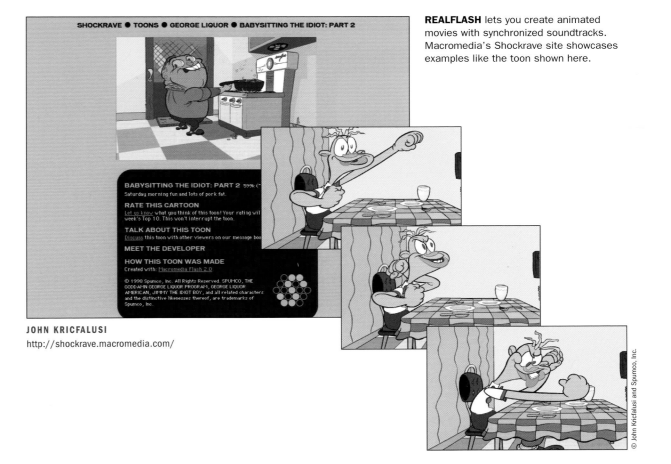

JOHN KRICFALUSI
http://shockrave.macromedia.com/

REALFLASH lets you create animated movies with synchronized soundtracks. Macromedia's Shockrave site showcases examples like the toon shown here.

You can't really use Flash as the user interface for navigating a Web site because nothing that's so core to the site experience should be presented with a plug-in. However, Flash is brilliant as a stand-alone Web presentation technology, and it's the smartest way to present full-screen motion.

PETER MERHOLZ, STUDIO ARCHETYPE

RealFlash

Macromedia and RealNetworks have collaborated to create a system, called RealFlash, that lets you combine Flash animation with a synchronized RealAudio track, to create more complex, streaming animations. Playing RealFlash animations requires a special server, available through RealNetworks. To view RealFlash animations, viewers must have the RealPlayer helper application.

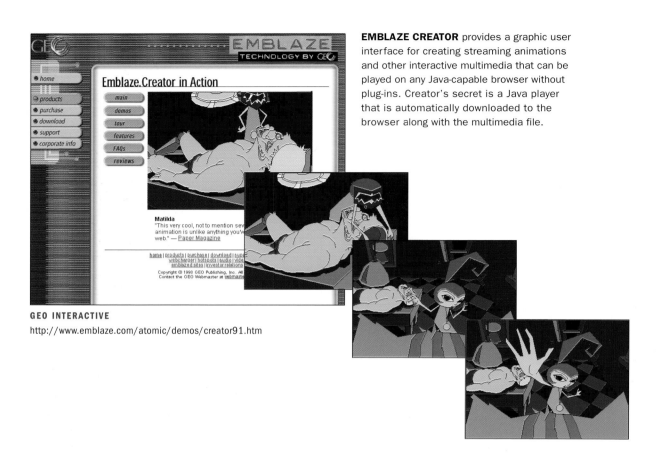

EMBLAZE CREATOR provides a graphic user interface for creating streaming animations and other interactive multimedia that can be played on any Java-capable browser without plug-ins. Creator's secret is a Java player that is automatically downloaded to the browser along with the multimedia file.

GEO INTERACTIVE
http://www.emblaze.com/atomic/demos/creator91.htm

Java Animation

Java (→**188**) is a programming language designed to create programs that run on any platform. Programmers can create Java programs that can do just about anything, and one thing they can do is create animations. Since version 2.0 of Navigator and 3.0 of Internet Explorer, the leading Web browsers have supported Java directly, just as they support HTML and GIF, so Java animations will run automatically in any recent browser; the user doesn't need to have a plug-in.

Several programs have been created to help Web designers create Java animations without knowing anything about Java. These programs, such as Emblaze Creator, PowerProduction's WebBurst FX, and PaceWorks' Object Dancer, offer a visual interface for creating animations. Then they either write the animation itself as a Java applet (→**188**), which is downloaded to the browser along with the HTML page (the most common method), or they download a separate Java applet that acts as a player for an animation saved in a proprietary format (an approach used, for instance, by Emblaze Creator). Often, such programs offer the ability to save in a number of other animation formats, as well (see sidebar).

Java is ubiquitous, but (there's always a but) the Java interpreters in most browsers are still pretty slow and unstable; if a plug-in is present, it could probably play your animation more reliably.

Java is a heavy-duty programming language. Using it for light-duty features like animation on the client is like using an elephant to squash a peanut.

MATTHEW BUTTERICK, ATOMIC VISION

JAVA PROGRAMMING SPINS this ASCII globe, featured on the home page of ASCII World, IO360's site featuring art made from alphabetic characters.

STEVE KANN
http://www.io360.com/v2/yo/asciiworld/

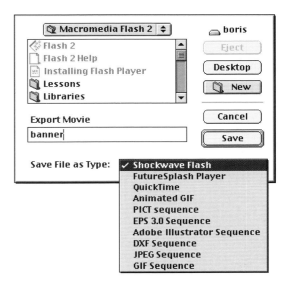

Whatever: Animation Packages That Don't Make You Choose a Format

The latest trend in Web animation tools is to allow animators to save their projects in their choice of formats: in a proprietary format that requires a plug-in, in Java, as dynamic HTML, or as an animated GIF. This approach has been adopted by Macromedia Flash (its Afterburner utility, whose interface is shown above, lets you save as Shockwave Flash, Java, or animated GIF) and Director (Shockwave for Director or Java), mBED Interactor (mBED, Java, or dynamic HTML), and PaceWorks' ObjectDancer (QuickTime, animated GIF, or Java). Each playback format has its advantages and disadvantages, described on these pages. Using scripts, you can figure out which format each visitor to your site can handle and make sure they get only those they can read.

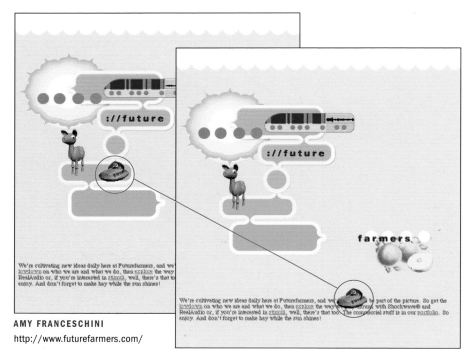

AMY FRANCESCHINI
http://www.futurefarmers.com/

JAVASCRIPT propels a GIF of a flying saucer around the browser window on this site for Web design company Future Farmers.

Animation With Dynamic HTML

The latest trend in animation is dynamic HTML (→**76**) HTML that moves. Creating animations with dynamic HTML involves using style sheets (→**98**) and CSS positioning (→**103**) along with JavaScript (→**186**). The idea is that you can use JavaScript to tell the browser to move and change HTML elements (including graphics and other embedded objects) in the browser window. Those JavaScript commands can make objects visible or invisible; change their color, size, and layering position on the page; and perform lots of other transformations.

Dynamic HTML has many good features. First, since you can achieve a lot of different effects by simply transforming an object's display characteristics (size, position, color, z-index, and so on), you can create animations with a single graphic; you don't need to download a different graphic for each position, color, or other state, as you do with GIF animation (→**152**), for example. Second, you can use it to animate HTML text; you no longer have to set text in graphics to animate it. And actions can be triggered in response to user choices, so you can use it to create interactive interfaces as well (→**172**). And last but not least, it requires no special plug-ins or players.

What it does require is support for style sheets, CSS positioning, and JavaScript—and these only began to be supported with Navigator and Internet Explorer 4.0, so it could be a while before the majority of browsers in use can display dynamic HTML effects.

DHTML animation will be important when it is supported consistently across browsers. As with any other kind of animation, though, the important thing is to use it because it enhances communication and not just because it's a novelty.

NATHAN SHEDROFF, VIVID STUDIOS

DYNAMIC HTML creates an interactive interface for the Fuse98 Web site. The timeline scrolls across the window when you click on the forward and back buttons.

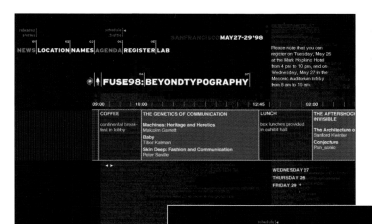

METADESIGN
http://www.fuse98.com/

The DOM: The Key to—and the Problem With—DHTML

In 1997, when Netscape and Microsoft were planning their implementations of dynamic HTML, there was no agreed-upon standard for how scripts should interface with HTML elements. Thus (surprise!) the two camps came up with two different methods. Netscape introduced the <LAYER> tag as a way to create objects that could be addressed by JavaScript. Microsoft came up with a more complex and complete plan—the document object model (DOM)—which described a general-purpose way to address any element within an HTML page.

The different models used by the two browsers becomes important when it comes to scripting. You refer to an HTML object using entirely different syntaxes depending on which model is used. (We won't go into the different syntaxes here, because understanding how they work requires a knowledge of how JavaScript works.)

Microsoft's DOM has gained acceptance by the W3C, and Netscape has pledged to support it in upcoming versions of its browser. Until that support is in place, though, programmers (and programs) creating dynamic HTML need to write separate scripts to support Netscape and Microsoft browsers.

RealPlayer: Zip Files

Title: Zip Files
Author: ZDTV
Copyright: ZDTV Copyright © 1998

Mono   00:29.2 / 00:41.4
Playing 19.5 Kbps network stream

http://www.zdnet.com/zdtv/cgi-bin/rmplay.cgi?/zdtv/channel/zipfile/zf_tilde.intro_56.rm

REALVIDEO, played via the RealSystems' RealPlayer plug-in or ActiveX control, is currently the most popular format for streaming video on the Web.

THIS QUICKTIME MOVIE, posted on Greenpeace's Web site, shows French commandos boarding the Rainbow Warrior as the ship monitored France's nuclear tests in the South Pacific.

http://www.greenpeace.org/

Video

Video can supply information that no other form can offer. Animation is great for eye-catching artist's effects and advertisements, but only video can show you people in action or convey what it's really like to be present at an event.

Video is also the biggest bandwidth hog on the Net. Even in compressed formats such as **MPEG**, **QuickTime**, and **AVI**, video files of more than a few seconds are commonly measured in megabytes, not the double-digit kilobyte sizes more acceptable on the Web.

It's possible to post video in any common digital format (such as those named above); plug-ins and ActiveX controls that support them are included with Microsoft's and Netscape's browsers. To avoid hours-long download times, though, it's usually best to use a streaming format (→**151**) for video. There are several streaming formats to choose from, including Xing Technologies' StreamWorks system, VDOnet's VDOLive, and others, and all have their benefits. But for Web publishing, where your first consideration is how likely it is that your visitors have the software they need to read your files, three formats deserve the spotlight: **RealVideo**, QuickTime 3.0, and NetShow.

RealVideo is the video format created by RealNetworks, which also created RealAudio, the most popular audio format (→**165**) and (with Macromedia) codeveloped RealFlash, an audio-enhanced version of the popular

Flash animation format (→**155**). All these formats are supported by a single player, the company's RealPlayer helper application, which is one of the most popular players on the Web. RealVideo authoring tools, player plug-ins, and server software are available free from the company's Web site. (The company does ask to be paid for more advanced versions of its software.)

The latest version of QuickTime, QuickTime 3.0, includes new Web-friendly features, including streaming and a new compression technology that offers higher-quality video, with lower file sizes, than earlier versions provided. QuickTime's small file sizes and cross-platform capabilities have already made it popular on the Web. These advances should make it even more so.

Microsoft's NetShow software may be on its way to becoming the most ubiquitous multimedia player on the Web, since it is distributed free with Microsoft Windows and Internet Explorer. (Players are also available for the Macintosh and for Unix machines.) In its next release, NetShow may also offer the most universal support; version 3.0 of the player will handle not only NetShow's **ASF** movies, but also RealVideo, RealAudio, QuickTime, AVI, and MPEG. Microsoft offers NetShow authoring software and servers.

With the help of special servers, all of these streaming formats allow publishers to broadcast live video as well as saved video files, allowing Web publishers to broadcast live events—press conferences and rock

QUICKTIME 3.0 offers tight compression and streaming playback.

APPLE COMPUTER, INC.
http://www.apple.com/quicktime/samples/interactive-mm/dratsam.html

ASF
Advanced Streaming Format, a format for streaming audio and video created by Microsoft and used in its NetShow products.

AVI
The standard video format for Microsoft Windows.

MPEG
A compressed video format, created by and named for the Motion Picture Experts Group of the International Standards Organization.

QuickTime
A video format created by Apple Computer and supported on the Macintosh and Windows platforms.

RealVideo
A streaming video format developed by RealNetworks.

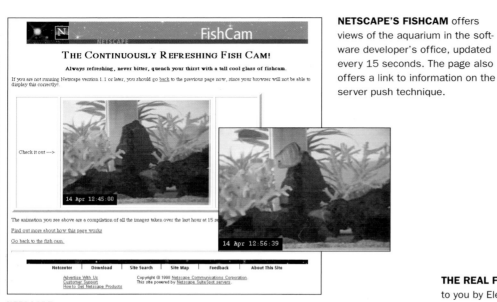

NETSCAPE

http://fishcam.netscape.com/fishcam/fish_refresh.html

NETSCAPE'S FISHCAM offers views of the aquarium in the software developer's office, updated every 15 seconds. The page also offers a link to information on the server push technique.

Eyes on the World: Web "Cams"

Combine an inexpensive digital video camera and "server push" (a method of automatically updating a portion of a page at regular intervals, introduced with Navigator 1.1), and you've got a way (if you want it) to put your life—or your pet, your lava lamp, your schoolroom, the wall of your apartment, whatever—on line. All over the Web, people have used this ability to offer a glimpse of their corner of the world to the world at large. The results range from the ridiculous to the sublime.

THE REAL FRIDGE CAM, brought to you by Electrolux in Sweden, snaps a shot each time one of the Essén family opens the fridge door for a snack.

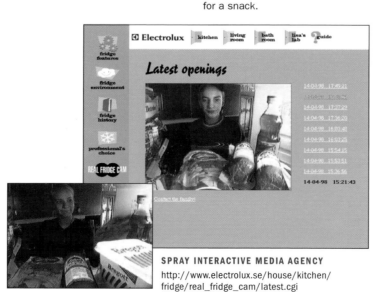

SPRAY INTERACTIVE MEDIA AGENCY

http://www.electrolux.se/house/kitchen/ fridge/real_fridge_cam/latest.cgi

concerts over the Internet and things like company meetings over office intranets.

While Web video is getting better all the time, no format can offer compression ratios or playback speeds sufficient to supply anything close to broadcast-quality video on the Web. When creating Web video, authors need to be mindful of factors such as busy backgrounds (which don't compress well) and must accept low frame rates and tiny window sizes for files that will be served over the Internet. A frame rate of about 5 frames per second (compared to the 15 to 24 frames per second of real-time video) is about all your visitors will see over a modem connection. The Web authoring systems mentioned here let you choose compression levels appropriate to different connection speeds.

If video does come into wide use over the Internet, publishers and Internet Service Providers will find their available bandwidth filling up fast: Even a T1 connection can handle only a few streams of real-time video at one time. To solve the problem, the Internet community is working on new ways to handle multimedia information on the Net. The most promising is called **multicasting**. Instead of sending out separate files to each client machine that requests one (the usual Web model), multicasting lets publishers send out just one stream. Strategically placed "reflectors" duplicate the stream as it is sent out, resulting in a geometric increase in the number of streams as it is passed from reflector to reflector. Users can "listen in" to a broadcast just as they would tune in to a TV or radio program.

To work, the system needs server software that can originate a multicast signal, enough reflectors in place to propagate the stream, and client software that can tune in. The server and client ends are being supported by new software such as Microsoft's NetShow, and the critical mass of multicast-enabled routers has been forming over the past few years. This virtual multimedia network, referred to as the **MBONE**, is almost ready for prime time.

On a smaller scale, wannabe broadcasters can test the waters with CU-SeeMe, a videoconferencing system developed at Cornell University and sold in commercial versions by White Pine Software. CU-SeeMe includes software for setting up reflectors on a Unix machine, and public-minded CU-SeeMe users have set up several public reflectors that anyone can use (with advance notice) to broadcast an event. We'll discuss CU-SeeMe more when we talk about videoconferencing in the Interactivity chapter (→**179**).

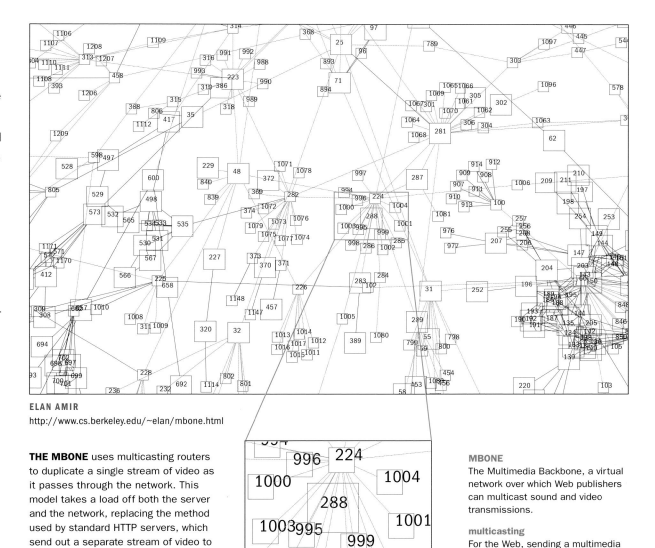

ELAN AMIR
http://www.cs.berkeley.edu/~elan/mbone.html

THE MBONE uses multicasting routers to duplicate a single stream of video as it passes through the network. This model takes a load off both the server and the network, replacing the method used by standard HTTP servers, which send out a separate stream of video to each user who asks for it.

MBONE
The Multimedia Backbone, a virtual network over which Web publishers can multicast sound and video transmissions.

multicasting
For the Web, sending a multimedia stream that can be read by multiple clients. (The stream is duplicated by multicast-capable routers along the way.) Client software "listens in" to a particular Internet address to receive the multicast stream.

REALAUDIO'S streaming format lets NPR post half-hour and longer radio broadcasts on its Web site.

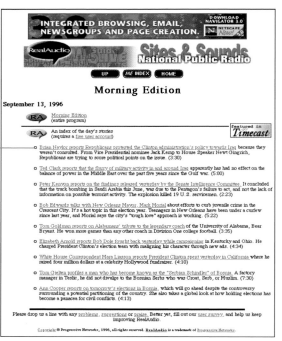

AIFF
Audio Interchange File Format, a cross-platform format for digital sound files.

.au
A sound file format commonly used on Unix computers.

Liquid Audio
An audio format designed to deliver CD-quality sound files over the Web.

MIDI
Musical Instrument Digital Interface, a standard for recording and playing synthesized sounds on electronic instruments.

RealAudio
A popular streaming sound format developed by RealNetworks.

Shockwave Audio
A streaming sound format that can be played through Macromedia's Shockwave player.

.wav
The native sound format for Microsoft Windows.

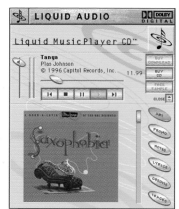

LIQUID AUDIO offers a system for selling CD-quality music over the net. The browser plug-in lets prospective buyers sample it first.

Sound

Sound can be part of almost any dynamic media format. We've already talked about animation formats, such as Shockwave for Director, and video formats, such as QuickTime and RealVideo, that can include sound. Sound is often also useful on its own, though: as a separate medium for broadcasting speeches, music, or other content without adding the bandwidth-hogging overhead of graphics. That's the use we'll talk about here.

Like video, sound can be added to the Web in standard digital formats, which are downloaded and then played through plug-ins or ActiveX controls, or served up in a special streaming format. Several sound-only file formats have been developed for digital multimedia. Some of the most common are **AIFF** (cross-platform, usually compressed), **.wav** (the standard format for Windows applications), **.au** (a common format for Unix software), and **MIDI** (a cross-platform standard used to record music from electronic instruments). MPEG and QuickTime, usually thought of as video formats, can also be used for audio alone. LiveAudio, a plug-in bundled with Netscape Navigator 3.0 and later, plays all these formats. Microsoft's browser handles them all but MIDI.

Except for MIDI, all these formats record sound by sampling it at frequent intervals and saving each value as a digital code. (MIDI records commands that create sounds in MIDI-capable instruments or sound boards.) The higher the sampling frequency (common frequencies are 11KHz, 22KHz, and 44KHz) and the greater the number of bits per sample (usually 8 bits or 16 bits), the better quality the sound: 44KHz, 16-bit sound is CD-quality. Of course, the higher the frequency and the higher the bit-depth, the larger the file, as well. One second of uncompressed CD-quality sound can result in a roughly 70K file (44,000 samples x 16 bits/second). As with video, most sound recording software offers a range of compression levels that trade off sound quality for smaller files.

As with video, RealNetworks has a compelling lead in the category of streaming audio with its **RealAudio** format, which can be played back via the popular RealPlayer or in the latest version of Microsoft's NetShow player.

Another popular sound format, also linked to a popular player, is **Shockwave Audio**. Streaming Shockwave Audio files can be created from Macromedia Director or via an Xtra available for Macromedia's SoundEdit 16 audio editing program. Shockwave Audio plays back via Macromedia's standard Shockwave plug-in or ActiveX control.

And if your business is selling music over the Internet, you'll want to look into **Liquid Audio**, a system for distributing CD-quality sound files. It's being used by record labels and online record stores to let Web visitors download files they can save on their own CDs.

Online: Multimedia

Animated GIF
http://www.builder.com/Graphics/Webanim/
http://member.aol.com/royalef/gifanim.htm

Cameras on the Web
http://www.yahoo.com/Computers_and_Internet/Internet/
Entertainment/Interesting_Devices_Connected_to_the_Net/
Spy_Cameras/Indices/

CU-SeeMe
http://cu-seeme.cornell.edu/
http://www.wpine.com/

Document Object Model
http://www.w3.org/DOM/

Dynamic HTML
http://www.dhtmlzone.com/
http://www.hotwired.com/webmonkey/dynamic_html/
http://www.insidedhtml.com/
http://www.microsoft.com/workshop/author/dhtml/
http://www.projectcool.com/developer/dynamic/
http://www.webdeveloper.com/categories/advhtml/
http://www.webreview.com/wr/pub/Dynamic_HTML/

Emblaze Creator
http://www.emblaze.com/

General Information and Tutorials
http://www.hotwired.com/webmonkey/collections/multimedia/

Liquid Audio
http://www.liquidaudio.com/

mBED Interactor
http://www.mbed.com/

MBONE
http://www.yahoo.com/Computers_and_Internet/
Communications_and_Networking/MBONE/

NetShow
http://www.microsoft.com/workshop/author/streaming/intro.htm

Paceworks Object Dancer
http://www.paceworks.com/

QuickTime
http://www.apple.com/quicktime/

RealNetworks
http://www.real.com/

Shockwave
http://www.macromedia.com/shockwave/

WebBurst FX
http://www.powerproduction.com/

With the evolution of the Web, what we now call a "page" will eventually evolve into a multimedia experience. But the point is not to duplicate MTV on the Web; it's not just a blast of stimulation. The users will be in control of the speed, duration, and depth of their involvement.

SABINE MESSNER, HOTWIRED

Interactivity

Instant Feedback: Mailto

Structured Input: HTML Forms

Interactivity With JavaScript

Interactivity With Plug-Ins and Java

User-to-User: Forums, Chat, and Videoconferencing

On the Web, people can ask questions and get answers, customize their views of pages, and follow lines of thought that they, and not the publisher, determine. They can buy airline tickets, software, tires, and almost anything else. Web users can even interact with each other, exchanging information with other people all over the world. All these types of behavior can be talked about under the heading of "interactivity"—ways in which a Web site can respond to a user's actions and choices.

The Web's interactivity might be thought of in three categories: users interacting with the Web site itself, users interacting with the site's publisher, and users interacting with each other. The first category includes the hyperlinking by which users navigate through the Web, as well as Web pages that interact with visitors by changing their form and displaying new information in response to the position of the cursor or to mouse clicks. E-mail feedback and online commerce fall into the second category; online games, chat rooms, and forums fall into the third.

Some simple types of interactivity are built right into HTML. And if you're willing to do some programming (or know someone who is), the possibilities are almost limitless.

Instant Feedback: Mailto

One of the simplest—and most useful—ways to open lines of communication with your site's users is by including an e-mail feedback form. It gives them a straightforward way to get information to the keepers of the site, and even more important, it keeps the site's creators in touch with the needs of its users.

Creating an e-mail feedback form with HTML is as easy as creating a hyperlink. Instead of supplying a URL for the link, however, you type *mailto:* plus the address to which the information should be sent. For users, clicking on the anchor text brings up an e-mail form addressed to the mailbox you specify.

Most sites take advantage of this simple way of keeping in touch with their visitors, and Web users have come to expect a feedback loop on every site. Of course, including a mail link also means you have to have someone on your end ready to answer and act on the messages you receive.

AN EASY WAY TO create a feedback loop from your site is the mailto feature built into HTML. Use *mailto:* and the e-mail address you want comments sent to, instead of a URL, in the *href=* attribute in an <A> tag. When the user clicks the link, an e-mail form for that address appears.

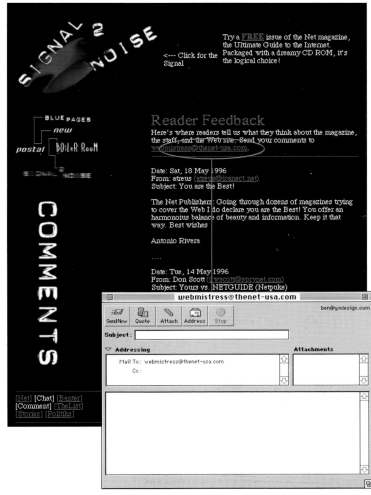

HEIDI SWANSON
http://www.thenet-usa.com/signal2noise/signal.html

START TAG	ATTRIBUTES	END TAG	EXPLANATION
<A>		</A>	
	href=mailto:"*address*"		Creates a link to an e-mail form addressed to the specified mailbox

HOTWIRED
http://www.hotbot.com/

HOTBOT'S EXPERT SEARCH option lets users choose search criteria from an array of buttons and menus.

ONLINE SHOPPING SITES, such as this one for the bookseller Amazon.com, present order forms in which users can indicate the items and quantities they want to buy.

SHEL KAPHAN
http://www.amazon.com/

Structured Input: HTML Forms

Mailto is a great way to give readers a voice, but it only generates an e-mail message form. If you want specific kinds of information or information that can be fed directly to a script or database, the way to get it is by creating fill-in forms.

Laying out a form is easy enough. It's all handled by standard HTML 2.0 code and by drag-and-drop controls in most WYSIWYG HTML editors. HTML's form commands can create a variety of controls, which anyone who works with Microsoft Windows or Macintosh computers will be familiar with. Mostly, they're the same ones you see in dialog boxes in all your software: text fields, radio buttons, checkboxes, drop-down lists, and buttons. The browser determines how each of these controls is displayed, but designers can use standard HTML structural tags and style tags to control the placement of the controls on the page and the layout of additional text within the form.

Once you've built the form in HTML, users have a place to supply information or specify preferences, but what happens when they click the button to submit that data? That's where HTML's features end and the need for programming begins. Form data is generally sent back to the Web publisher via CGI (→**183**), for processing by a script on the server. The *action=* attribute of the <FORM> tag provides a URL for the script. The tags that create each form control (<INPUT> is the most common) each have a *name=* attribute, which tells the script which variable that input should be applied to.

JavaScript (→**186**) can be used to handle interactions that don't require information on the server. For example, you might use JavaScript to check the form before it's submitted to make sure any required fields are filled in or to ask for additional information based on user input. JavaScript event handlers (→**172**) can be used with any form element to trigger interactions. And HTML 4.0 introduces an attribute, *disabled,* specially designed to be controlled by JavaScript. When used in the HTML describing a form control, *disabled* makes the control inactive; a JavaScript function can activate it when certain criteria are met; for instance, to activate a Submit button when all required fields are filled in.

As HTML's main method for gathering input from a site's users, form controls are used for many kinds of interactivity. What happens to the information— whether it's posted to a customer database, sent as e-mail to a feedback address, used to determine which information the user will see next, or any other result—is determined by the program to which you send it. The illustrations on these two pages show some examples of different ways Web designers have used this capability.

ATOMIC VISION
http://www.excite.com/

EXCITE and other Web search services offer a simple text field and a Submit button to allow users to quickly search their site indexes.

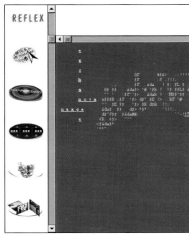

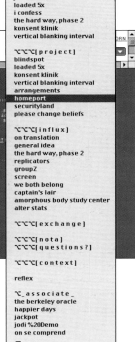

FORM CONTROLS can also be used for navigation. Here, äda 'web, an online magazine, offers its table of contents in a drop-down menu.

WP-STUDIO
http://www.adaweb.com/home.shtml

START TAG	ATTRIBUTES	END TAG	EXPLANATION
\<FORM>		\</FORM>	Surround all the tags that create the form
	action="*URL*"		The script that should be run, and that the form data should be sent to, when the user clicks the Submit button
	enctype="*MIME-type*"		The format in which the information should be sent (used only with *method="post"*)
	method="get" OR "post"		Specifies a method for sending the data to the server: "get" uses a default MIME type created specially for forms; "post" uses the MIME type specified with the *enctype* attribute
	target="*frame*" OR "_blank" OR "new" OR "_parent" OR "_self" OR "_top"		Used with frames, names the frame or window in which the results of the form should be displayed
\<INPUT>			Creates input controls within a form
	type="button" OR "checkbox" OR "file" OR "hidden" OR "image" OR "password" OR "radio" OR "reset" OR "submit" OR "text"		The type of control to be created. (See the illustrations for examples.)
	checked		For *type="checkbox"* or *type="radio"*, specifies that the box or button should be chosen as a default
	disabled		Used to disable the control. (The control can be enabled via a JavaScript command in response to user actions.)
	maxlength="*length*"		For *type="text"*, the maximum length of an entry, in characters
	name="*name*"		A name for the control, used as a variable name when input is sent to a script for processing. (Used for all input types.) For *type="radio"*, all the radio buttons in a group have the same name.
	size="*size*"		For *type="text"*, the length of the text box
	src="*URL*"		For *type="image"*, names an image to use as a Submit button
	value="*text*"		For *type="checkbox"*, a variable value to be sent when the box is checked. For *type="text"*, the default entry in the text field. For *type= "submit"*, *type="reset"*, or *type="button"*, the text displayed on the button. For *type="file"*, the name of a default file.
\<BUTTON>		\</BUTTON>	Creates a button
	disabled		Used to disable the control. (The control can be enabled via a JavaScript command in response to user actions.)
	name="*name*"		The name displayed on the button and used as the button's name by the script that determines its behavior
	type="button" OR "reset" OR "submit"		Determines the action of the button. *"Submit"* and *"reset"* act like buttons created with the \<INPUT> tag with a *type=* attribute of these types; "button" creates a button with the name given by the *name=* attribute, whose behavior is created via JavaScript.
	value="*text*"		The default value for the variable named with the *name=* attribute

```
<INPUT type="text">
<INPUT type="password">
```

```
<INPUT type="checkbox">
```

```
<INPUT type="radio">
```

```
<INPUT type="submit">
<INPUT type="reset">
<INPUT type="button" value="Text">
<BUTTON>
```

START TAG	ATTRIBUTES	END TAG	EXPLANATION
<SELECT>		</SELECT>	Creates a menu of choices, either a pulldown menu (the default) or a scrolling menu
	disabled		Used to disable the control. (The control can be enabled via a JavaScript command in response to user actions.)
	multiple		Allows multiple selections from a scrolling menu
	name="*name*"		A name for the menu, used as a variable name when the input is sent to a script for processing
	size="*size*"		Creates a scrolling menu of the depth specified
<OPTGROUP>		</OPTGROUP>	Used with <SELECT> to group menu options. The browser may display option groups as submenu entries.
	disabled		Used to disable the control. (The control can be enabled via a JavaScript command in response to user actions.)
	label="*text*"		A label for a group of menu options. If the group is displayed as a set of submenu entries, the <OPTGROUP> label is the name of the menu.
<OPTION>		<OPTION>	Used with the <SELECT> tag to create an option in a menu
	disabled		Used to disable the control. (The control can be enabled via a JavaScript command in response to user actions.)
	label="*text*"		An alternate name to be displayed in the menu
	selected		Specifies that the option should be selected by default
	value="*text*"		The value to be sent if the option is selected
<TEXTAREA>		</TEXTAREA>	Creates a multiline text field
	cols=*n*, rows=*n*		The width (cols) and height (rows) of the text area, in characters
	disabled		Used to disable the control. (The control can be enabled via a JavaScript command in response to user actions.)
	name="*name*"		A name for the text area, used as a variable name when the input is sent to a script for processing
	wrap="off" OR "virtual" OR "physical"		Specifies how text lines wrap in the control. "Off" (the default) means no word wrap; "virtual" means the text wraps in the browser window but is sent to the processing script as a single line; "physical" means the text wraps in the window and is sent to the script with line breaks.

`<INPUT type="image">`

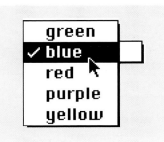

`<SELECT>`

`<SELECT size=>`

`<TEXTAREA>`

MANY TYPES OF FORM CONTROLS can be created using the <INPUT> tag; others can be created with <BUTTON>, <SELECT>, and <TEXTAREA>.

HANDLER	USED WITH
GENERAL EVENT HANDLERS	
onclick ="*script*"	all elements
ondblclick="*script*"	all elements
onkeydown="*script*"	all elements
onkeypress="*script*"	all elements
onkeyup="*script*"	all elements
onmousedown="*script*"	all elements
onmousemove="*script*"	all elements
onmouseover="*script*"	all elements
onmouseout="*script*"	all elements
FORM CONTROL EVENT HANDLERS	
onblur="*script*"	<BUTTON>, <INPUT>, <LABEL>, <SELECT>, <TEXTAREA>
onchange="*script*"	<INPUT>, <SELECT>, <TEXTAREA>
onfocus="*script*"	<BUTTON>, <INPUT>, <LABEL>, <SELECT>, <TEXTAREA>
onreset="*script*"	<FORM>
onselect="*script*"	<INPUT>, <TEXTAREA>
onsubmit="*script*"	<FORM>
NONINTERACTIVE EVENT HANDLERS	
onload="*script*"	<BODY>, <FRAMESET>
onunload="*script*"	<BODY>, <FRAMESET>

event handlers
Commands that trigger actions when a certain event occurs—either an interactive event, such as the user clicking a button, or a noninteractive event, such as a page loading. In HTML 4.0 and recent browsers, event handler attributes can be added to many tags and generate scripted actions.

HTML 4.0's EVENT HANDLER ATTRIBUTES can call scripts in response to a number of common events. In browsers that support HTML 4.0, many of these attributes can be used with almost any HTML element. Others are used only with form controls or triggered when a page or frameset loads or unloads. Earlier browsers, beginning with Navigator 2.0, supported a smaller set of event handlers and supported them for a smaller set of elements: mostly for form controls and (in Navigator) for images.

Interactivity With JavaScript

When Netscape introduced JavaScript (→**186**) with Navigator 2.0, it also built in support for a set of standard **event handlers**: commands that trigger actions whenever a certain event occurs. Those events might be user actions (such as clicking the mouse button) or browser actions (such as loading the page). When the event happens, the event handler can be used to run a JavaScript function in response to it.

Event handlers can be used in a couple of ways. They can be defined in scripts that are added to HTML pages with the <SCRIPT> tag (→**187**), or they can be called via attributes added to an HTML structural tag. For example, to substitute an alternate graphic to provide user feedback when a visitor rolls over an on-screen button, you could include the event handler *onmouseover=switch()* in the <BUTTON> tag (→**170**). (You would also, of course, need to write the JavaScript *switch()* function that would do the actual graphic switching.)

As with everything else on the Web, the ability to process JavaScript event handlers varies from browser to browser. A standard set has been added to the HTML 4.0 spec, but even earlier browsers (beginning with Navigator 2.0) can handle a subset of these. In fact, every new browser version handles a slightly different set. Internet Explorer didn't begin supporting JavaScript event handlers until version 4.0, so these techniques should be used with care and tested in your target browsers.

HTML 4.0 specifies that the entire set of event attributes can be used with just about any HTML element. This also assumes a document object model (DOM) (→**159**) that allows JavaScript to address any element on a page. In earlier browsers, JavaScript could address only a subset of elements: certain form controls, graphics embedded with the <IMG> tag, and browser entities such as windows and frames. For the most part, then, JavaScript event handlers have been used to show active states of buttons (by switching out graphics as we described above), to handle form input (→**168**), and to run scripts when an HTML page was loaded into the browser.

In new browsers—those that support HTML 4.0 and a more powerful DOM—these event handlers become really powerful. This is where dynamic HTML (→**76**) becomes really dynamic, and really interactive. Any object on a page can react to user actions, as event handlers do things like trigger sounds and animation or even, using the formatting powers of dynamic HTML, re-layout the page. And since JavaScript uses client-side processing (→**181**), this can all happen on the user's own machine—users don't need to wait for each new state of the page to be downloaded from the server.

NETSCAPE'S COMPANY TIMELINE uses JavaScript and dynamic HTML to let the visitor see different views of the company's history. Clicking on the floating control (an onMouseUp event) changes the view of the data, showing business events (blue), product news (orange) or Web site statistics (green).

NETSCAPE
http://www.netscape.com/company/timelines/1997/

COUNTERSPACE teaches typographic terminology with Shockwave Flash. Rolling your mouse over names of letterform parts highlights the item in the type sample and displays a definition of the term.

ROBERT ABBOTT/BRETT COLLINS/STUDIOMOTIV
http://www.studiomotiv.com/counterspace/space.htm

Interactivity With Plug-Ins and Java

In our chapters on alternate formats and multimedia, we've already talked about VRML (→**148**), Shockwave for Director (→**153**), and Shockwave Flash (→**154**): tools for creating interactive environments. Shockwave for Director and Shockwave Flash can also be used to create small interactive elements in Web pages, such as navigation tools that feature user-triggered actions such as rollovers and sound-effect feedback.

Shockwave offered these effects as early as Navigator 2.0—long before JavaScript offered rollovers via graphics in Navigator 3.0 and dynamic HTML became available in the 4.0 browsers—and they still offer the benefits of a graphical authoring environment for sophisticated interactive effects. The drawback, as we've mentioned, is that depending on these formats assumes that visitors will have the plug-ins they need or will be willing to spend time downloading them, and the files can be large.

In our chapter on multimedia, we also talked about Java as a tool for animation (→**156**), and Java can likewise be used for interactivity (and just about anything else). Programs we mentioned there, such as mBed Interactor and PowerProduction WebBurst FX let you add interactive features to your animations, and general-purpose Java tools let you create even more elaborate interactive environments.

Java programs can play in any browser that supports Java (anything after Navigator 2.0 or Internet Explorer 3.0)—no plug-ins required. The problem again, though, is download time and response speed. The files are large, and the Java engines in most browsers are still pretty sluggish.

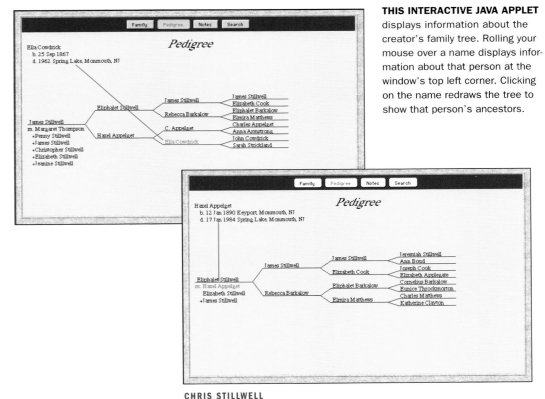

THIS INTERACTIVE JAVA APPLET displays information about the creator's family tree. Rolling your mouse over a name displays information about that person at the window's top left corner. Clicking on the name redraws the tree to show that person's ancestors.

CHRIS STILLWELL
http://ourworld.compuserve.com/homepages/cstillwell/pafinit.htm

The best kind of interactivity does something meaningful and responds within a second or two. I don't want to click and see something go "Pow." I want to see something usable.

JOHN GROTTING, STUDIO ARCHETYPE

THE GUEST BOOK at The Blue Dot allows visitors to comment on work displayed in the online gallery. The list of messages is enhanced by graphic bullets showing which artist each message pertains to.

CRAIG KANARICK
http://www.thebluedot.com/

chat
A system that allows Internet users to exchange text messages with other visitors to a site in real time.

forum
A Web site feature that lets users post messages, which are saved in a public space where they can be read and responded to by others. Forums are often based on the Internet's newsgroup protocol (NNTP) and tied into Web sites via back-end engines that write the resulting pages as HTML.

Internet Relay Chat (IRC)
The standard Internet protocol for chat.

User-to-User: Forums, Chat, and Videoconferencing

Potentially the most powerful feature of Web publishing is its ability to create community. As with any other publication, visitors to a Web site are brought to it by a common interest. Unlike any other kind of communication, though, Web sites are published on a medium—the Internet—that those visitors can also use to communicate with one another.

The Internet has long included bulletin board services, called newsgroups (also called conferences or **forums**), in which users can post messages in a public place where other users can read them and respond. Likewise, the Internet has hosted **chat** sessions, through a technology called **Internet Relay Chat (IRC)**. These sevices, though, have been based on their own protocols and so have not been available via a standard Web browser (though Netscape and Microsoft have both built news and chat capabilities into enhanced versions of their browsers). Such services are still available and widely used. (With Communicator 4.0, Netscape added a chat client and newsgroup reader to its browser package, as Microsoft did with Internet Explorer 4.0.) But here, we'll talk about how such services can be integrated into a Web publication, offering the HTML, click-to-choose interface familiar to Web users.

Many software packages are now available for adding forum services to your Web page. They may use standard NNTP software for creating the forums, but they do some back-end processing that outputs the pages as HTML. These tools also let Web publishers customize the layout of the resulting pages.

The chat situation is a bit more complex, since the displayed pages change in real time, and aren't static like those for a forum. Chat software for Web publishing offers a variety of approaches. Some provide a player in the form of a plug-in or ActiveX control, which puts a modified IRC interface within your browser window. More handily, some provide a Java player, which automatically adds the ability to handle chat to your standard Web browser.

Most chat environments use a text-based interface, in which users type messages to one another in a standard ASCII format. Newer systems are providing sound capabilities as well. Others offer graphic stand-ins called **avatars**—which users can use to represent themselves on line. Some services use VRML (→**148**) to create interactive 3D spaces in which your avatar can actually walk up to other users (or to their avatars) and exchange conversation (again, usually as text strings displayed in the window).

Fanciful 3D environments are fine for cocktail-party chatter. For business users and for others who want to see each other face to face, the best communication

CHAT ROOMS offer visitors the ability to exchange comments with others who are on line at the same time. Usually less topic-oriented than forums, chat sites usually let visitors choose among several "rooms," where they exchange pleasantries.

THE LATEST TREND in chat sites uses 3D interfaces and avatars (below), creating worlds in which visitors can take on new personalities and interact in fantasy situations.

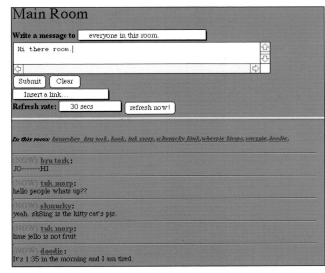

http://www.firefly.com/

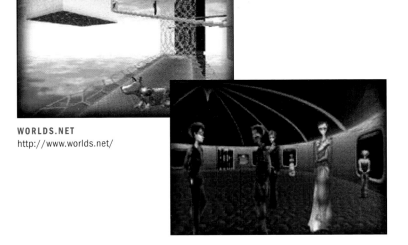

WORLDS.NET
http://www.worlds.net/

avatar
In graphics-based chat systems, a figure that represents a participant.

•TIMED OUT•	
2.3 fps	20 Kbps
.1 fps	15 Kbps
0.0 fps	0 Kbps

CU-SEEME is designed to let anyone with a digital video camera send messages—and his or her image—out over the Internet. Sessions can be as private as a telephone call, or the video and chat sessions can be bounced off public "reflectors" that broadcast the message to anyone who wants to participate. (Lurkers need only the free CU-SeeMe helper app to tune in.) The pictures are transmitted in discrete segments, creating an arty "pixellated" effect.

0.0 fps	4 Kbps
.2 fps	1 Kbps
.3 fps	7 Kbps
2.3 fps	20 Kbps

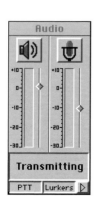

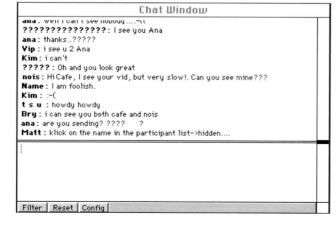

Audio

Transmitting

PTT | Lurkers ▷

Chat Window

ana : well I can t see nobody....•((
??????????????? : I see you Ana
ana : thanks..?????
Vip : i see u 2 Ana
Kim : i can't
????? : Oh and you look great
nois : Hi Cafe, I see your vid, but very slow!. Can you see mine???
Name : I am foolish.
Kim : :-(
t s u : howdy howdy
Bry : i can see you both cafe and nois
ana : are you sending? ????   ?
Matt : klick on the name in the participant list->hidden....

Filter | Reset | Config

Participant List

	Ran
	Martin
	nois
	t s u
	Ken
	Pete
	Bry
	Vip
	Matt
	?????

▽ **Lurkers (7)**

	page	✕
	Charlie	✕
	Tom	✕
	MrC	✕

23 participants ⬇ ⬆

interface is provided by **videoconferencing** systems, which send video images of conference participants over the Net. Though they're not really part of the Web yet (they require separate software and use different protocols), they're good to know about for those who are thinking about ways to tie face-to-face communications into their Web services. Videoconferencing applications can be launched as helper applications or as browser plug-ins.

Videoconferencing, like any other video application, is hobbled by the Net's limited bandwidth, but it is getting lots of attention lately as corporations install more Web-based intranets, connected by fast dedicated lines. In such environments, videoconferencing can save money and time, as meetings with colleagues across the world can take place on a desktop.

Online: Interactivity

Chat, Forum, and Videoconferencing Applications
http://www.serverwatch.com/dtdiscussion.html
http://www.zdnet.com/products/chatuser.html

CU-SeeMe
http://cu-seeme.cornell.edu/
http://www.wpine.com/

Forms
http://robot0.ge.uiuc.edu/~carlosp/cs317/cft.html
http://www.hotwired.com/webmonkey/html/97/06/index2a.html

Java
http://java.sun.com/
http://www.hotwired.com/webmonkey/collections/java.html

JavaScript Event Handlers
http://developer.netscape.com/docs/technote/javascript/
    eventhandler/eventhandler.htm
http://www.hotwired.com/webmonkey/collections/java.html
http://www.javaworld.com/javaworld/jw-06-1996/
    jw-06-javascript.html
http://www.netscapeworld.com/netscapeworld/nw-12-1996/
    nw-12-javascript1.html

mBED Interactor
http://www.mbed.com/

PowerProduction WebBurst FX
http://www.powerproduction.com/

Shockwave
http://www.macromedia.com/shockwave/

A lot of businesses approach the Web with a print media standard of design. They're missing the capabilities of feedback and interaction, which are 90 percent of what makes the Web powerful.

ANNETTE LOUDON, CONSTRUCT

videoconferencing
Systems in which video images of the participants are displayed on the other participants' screens in real time. Conversations may be held via text or audio, depending on the system and the available bandwidth.

Programming the Web

Client-Side and Server-Side Processing

Programming the Server: CGI and APIs

Client-Side Scripting: JavaScript and Visual Basic Scripting Edition

Java

ActiveX

The computers that host Web sites and read Web pages can do a lot more than interpret HTML and handle hyperlinks. You can put all that power to work creating pages that react to user input or creating systems that build HTML pages automatically from company databases, handle credit card purchases, or carry out countless other types of tasks. To do all that, though, you need to do some programming.

Earlier in the book, we talked about tools that let designers create interactive, animated interfaces with Java and JavaScript-driven DHTML, but Web programming can go far beyond that. The purpose of this chapter isn't to teach you programming, however, or even suggest that you learn it (though designers who do their own HTML coding might very well want to learn some basics of JavaScript). Instead, it's to introduce you to terms like *API* and *CGI* and to provide an overview of how Web programming works.

Client-Side and Server-Side Processing

Web programs can be thought of in two categories: those that run on the client machine and are executed by the Web browser, and those that run on the server computer and are executed by server or database software.

Client-side programs are used to handle any tasks that don't require access to data on the server. For example, you might use a client-side script to switch between the active and nonactive states of onscreen buttons or to validate form data before it is sent to the server. Client-side scripts can also be used to test which browser has requested a page and then show different content depending on the capabilities of that browser.

Server-side programs handle jobs that require access to information that isn't on the user's machine. Say a Web user is shopping for CDs at on online record store. On the site's home page is a form allowing the visitor to specify the name of an artist he or she would like to find music by. The visitor fills in "Spice Girls" and clicks Submit.

The message sent from the client's browser to the server includes the information ("Spice Girls") submitted in the form. To pull together the right list of CDs for the shopper, though, the server needs to

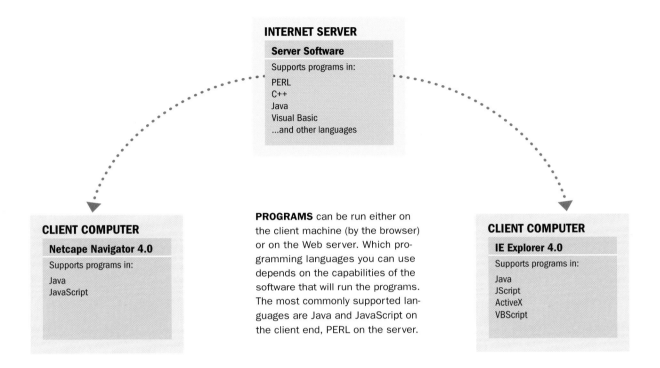

PROGRAMS can be run either on the client machine (by the browser) or on the Web server. Which programming languages you can use depends on the capabilities of the software that will run the programs. The most commonly supported languages are Java and JavaScript on the client end, PERL on the server.

We're seeing a powerful shift in capabilities on the Web from the server to the client. In the past, we had to do all the processing on the server side—databases pushing custom content, style encapsulated in images, and search engines indexing massive amounts of content. Now much of that functionality can be done on the client.

JEFF VEEN, HOTWIRED

> Lately, we've used JavaScript to handle things that would usually be handled by CGI—things like keeping track of RealAudio files that the user wants to hear.

PETER SEIDLER, AVALANCHE

call a program that accesses the record store's database, creates an HTML page that includes the information it finds there, and hands that page back to the server so it can send it back to the shopper.

In the next sections, we'll talk about how programs are executed by browsers and by the server software, and we'll introduce the common programming languages used on the Web.

Scripts vs. Programs

For the sake of simplicity, we usually just refer to "programs" when we talk about a set of instructions that tell the server or browser what to do, but programmers and Web software vendors often break that concept down into two groups: traditional programs and scripts.

The distinction between the two isn't clear-cut: Both provide a set of commands for the computer to follow. The difference is in the type of language used to write them—full-featured programming languages like Visual Basic, C++, or Java or scripting languages like PERL or JavaScript—and how the computer handles them.

As a rule, scripting languages are more specialized than full-fledged programming languages. Their range of capabilities is usually focused on the particular environment in which they will be used—JavaScript, for example, is designed for use on the Web and so includes commands for things like

checking for particular plug-ins and handling browser tasks. PERL was designed as a tool for managing Unix systems and so includes commands for Unix file management, while AppleScript includes calls to the MacOS and standard Mac application code.

As they're being processed by the computer, scripts are generally executed line by line by a piece of software called a script "interpreter"; programs are first sent to a "compiler," which parses the program code into a more quickly executed form, called machine language, that can be directly handled by a computer's processing chip, resulting in faster processing for complex programs.

Although programming languages are designed to give programmers maximum control, scripting languages are designed to help them get a given task done easily. Consequently, scripting languages are fairly easy to learn, even for people who have no programming experience.

Programming the Server: CGI and APIs

In the Web's earliest days, all programs for the Web were run on the server. When special actions were required or decisions had to be made based on user input, the browser handed the job to the server for processing and waited for a file based on the program's results to be sent back.

This method is a rather ingenious way to get around the problem that would otherwise stymie Web publishers: that, in general, programs must be written specifically for the type of computer they will be run on. Distributing programs to all the different types of computers that access the Web would require writing several versions of each program (one for each platform) and then somehow developing a system to make sure each reader gets the correct version.

Instead, the creators of the Web designed a method by which a server can offer access to its processing power, just as it offers access to its files, to every computer on the Net. The browser just needs some way to ask the server to execute the right program and a way to pass on any user input. That's the purpose of the **common gateway interface (CGI)**. Just as the HTTP specification sets standards for the way browsers and servers request and transmit files, CGI sets standards for the way they handle requests for programs.

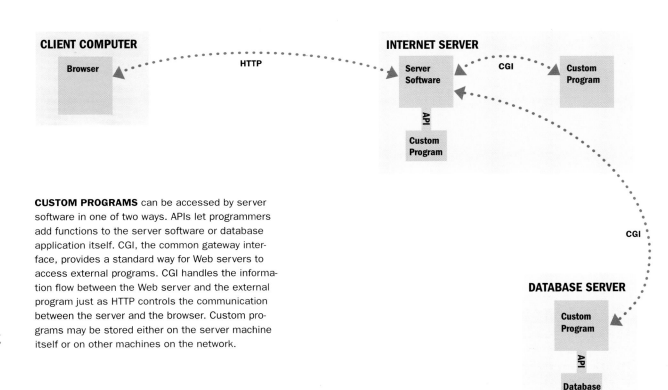

CUSTOM PROGRAMS can be accessed by server software in one of two ways. APIs let programmers add functions to the server software or database application itself. CGI, the common gateway interface, provides a standard way for Web servers to access external programs. CGI handles the information flow between the Web server and the external program just as HTTP controls the communication between the server and the browser. Custom programs may be stored either on the server machine itself or on other machines on the network.

common gateway interface (CGI)
A set of specifications that provide rules for the way Web clients and servers handle requests for executing and sending the results of server-based programs.

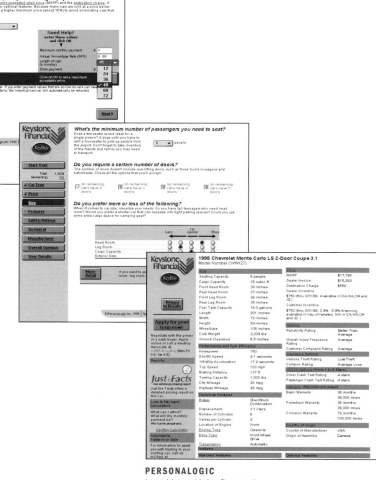

USER'S CHOICES on each screen of this new car selector create a mathematical profile, which is sent to a server-side program written in C. The program results are sent to a Java program, which builds the customized page.

PERSONALOGIC
http://www.kb.keyfin.com/

AppleScript
A scripting language developed by Apple to offer a standard method of controlling Macintosh programs.

Frontier
A scripting language developed by UserLand, used as an alternative to AppleScript to script actions in Macintosh programs.

PERL
A scripting language often used to create scripts for Web servers.

variable
In programming, a placeholder for a value that can be reassigned based on user input or other changing conditions.

Visual Basic
A programming language developed by Microsoft especially for creating Windows programs.

The rules set out by CGI are simple. The request to run the program can be sent to the server from a client-side script or from an <A> tag (→**78**) or a form's Submit button (→**168**). Making the request is easy; you simply name the script you want to run. (For a Submit button, that's done with the *action=* attribute of the <FORM> tag (→**168**).)

Often, the browser will also need to send **variable** information to the program: information about the reader's input into a form or clicks on an image map, for example. CGI provides two easy ways to do that: via GET or POST. Using GET, the browser appends a question mark to the script name it sends to the server, followed by the values for any variables. On receiving the CGI request, the server launches the script and passes the variables to it. Using POST, the browser sends the variable information as a separate transmission. Using either method, the script, once called, carries out its process using the provided variables and spits out a file or file reference, all in the form specified by CGI, to send back to the browser.

The CGI programs themselves can be written in any language that can be run on the server. For Unix servers, the most common language has been the Unix scripting language **PERL** (Practical Extraction and Report Language); Windows servers usually use PERL or **Visual Basic**; for Macintoshes, it's PERL, **AppleScript**, or **Frontier**. Programming languages, such as C or Java, can also be used. Prebuilt scripts for many commonly used functions, such as counting the number of hits on a Web page, are freely available over the Web. Others, such as systems for buying and selling on line, are available for purchase from Web software vendors. Programs that call for information from a proprietary database or for other custom needs must be written specifically for the task.

As Web servers matured, a second, similar method became available. Instead of being launched via CGI, custom programs can be linked directly into Web server and database software via an **API** (application programming interface). APIs usually work faster than CGI because the server doesn't need to start a new program each time a request needs processing. Different servers support different APIs and links to different programming languages.

CGI and APIs can handle any type of programming you need done on the Web: any request can be handed off to the server. Unless your program needs access to a database, though, that's probably not the best way to handle many tasks, since sending a request to the server and waiting for a response takes time, especially on heavily trafficked servers. For other tasks, you'll want to use scripts that run on the client side of the connection, which we'll talk about next.

```perl
#!/usr/local/bin/perl
# PERL script to generate html for unread mail

$user = "demo";
$mbox = "/usr/spool/mail/$user";
$title = "Mail for $user";

# Subroutine to print out a mail message (called below)
sub print1Message {
                local($from, $subject) = @_;
                print "<DT>From: $from ";
                if (defined($subject)) {
                                print "<DD>Subject: $subject \n";
                }
}

# Static HTML title
print "Content-type: text/html\n\n";
print "<HEAD>\n<TITLE>$title</TITLE>\n</HEAD>\n";
print "<BODY>\n<H1>$title</H1>\n";
print "Here is a listing of mail we are storing for you:\n";

# Open the mailbox, if no mailbox file is found, indicate
open(MBOX, $mbox) || print "<B> \nNo Mailbox found</B>\n";

print "<DL>\n";

# Pull apart the mail headers, find "From:" and "Subject:"
# Call print1Message whenever a message separator is found
while ( <MBOX> ){
                if ( /^From:\s*(.*)/ && !defined($from)) {
                                $from = $1;
                }
                if ( /^Subject:\s*(.*)/ && !defined($subject)) {
                                $subject = $1;
                }
                if ( /^From \s*(.*)/ && defined($from)) {
                                &print1Message($from, $subject);
                                undef $from;
                                undef $subject;
                }
}

# Print out the last message (if any)
if (defined($from)) {
                &print1Message($from, $subject);
}

print "</DL>\n</BODY>\n";
```

SCRIPTS can carry out simple programming tasks on the Web. This one, written in PERL and suitable for access via CGI, looks for unread mail in the user's account and sends an HTML file listing the mail back to the client. Phrases preceded by # are comments—lines that are embedded in the script to explain its use to humans but aren't processed by the script interpreter.

API
Application programming interface, a method of hooking custom programs into existing applications. By calling the API, custom programs can run processes within the first application.

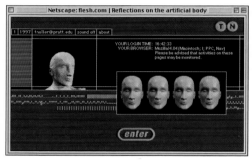

JAVASCRIPT in the HTML page shown at right checks which browser is requesting the page, then sends a dynamic HTML page to Navigator 4.0 users, a static page to others. Comments in the script (marked by //) explain each section.

```
<script>
<! - - (c) flesh.com, 1997

//split browsers

version = navigator.appVersion
name = navigator.appName
var nav4, ie, oldnav

if (version.charAt(0) == "4"){ //4.x Browsers
            if (name == "Netscape"){
                            nav4 = true
            }else
            if (name == "Microsoft Internet Explorer"){
                            ie = true
                            }
}

if ((version.charAt(0) == "3") || (version.charAt(0) == "2")) {
                    if (name == "Microsoft Internet Explorer"){
                            ie = true
                    }else{
                            oldnav = true
                            }
}

            function partIt(){
            // send Netscape 2,3 browsers to this page
            if (oldnav) {
                            var win = ""
                            // double call is to get around a bug in Netscape 2/Mac
win=window.open("sorry[f].html","sorry","width=500,height=300");

win=window.open("sorry[f].html","sorry","width=500,height=300");
            }

            if (ie) {
            // send Explorer browsers to this page
                            var win = ""
win=window.open("ie4.html","ie4","width=500,height=300");
            }

            // Netscape 4 passes here
            if (nav4) {
                            var win = ""
win=window.open("gate.html","gate","width=500,height=300");
            }

}

//wake up again - ->
</script>
```

THOMAS NOLLER
http://www.typospace.de/

Client-Side Scripting: JavaScript and Visual Basic Scripting Edition

Client-side scripts are embedded right in the HTML file that uses them, embedded between <SCRIPT> and </SCRIPT> tags in the head of the document. (Putting them in the document head ensures that they're read into the client machine's memory before the rest of the HTML page.) A script's functions can be executed as they're read (if, for example, they're checking which browser is being used) or when a particular event (→**172**), such as a mouse click, occurs.

For client-side scripts to work, of course, the scripting language you use has to be understandable by the user's browser. The most common client-side scripting language for the Web is **JavaScript**, developed by Netscape and supported in its browsers. (Despite the name, JavaScript has nothing to do with Java, the programming language we'll describe in the next section.) Microsoft browsers support a JavaScript-compatible scripting language called **JScript**. You might also hear the term **ECMAScript** associated with these languages; it's a scripting standard based on JavaScript, overseen by a European standards organization called ECMA. Microsoft (but not Netscape) also supports a second scripting language called **Visual Basic Scripting Edition** (often called Visual Basic Script or VBScript).

JavaScript was created to let Web programmers handle common Web tasks without depending on the server. It has built-in commands, for instance, for controlling the navigation and appearance of browser windows, checking for plug-ins, and other actions that make it especially useful on the Web. Additional features can be defined by programmers.

JavaScript and JScript have been supported in browsers since Navigator 2.0 and Internet Explorer 3.0; VBScript has been supported by Internet Explorer since version 3.0. However, Web authors still can't count on those browsers running scripts automatically. That's because, as a security measure, users can turn off the browser's ability to run scripts (→**188**). For that reason, any page designer depending on client-side scripting should also create a fall-back position for users who have scripting turned off. Alternate content for browsers that don't understand scripts can be embedded between <NOSCRIPT> and </NOSCRIPT> tags.

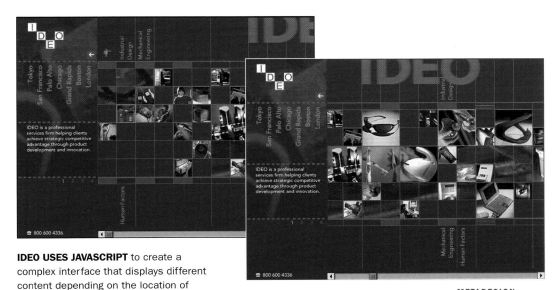

IDEO USES JAVASCRIPT to create a complex interface that displays different content depending on the location of the visitor's mouse pointer.

METADESIGN
http://www.ideo.com/

ECMAScript
A scripting standard overseen by the standards organization ECMA. JavaScript and JScript are based on ECMAScript.

JavaScript
A scripting language, developed by Netscape, specialized for controlling Web browser processes.

JScript
A JavaScript-compatible scripting language developed and supported by Microsoft.

Visual Basic Scripting Edition
A scripting language, based on Microsoft's Visual Basic programming language, designed to control Web processes and ActiveX controls and passing information to Java programs.

START TAG	ATTRIBUTES	END TAG	EXPLANATION
<SCRIPT>		</SCRIPT>	Marks a client-side script
	language="*name*"		Names the language the script is written in
	src="*URL*"		Names an external script file
<NOSCRIPT>		</NOSCRIPT>	Marks material that should be displayed in browsers that don't support the scripting language

> Java is everything it's cracked up to be and more. It's a new operating system. It's awesome. We're in this completely new medium with great tools and no rules. Now it's up to us to figure out what to do with them.
>
> JONATHAN NELSON, ORGANIC

Security for Client-Side Processing

The client-side processing used by Java, ActiveX, JavaScript, and Visual Basic Scripting Edition is a breakthrough for Web programmers aiming for more extensive programming possibilities, but it's also ringing some alarms among Web users and system administrators worried about the security of files on the client machines.

When you think about it, downloading programs to run on your own computer is a risky business. The same capabilities that let local programs carry out useful functions can also be used to plant viruses or play "practical jokes" like erasing your hard disk. Some Web users are also worried about the ability of client-side programs to dig around their systems and send information about them, undetected, back to distant Web sites.

To answer these concerns, Sun Microsystems, the developer of Java, built certain limitations into the language. Programs written with Java cannot read files from or write files to the client computer's disks; can't run other programs; and can't make any network connections, except back to the server that

sent them. The same kinds of limitations also apply to JavaScript.

ActiveX and Visual Basic Script use a different security approach. Instead of hobbling ActiveX applications by restricting their access to the client computer's file systems, Microsoft has instituted a security system based on "code signing," which allows readers to find out who wrote each downloadable program and verify that it has not been tampered with since the developer put its seal on it. Code-signing ensures that practical jokers can't intercept software to carry out their own nefarious agendas, but it doesn't safeguard against faulty or mischievous software. In the latest versions of JavaScript, scripts that want to work with the user's file system may ask for those privileges by offering signed code as security.

Recognizing that many users don't feel safe running client-side programs, browser manufacturers offer controls that let users deny the downloading of ActiveX progrrams and turn off execution of Java and JavaScript.

Java

JavaScript is great for controlling HTML functions and HTTP events. Going beyond such tasks, though, requires a stronger, less specialized tool—a programming language such as **Java**, a cross-platform programming language developed by Sun Microsystems. Unlike traditional programming languages, which require compiling separate versions of a program for each machine it is to run on, Java programs—usually called **applets**—can be compiled just once to run on a **Java Virtual Machine**, a software base that acts as a Java-specific processor. The ability to run, just like HTML, on any computer makes Java a natural for creating applications that are to be distributed over the Web. The fact that Java programs can be run on any kind of computer also makes it handy for webmasters who may have many types of server software running their systems. Custom server-side programs can be written just once and then used on any server that supports Java.

As a full-featured programming language, Java can be used for just about anything, from onscreen animations to building a back-end database. Since it is a full-featured programming language, though, it also requires a good deal of expertise to use. For custom uses of Java, you'll need the services of a programmer. But Java interactivity and animations can be created with WYSIWYG tools (→**156, 174**), and premade Java programs are available freely on the Web and

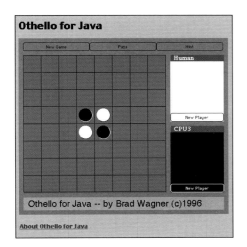

Othello for Java

Othello for Java -- by Brad Wagner (c)1996

About Othello for Java

BRAD WAGNER
http://www.cs.wisc.edu/~bradw/Othello/

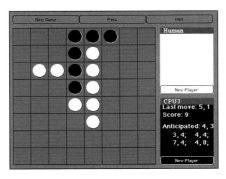

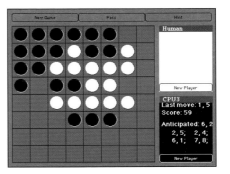

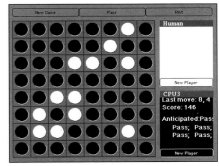

IN THIS JAVA-BASED Othello game, users move their own pieces and the Web site responds with its move.

THE JEROME WEISNER SITE at MIT's Media Lab uses Java to create a dynamic interface. Clicking on a tile in the grid calls up a custom menu of topics. Clicking on one of the topics brings it to the top of the list and displays the related text in the right-hand frame.

MICHAEL MURTAUGH/M.I.T. MEDIA LAB INTERACTIVE CINEMA GROUP
http://ic.www.media.mit.edu/JBW/

applet
A name often used for Java programs designed to be used on the Net.

Java
A cross-platform programming language developed by Sun Microsystems.

Java Virtual Machine
A software layer that executes compiled Java code. The existence of the "virtual machine" is the key to Java's cross-platform capabilities.

START TAG	ATTRIBUTES	END TAG	EXPLANATION
<APPLET>		</APPLET>	Embeds a Java applet in the page
	align="left" OR "right" OR "top" OR "middle" OR "bottom"		The alignment of the applet's output in the window
	alt="*text*"		Text that will be displayed if the applet doesn't load correctly
	code="*URL*"		The name of the Java applet
	codebase="*URL*"		The directory the applet is stored in
	height=*n*, width=*n*		The height and width of the applet's output, in pixels
	hspace=*n*, vspace=*n*		The horizontal space, in pixels, set between the applet and surrounding text
	name="*name*"		A name by which other applets on the page can refer to this one
<OBJECT>		</OBJECT>	Inserts an object (e.g., an image, media file, or program) into the page
	align="left" OR "right" OR "center" OR "top" OR "middle" OR "bottom" OR "baseline" OR "texttop" OR "absmiddle" OR "absbottom"		The alignment of the object in the window
	border=*n*		The width of the border around the object, in pixels
	classid="class-identifier"		A unique identifier for the plug-in or program. (The syntax depends on the type of object being inserted.)
	codebase="*URL*"		The directory that holds the program
	codetype="*MIME-type*"		The MIME type of the program
	data="*URL*"		The URL for the object to be inserted
	height=*n*, width=*n*		The height and width of the object, in pixels
	name="*name*"		A name by which other programs can refer to the object
	standby="*text*"		Text that displays while the object is loading
	type="*MIME-type*"		The object's MIME type. The browser uses this to determine whether it can display the object.
<PARAM>		</PARAM>	Used with the <OBJECT> or <APPLET> tag to pass parameter values to a program
	name="*name*"		The parameter the value should be assigned to
	type="*MIME-type*"		The MIME type of the data
	value="*value*"		A value for the parameter
	valuetype="data" OR "ref" OR "object"		Describes how the value should be interpreted: as data (the default), as a URL (ref), or as the URL of an object in the same document (object)

from commercial distributors. A central Java program repository hosted by developer.com offers access to thousands of Java programs in categories such as Arts and Entertainment (Java games, drawing applications, even a Java piano you can play from your computer keyboard), Special Effects (e.g., animated text and graphic banners), and Utilities (calculators, calendars, and clocks for Web page, and the like).

Java programs work, of course, only if the Java Virtual Machine is present. Java support has been built into Netscape's browser software starting with version 2.0 and in Microsoft's starting with version 3.0, and it is built into Netscape's and others' server software. Major operating system vendors, including Microsoft and Apple, are also beginning to support Java directly in their operating systems, and Sun has even announced plans to release a full operating system built with Java.

Calling programs from Web pages was one of those areas not covered by the original HTML specifications, so it was dealt with ad hoc by browser manufacturers as they added the capabilities to their software. The <APPLET> tag was introduced for the task by Netscape with version 2.0 of its browser, and that method has been picked up by every browser that supports Java. In newer browsers supporting HTML 4.0, Java applets can also be called with the <OBJECT> tag.

SADISTS AT VIRTUAL DESIGN, a Web design company in Atlanta, Georgia, created Virtual Voodoo, a Java applet that lets you manipulate knives, candles, and pins to torture a stand-in for your enemies.

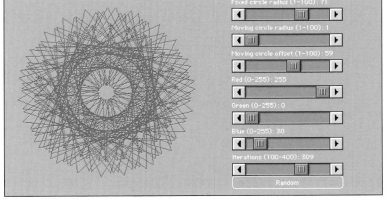

THIS INTERACTIVE SPIROGRAPH, built with Java, lets users experiment with colors, different-length radii, and other controls.

Faster processors and better Java Virtual Machines will make client-side Java viable eventually, and until then it will continue to pick up momentum as a language for servers. But as a general tool for dislaying Web content, it will never be as fast or compatible as HTML.

MATTHEW BUTTERICK, ATOMIC VISION

BEN & JERRY describe their ice cream in an animation created with ActiveX.

NARRATIVE
http://www.narrative.com/benjerry.htm

ActiveX
Microsoft's set of technologies for Web programming.

ActiveX control
A program, based on ActiveX technology, that adds new features to an ActiveX-compatible program.

ActiveX

In early 1996, Microsoft announced its own programming technology for the Web, called **ActiveX**. ActiveX is an extension of Microsoft's popular OLE (Object Linking and Embedding) technology, invented several years ago as a way to tie application programs together (Microsoft uses it within its Office suite—Microsoft Word, Excel, PowerPoint, and so on—to make it possible to open one program's files from within another's). ActiveX simply adds Internet hooks to this idea. **ActiveX controls** are like Java applets: programs that are downloaded to the browser to add new capabilities.

Like Java and JavaScript, ActiveX controls won't work unless the technology is supported by the browser they're downloaded to, and ActiveX has far less support than Java in the Web world. The only browsers that really support ActiveX are Microsoft's browsers for Windows machines. (A plug-in can add ActiveX support to Netscape Navigator and Netscape Communicator for Windows.) If you're designing an intranet site whose pages are meant to be read only inside a corporation, and you know that all the machines inside that company are Windows machines running Internet Explorer, that's not a problem. For publishing over the Internet, it's a bigger problem, and ActiveX isn't widely used.

Outside of intranets, ActiveX controls are mainly used to support additional formats in Internet Explorer. Many popular plug-ins (→**11**) are also available for Windows machines as ActiveX controls.

Like Java programs, ActiveX controls can carry out pretty much any kind of task, from single processes, such as running an animation, to complete applications. Like Java applets, too, ActiveX controls can be custom-programmed or obtained from shareware sites and commercial software publishers. ActiveX controls you'll find at ActiveX.com, an ActiveX repository hosted by CNET, include programs that create interactive buttons, create and display a variety of chart types, display text at a variety of angles, play Microsoft PowerPoint animations, and set a special "New" icon to display until a given date within a Web page.

Like other non-HTML objects, ActiveX controls can be embedded in HTML documents through the <OBJECT> tag (→**190**).

Online: Programming the Web

ActiveX
http://www.microsoft.com/com/

ActiveX Controls
http://www.activex.com/
http://www.developer.com/directories/pages/dir.activex.html

CGI
http://hoohoo.ncsa.uiuc.edu/cgi/intro.html
http://www.yahoo.com/Computers_and_Internet/Internet/
    World_Wide_Web/CGI_Common_Gateway_Interface/

ECMAScript
http://www.ecma.ch/stand/ecma-262.htm

General Information
http://www.builder.com/Programming/

Java
http://java.sun.com/
http://www.hotwired.com/webmonkey/collections/java.html
http://www.javaworld.com/javaworld/
http://www.webdeveloper.com/categories/java/

Java Applets
http://www.developer.com/directories/pages/dir.java.html

JavaScript
http://developer.netscape.com/docs/manuals/javascript.html
http://developer.netscape.com/tech/javascript/
http://www.hotwired.com/webmonkey/collections/javascript.html
http://www.netscapeworld.com/ned-ti/ned-ti-javascript.html
http://www.webdeveloper.com/categories/javascript/

JScript
http://www.microsoft.com/scripting/jscript/

Visual Basic Scripting Edition
http://www.microsoft.com/scripting/vbscript/

ActiveX is excellent for intranet sites, where you know that users will be using Internet Explorer.

STEPHAN FIELEDING-ISAACS, ART & SCIENCE

Keeping the Site Fresh

Designing for Change

Contracting for Change

Imagine publishing in a medium where nothing is ever final, where designs can be changed at will and new information can be published within minutes of hearing it, where ideas can be tested and discarded—or built upon—as soon as you test your audience's reaction to them, and to which readers can return time and time again and find new information at each visit. That's the world of the Web. For many designers, it's a world that takes a little getting used to, but understanding the fast pace of the Web is an important key to success in the medium.

On the Web, changing information, even after publication, is easily done. Unlike print, CD-ROM, video, or any other form of publishing, Web publications are never really "final." Making changes requires revising only one copy—the original on the server. A simple change can be made, and be available to the reader, within moments.

Web publications continue to live and breathe after they're published. Changes aren't limited to refinements on the original content, though that's one benefit you'll quickly learn to appreciate. You can post new features in response to reader requests, add new content as your company grows or launches new products, decorate your site for the holidays—even post content that changes minute by minute. Such changes are important to the character of the Web, and Web publications, like magazines, need to constantly refresh their look and their content, both to stay up to date and to keep their readers interested and coming back for more.

The swift-moving pace of Web technology is another strong motivation for revamping a Web site's design regularly. In other media, the set of possible effects remains fairly constant, and technological advances mostly affect the ease with which those effects can be achieved. On the Web, new advances change the way pages can look and act, and Web sites that haven't changed in six months or so can look creaky and dated.

This capability for continuous change and refinement can't be overlooked when planning a Web site; it has repercussions for how you design your site, what features you include, and how you plan your contracts with clients or the scheduling and staffing requirements for in-house projects. In this final chapter, we'll go through some of the ways you can plan for and take advantage of this unique quality of the Web.

A "WHAT'S NEW" SECTION is a popular way to highlight new content on a site. At the Internet Underground Music Archive, a What's Brewin' button sends users to a list of upcoming events and new recordings.

BRANDEE AMBER SELCK
http://www.iuma.com/IUMA-2.0/brew/

When I first started designing for the Web, I had to totally change my attitude about the work. I was used to print, where I would get this moment of relief when I had the final product in my hands. But on the Web you're never done.

SABINE MESSNER, HOTWIRED

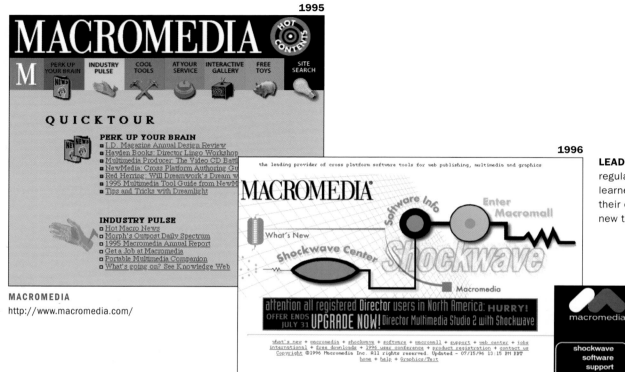

1995

1996

LEADING WEB SITES change their look regularly to take advantage of what they've learned from reader responses and from their own hard-won experience, as well as new technology.

1998

MACROMEDIA
http://www.macromedia.com/

When you're developing the look of a magazine, it's a really big deal to change something about it. On the Web, it's not, and we can experiment. In fact, we should feel responsible to experiment and push the possibilities forward.

BARBARA KUHR, HOTWIRED

PETER BRAY/JOE WAKER
http://www.cybersight.com/

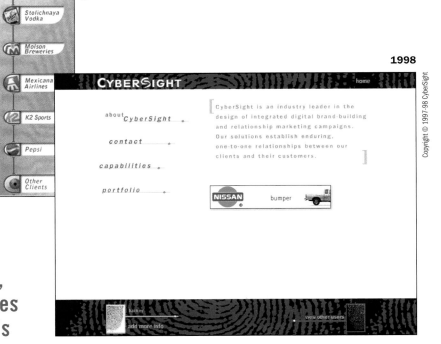

The idea is that you have to keep the information current, so you have repeated opportunities to redesign. Sometimes we say to our clients, "Here's what you can do now; here's something we may be able to do in the future."

JONATHAN NELSON, ORGANIC

1990...

World Wide Web invented

1993

Mosaic
First graphical browser

MOSAIC

NEW WEB DESIGN TECHNOLOGIES started exploding after the invention of Mosaic, the first graphical browser, in 1993. As the importance of the Web as a publishing medium became more apparent, software companies vied to create tools, and the pace of development has been explosive, changing what's possible on the Web every few months. Keeping your Web pages *au courant* requires constant study of new technologies and rethinking your sites to take advantage of them.

1994

Netscape Navigator 1.0
JPEG support, simultaneous download of text and images

Microsoft Internet Explorer 1.0
Font face and color

RealAudio
Streaming audio

Netscape Navigator 2.0
Java, JavaScript, plug-ins, frames, animated GIF

NETSCAPE 2.0

1995

Netscape Navigator 1.1
Background colors, table layouts, server push

VRML 2.0
Interactive 3D

Liquid Motion/WebBurst
WYSIWYG Java animation tools

Microsoft Internet Explorer 3.0
ActiveX controls, style sheets

Netscape Navigator 3.0
Column layouts, streaming QuickTime, VRML plug-ins

WebTV
Set-top boxes to receive Web pages on TV

INTERNET EXPLORER 3.0

1996

Shockwave
Interactive multimedia on Web pages

1997

Microsoft Internet Explorer and Netscape Navigator 4.0
Dynamic HTML for exact placement of text and graphics, layered layouts, and animation of HTML elements; downloadable fonts

High-quality, low-bandwidth sound
Shockwave audio and RealAudio 3.0 offer CD-quality sound over 28.8Kbps modems

Shockwave Flash
Tiny file sizes for high-quality vector animation

INTERNET EXPLORER 4.0

1998

XML
The extensible markup language, enabling designers and industries to define their own markup languages

Style sheet–based Web layout applications
HTML authoring applications offering the control and WYSIWYG ease of page-layout programs

The Internet desktop
Internet access built into desktop software and operating systems

Bandwidth breakthroughs
New communication technologies, such as DSL and cable modems, offering fast connections to homes and small businesses

I think you need to rethink a site every six months. The function of a site changes as the environment changes and the abilities of the technology change.

PETER SEIDLER, AVALANCHE

Designing for Change

Now that you know your site will be a living and breathing entity, your first task is to make sure it has room to breathe. When we talked about structuring a site, we discussed the need to plan for change by setting up departments that could house categories of content rather than a particular piece of information (→**55**). Planning for change has other aspects as well. Careful up-front thinking about your site's directory structure and filenames will ensure that files will be easy to find and weed out at update time. By considering the maintenance effects of every decision, you will guard against implementing solutions—such as different versions of your page for each type of browser—that will be too costly or time-consuming to keep up over the long run. Technology can also help you automate the updating of your site. Java, ActiveX, and Unix file management programs can be set up to swap out pages, or portions of pages, on regular schedules. More and more, entire sites are created from databases, which can automatically churn out up-to-date HTML-formatted pages in various views and with constantly updated information from company databases.

In our chapter on interactivity, we talked about ways to use HTML forms (→**168**) and the mailto feature (→**167**) to elicit feedback from readers. Wise designers take advantage of these features to create a partnership

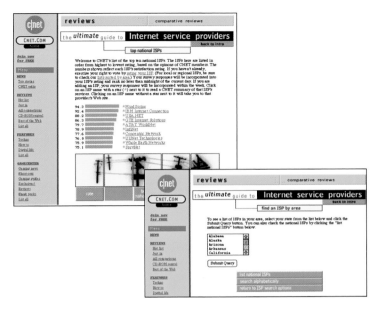

DATABASE-DRIVEN PAGES can be updated with each click of the visitor's mouse. CNET's comparative review of Internet Service Providers keeps a running tally of the top-rated ISPs in the country, based on users' ratings (top). Readers can search the listings for the top-rated services in their area (center) and add their own ratings to the database (right).

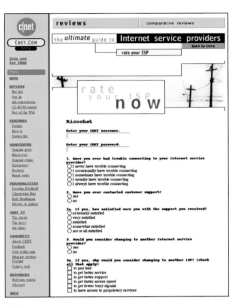

CNET
http://www.cnet.com/Content/Reviews/Compare/ISP/

The idea of the Web is that it's always new and updated. We publish new stories every day, and we can't reinvent the wheel every time. We're starting to work on a more template-based program. On a feature story, the only change we make to the design is updating the graphic.

FRED SOTHERLAND, CNET

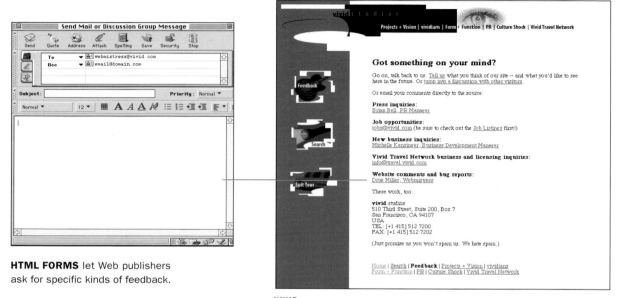

HTML FORMS let Web publishers ask for specific kinds of feedback.

VIVID
http://www.vivid.com/

Server Stats: Gathering Intelligence Behind the Scenes

Direct feedback from readers in the form of e-mail and HTML forms is just one way to find out what's working the way you want it to, and what isn't, on your site. You can also use software on the server to compile site-usage statistics that report what pages are visited most often and from what domains the visitors are arriving. Such statistics can provide valuable information about whether readers are using your site as you expected and whether the pages you want your readers to see are actually getting attention. It's a kind of information available from no other medium.

with readers in the ongoing development of the site. You can use these methods to elicit feedback that will help you learn what works and what doesn't work on the site and to find out what readers want to see more of. Many sites have a mailto feedback link at the bottom of every page, encouraging readers to mail off their impressions as soon as they think of them. Using a form instead of mailto at the link allows publishers to pre-sort reader comments into categories, depending on the way the mail will be handled when it is received. Requests for new content can be sent to one mailbox and reports of broken links to another, for example. A series of questions can elicit the specific information the publisher is most interested in getting. If you have questions about your readers' preferences, put those into a feedback form. Visitors are usually happy to answer them, knowing that their answers will go toward creating a site that will more closely suit their needs.

The knowledge that change is inevitable and feedback will be swift also frees designers to take some chances they might not take in a less elastic medium. Trying a new layout, button design, department title, front page, or any novel approach has fewer risks on a Web site than in any other medium. If it doesn't work, your readers will let you know, and you can change it at great speed and comparatively little cost.

Contracting for Change

For freelance designers, the lack of an irrevocable end to their responsibilities—traditionally provided by the printing of the job—can lead to some confusing situations between the design shop and the client unless the situation is wisely prepared for. Above all, designers should make sure that the extent of their responsibilities is spelled out in the contract and understood by all parties. Knowing something about the evolutionary process of Web sites can help craft a contract that meets both the designer's and the client's needs.

The first order of business is to make sure both parties understand the need for **design specifications** and **design templates**, documents that are drawn up to explain and codify decisions made during the initial design process. Such specifications spell out things such as what font sizes, colors, and special fonts are used, and under what conditions. For a Web publication, these documents might also specify HTML coding styles (e.g., "all HTML tags typed in uppercase"). Such documents will help the production department and any designers who do work on future editions of the site keep the look of the site consistent as it evolves. In the days when production departments and typesetters carried out a designer's plans, such written specifications were a common part of a designer's contract, but they are rarer now that

It's crucial to do a real thought transfer when you hand over the design. It has to be in documents.

NATHAN SHEDROFF, VIVID STUDIOS

PROVIDING DOCUMENTATION of a site's structure and design specifications helps your client keep the site in shape after your part is done. These specifications show which documents go where on a complex frame-based site.

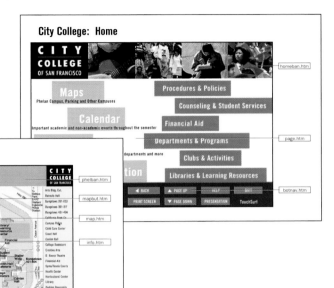

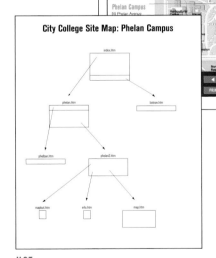

HOT
City College Student Information Kiosk

design specifications
Documentation showing what design styles (typeface, size, indentation, and so forth) are to be used for each element of a publication.

design templates
Electronic documents that serve as starting points for new files. Templates include standard elements, styled according to the design specifications, that can be used or copied as a model for similar elements in the publication.

Push Channels: In-Your-Face Updates

If you want to publish content that depends on always being fresh—news, sports scores, stock quotes, or even just what's new on your Web site—you might consider publishing it as a Web "channel": a set of Web pages that are sent out (or "pushed") to Web users on a regular schedule. Channel pages are saved on users' own computers, allowing them to browse the pages at their leisure; once the pages are downloaded, users don't even need to be connected to the Internet to read them.

Channels appeared on the scene with the 4.0 releases of Netscape's and Microsoft's browsers, which built in special interfaces for receiving and organizing channels. (Netscape's channel-browser component is called Netcaster; Microsoft's is referred to as its "channel bar.") And in Windows 98, Microsoft will put its channel bar on every Windows desktop, so the technology may quickly become mainstream.

On the content provider's side, developing a channel is just like developing a regular Web site: Channel pages are created in HTML. Turning those pages into a channel simply requires supplying code that will identify the site to Internet Explorer's channel bar or Netscape's Netcaster. The way you do that is (you guessed it!) different for Netscape and Microsoft browsers. Microsoft's method includes creating a special file in a format called CDF that describes the channel and its update schedule. Netscape's method uses special JavaScript commands to do the same thing. (Documentation for each method is available on the browser makers' Web sites.) In keeping with the television metaphor, Netscape and Microsoft encourage publishers to use dynamic HTML to create lively animated interfaces for channels, but there's nothing about the technology that requires it.

To receive a channel, Web users "subscribe" using their browsers' channel controls. A certain set of channels are automatically supplied in Microsoft's channel bar and Netscape's Netcaster window. These are companies that have made multimillion-dollar deals with the browser companies, so yours probably won't be among them. Both companies also offer a channel guide, available from the main channel controls, on which you can list your channel. But in most cases, users will find out about your channel by visiting your main Web site. You can add links and some code that set up channel subscriptions on your regular Web pages.

Think of channels as an adjunct to your regular Web site: a way to keep your readers up to date on topics that are of special interest to them or have timely news value. You can even create separate channels for separate audiences, targeting special interests.

designers do their own production using desktop publishing. Creating a good set of specifications can take significant time and skill, in addition to the time and skill needed to create the design itself, and designers should make sure their contracts include sufficient payment for this extra step.

Designers should also be sure that their clients expect and have a plan for dealing with the inevitable design feedback that will occur once the site is on line. If the contract is not clear, clients may expect the designers to fix "mistakes" pointed out by visitors to the site. In some cases, that may be appropriate, of course, but in many others, the "mistake" may simply be one reader's opinion. One way of dealing with the situation is to expect a certain number of requests for revisions and include a price for changes after publication in your bid.

New design work will also be required, of course, when new types of content are added to the site over time. Some sites will be taken over by in-house teams after the initial edition is complete, but some designers may want to be involved in the continued development of the sites they design. Having a hand in the evolution of your own design can be a great opportunity to learn about what works and what doesn't work in Web design, as well as a way to make sure that work you're proud of doesn't deteriorate once it leaves your hands.

Of course, the constant change required of Web sites can create exciting opportunities as well as a few contractual pitfalls. No other medium gives designers a chance to experiment so freely with new approaches; collaborate so closely with their readers; know so surely, from instant feedback, what works and what doesn't in their designs; be so close to the forefront of the newest communication technology; and pioneer, so excitingly, new approaches to communicating in a brand new, interactive, animated medium.

Welcome to the World Wide Web.

Keeping the Site Fresh

Channels

http://developer.netscape.com/docs/manuals/netcast/
  devguide/

http://www.microsoft.com/workshop/prog/ie4/channels/
  cdf1.htm

Database-Driven Sites

http://www.hotwired.com/webmonkey/97/50/index1a.html

Server Statistic Analysis

http://www.webdeveloper.com/categories/management/
  management_log_analysis.html

Web design never gets old. The minute you think something is proven, the rules change and you start over.

ERIC EATON, HOTWIRED

HTML
Reference

This reference provides a guide to the HTML tags you'll use to take advantage of the Web design features we've described in this book. Rather than try to settle on any "official" version of HTML, we've tried to include the tags and attributes that are most useful for designers and supported by today's browsers, whether or not they're part of HTML 4.0.

This reference is a bit different from the HTML boxes you've see throughout the book. Here, we list all the tags in alphabetical order for quick access and add some extra information.

If an end tag or attribute is in boldface, that means it is required: If you use the tag, you must include it.

A "Support" column lists the first version of Netscape Navigator and Microsoft Internet Explorer to support the tag or attribute. (You can assume that later versions support it, too.) If the Support column for a tag or attribute is blank, that means the code wasn't yet supported in version 4.0 of the browser, the latest available when this book went to press.

Last but not least, the "Page" column shows where you can find more information about the tag or attribute in the book.

Universal Attributes

HTML 4.0 includes some attributes that can be used with almost any tag. Rather than repeat them for every tag in the table, we've listed them here.

STYLE

Used to add CSS style properties to an element

ATTRIBUTE	EXPLANATION	SUPPORT NS	MS	PAGE
style="*property : value*"	Assigns layout styles to the element. The styles are specified in CSS syntax.	4.0	3.0	99

IDENTIFIERS

Used to add identifiers to elements, which can be used to address the element from scripts or style sheets

ATTRIBUTE	EXPLANATION	SUPPORT NS	MS	PAGE
class="*name*"	Identifies the element as one of the named class	4.0	3.0	100
id="*name*"	Creates a unique identifier for the element	3.0*	3.0	

EVENT HANDLERS

Used for interactive interfaces, to call scripts when certain events occur

ATTRIBUTE	EXPLANATION	SUPPORT NS	MS	PAGE
onclick="*script*"	Activates a script when the mouse button is clicked on the element	2.0*	3.0*	172
ondblclick="*script*"	Activates a script when the mouse button is double-clicked on the element		4.0	172
onkeydown="*script*"	Activates a script when a keyboard key is pressed		4.0	172
onkeypress="*script*"	Activates a script when a keyboard key is pressed and released		4.0	172
onkeyup="*script*"	Activates a script when a keyboard key is released		4.0	172
onmousedown="*script*"	Activates a script when the mouse button is pressed on the element		4.0	172
onmousemove="*script*"	Activates a script when the mouse pointer moves over the element		4.0	172
onmouseout="*script*"	Activates a script when the mouse pointer leaves the element	3.0*	4.0	172
onmouseover="*script*"	Activates a script when the mouse pointer is over the element	2.0*	3.0*	172
onmouseup="*script*"	Activates a script when the mouse button is pressed and released on the element		4.0	172

*Note: In browser versions before 4.0, supported only for selected elements.

START TAG	ATTRIBUTES	END TAG	EXPLANATION	SUPPORT NS	MS	PAGE
\<A>		\</A>	Creates a hyperlink	1.0	1.0	78
	accesskey=*x*		A key that can be pressed to access the hyperlink		4.0	
	coords="*coord1, coord2, coord3 . . .*"		The coordinates of the area's boundaries. (Each shape has its own rules for specifying coordinates.)			128
	href="*URL*"		The file to be called by the hyperlink	1.0	1.0	78
	name="*name*"		Names a section of an HTML document. That name can then be used in the *href=* attribute of another \<A> tag.	1.0	1.0	
	tabindex=*x*		The order in which the link is accessed when the page is navigated using the Tab key		4.0	
	shape="default" or "rect" or "circle" or "poly"		The type of shape being defined			
	target="frame" or "_blank" or "new" or "_parent" or "_self" or "_top"		Used with frames, names a frame or window in which the file should be displayed	2.0	3.0	94
\<ABBR>		\</ABBR>	Marks text that should be set as an abbreviation			128
\<APPLET>		\</APPLET>	Embeds a Java applet in the page	2.0	3.0	190
	align="left" OR "right" OR "top" OR "middle" OR "bottom"		The alignment of the applet's output in the window	2.0	3.0	
	alt="*text*"		Text that will be displayed if the applet doesn't load correctly	3.0	3.0	
	code="*URL*"		The name of the Java applet	2.0	3.0	
	codebase="*URL*"		The directory the applet is stored in	2.0	3.0	
	height=*n*, width=*n*		The height and width of the applet's output, in pixels	2.0	3.0	
	hspace=*n*, vspace=*n*		The horizontal and vertical space, in pixels, set between the applet and surrounding text	2.0	3.0	
	name="*name*"		A name by which other applets on the page can refer to this one	2.0	3.0	
	onblur="*script*"		A script to be run when the control loses focus	2.0	3.0	
	onfocus="*script*"		A script to be run when the control gains focus	2.0	3.0	
	tabindex=*n*		The order this control should be accessed in when a user navigates the form using the Tab key	2.0	3.0	
\<AREA>			Creates a hyperlink area within a client-side image map created with the \<MAP> tag	2.0	3.0	128
	accesskey=*x*		A key that can be pressed to access the control			
	alt="*text*"		Text to be displayed in nongraphics browsers	3.0	4.0	

START TAG	ATTRIBUTES	END TAG	EXPLANATION	SUPPORT NS	MS	PAGE
	coords="*coord1, coord2, coord3 . . .*"		The coordinates of the area's boundaries. (Each shape has its own rules for specifying coordinates.)	2.0	1.0	128
	href="*URL*"		The URL of the linked file	2.0	1.0	
	nohref		Defines the area as having no hyperlink	2.0	1.0	
	onblur="*script*"		A script to be run when the linked area loses focus			172
	onfocus="*script*"		A script to be run when the control gains focus			172
	shape="default" OR "rect" OR "circle" OR "poly"		The type of shape being defined	2.0	1.0	128
	tabindex=*x*		The order in which the link is accessed when the page is navigated using the Tab key		4.0	
	target="*frame*" OR "_blank" OR "new" OR "_parent" OR "_self" OR "_top"		Used with frames, names a frame or window in which the linked file should be displayed	2.0	3.0	94
\<B>		\</B>	Marks text to be set in boldface type	1.0	1.0	108
\<BASE>			Sets default locations for the document	1.0	1.0	
	href="URL"		A base URL to be used for all relative links in the document	1.0	1.0	
	target="*frame*" OR "_blank" OR "new" OR "_parent" OR "_self" OR "_top"		Used with frames, names a frame or window in which linked files from this document should be displayed	2.0	2.0	94
\<BASEFONT>		\</BASEFONT>	Names default font settings (used in the head of an HTML document)	1.1	2.0	112
	color="#*RRGGBB*" OR "*name*"		A color for the text, using an RGB value expressed in hexadecimal or a color name		2.0	112
	face="*name*"		The name of a typeface		2.0	112
	size="*size*"		A type size, from 1 to 7; 3 is the default. The number can be an absolute number from 1 to 7 or a relative size from –1 to +3.	1.1	2.0	112
\<BGSOUND>			Plays a .wav (sound) file when the file is loaded		2.0	
	loop=*n* OR "infinite"		The number of times the sound clip will loop		2.0	
	src="URL"		The URL of the sound file		2.0	
	volume=*n*		Sets the volume, in values from 0 (full) to -10000 (no volume)		4.0	
\<BIG>		\</BIG>	Marks text to be set in a large size	1.1	3.0	108
\<BLOCKQUOTE>		\</BLOCKQUOTE>	Marks text to be set as an indented quotation	1.0	1.0	84-6
	cite="*URL*"		A URL that holds a file containing the source for the quotation			

KEY

NS=Netscape

MS=Microsoft

End tags and attributes in **boldface** are required

START TAG	ATTRIBUTES	END TAG	EXPLANATION	SUPPORT NS	SUPPORT MS	PAGE
<BODY>		</BODY>	Marks the text to be displayed in the browser window	1.0	1.0	71
	alink="#*RRGGBB*" OR "*name*"		A color for the active links (links being clicked on), using an RGB value expressed in hexadecimal or a color name	1.1	4.0	130
	background="*URL*"		A graphics file to be used as the background	1.1	1.0	130
	bgcolor="#*RRGGBB*" OR "*name*"		A background color	1.1	1.0	130
	bgproperties="fixed"		Specifies that the background image should not scroll		2.0	
	leftmargin=*n*		Sets a left margin, described as a number of pixels		2.0	88-9
	link="#*RRGGBB*" OR "*name*"		A color for hyperlink anchors	1.1	1.0	130
	onload="*script*"		A script to be run when the document is loaded into the browser	2.0	3.0	172
	onunoad="*script*"		A script to be run when the document is unloaded (i.e., when another page is loaded)	2.0	3.0	172
	scroll="yes" OR "no"		Whether or not a scrollbar appears on the window		4.0	
	text="#*RRGGBB*" OR "*name*"		A color for nonlinked text	1.1	1.0	130
	topmargin=*n*		Sets a left margin, described as a number of pixels		2.0	88-9
	vlink="#*RRGGBB*" OR "*name*"		A color for visited links	1.1	1.0	130
** **			Creates a line break	1.0	1.0	
<BUTTON>		</BUTTON>	In a form, creates a button control		4.0	170
	accesskey=*x*		A key that can be pressed to access the control		4.0	
	disabled		Indicates that the button should be disabled by default		4.0	169
	name="*text*"		A name for the button, so that scripts can refer to it		4.0	169
	onblur="*script*"		A script to be run when the control loses focus		4.0	172
	onfocus="*script*"		A script to be run when the control gains focus		4.0	172
	type="button" OR "reset" OR "submit"		The type of button: a push button (which runs a script), a reset button (which deletes all entered information), or a submit button (which submits the form information)		4.0	
	usemap="*name*"		A map to be used if the button is an image map		4.0	126-7
	value="text"		A default value to be submitted when the button is clicked; also the text displayed on the button		4.0	
<CAPTION>		</CAPTION>	Provides a caption for a table	1.1	2.0	
	align="top" OR "bottom" OR "left" OR "right"		The alignment of the caption	1.1	2.0	
<CENTER>		</CENTER>	Marks elements that should be centered in the window	1.0	1.0	88-9

START TAG	ATTRIBUTES	END TAG	EXPLANATION	SUPPORT NS	MS	PAGE
<CITE>		</CITE>	Marks text that should be set as a citation	1.0	1.0	108
<CODE>		**</CODE>**	Marks text that should be set as computer code	1.0	1.0	108
<COL> <COLGROUP>		</COLGROUP>	Supply specifications for groups of columns in tables; the <COLGROUP> element can contain one or more <COL> elements, which supply particular specifications for individual columns		3.0	
	align="left" OR "center" OR "right"		The horizontal alignment of the column or column group		4.0	
	span=*n*		The number of columns the specification applies to		*3.0*	
	width=*n* OR "*n*%"		The width of the specified column or column group, specified in pixels or as a percentage of the window		3.0	
	valign="top" OR "middle" OR "bottom" OR "baseline"		The vertical alignment of text in the column or column group's cells		4.0	
<DD>		</DD>	Marks text that should be set as a definition in a definition list (used with <DL> and <DT>)	1.0	1.0	84–6
<DEL>		</DEL>	Marks text as deleted (usually with strikethrough)		4.0	108
<DFN>		</DFN>	Marks text that should be set as a definition		1.0	108
<DIR>		</DIR>	Creates a columnar list (up to 20 items)	1.0	1.0	84–6
<DIV>		</DIV>	Groups a set of elements, applying the attributes to all of them	2.0	3.0	104–5
	align="left" OR "right" OR "center" OR "justify"		The alignment of the elements in the division	2.0	3.0	
<DL>		</DL>	Creates a definition list	1.0	1.0	84–6
<DT>		</DT>	Marks text that should be set as a term in a definition list (used with <DL> and <DD>)	1.0	1.0	84–6
<EM>		</EM>	Marks text that should be emphasized	1.0	1.0	108
<EMBED>		</EMBED>	Embeds a plug-in or ActiveX control into the page	2.0	3.0	
	height=*n*, width=*n*		The height and width of the media, in pixels	2.0	3.0	
	name="*name*"		A name by which other objects can refer to this one	2.0	3.0	
	param="*value*"		Values to be passed to any parameters of the program	2.0	3.0	
	src="*URL*"		The file to be displayed by the plug-in or ActiveX control	2.0	3.0	
<FIELDSET>		</FIELDSET>	Groups form fields into a set		4.0	
<FONT>		**</FONT>**	Marks text to be set with special font attributes	1.1	1.0	112
	color="#*RRGGBB*" OR "*name*"		A color for the text, using an RGB value expressed in hexadecimal or a color name	2.0	1.0	112

START TAG	ATTRIBUTES	END TAG	EXPLANATION	SUPPORT NS	MS	PAGE
	face="*name*"		The name of a typeface	3.0	1.0	112
	size="*size*"		A type size, from 1 to 7; 3 is the default. The number can be an absolute number from 1 to 7 or a relative size from –1 to +3.	1.1	2.0	112
<FORM>		</FORM>	Surround all the tags that create a fill-in form	1.0	1.0	168–71
	action="*URL*"		The script that should be run, and that the form data should be sent to, when the user clicks the Submit button	1.0	1.0	168
	encytype="*MIME-type*"		For *method="post"*, the encoding method of the information sent	1.0	1.0	
	method="get" OR "post"		Specifies a method for sending the data to the server	1.0	1.0	
	name="*text*"		A name for the form, so that it can be manipulated by scripts	2.0	3.0	
	onreset="*script*"		A script to be run when the user resets the form	3.0	4.0	172
	onsubmit="*script*"		A script to be run when the user submits the form	2.0	3.0	172
	target="*frame*" OR "_blank" OR "new" OR "_parent" OR "_self" OR "_top"		Used with frames, names a frame or window in which the file should be displayed	2.0	3.0	94
<FRAME>			Specifies the attributes of an individual frame within a frameset	2.0	3.0	94–7
	bordercolor="*#RRGGBB*" OR "*color*"		A color for the frame's border, expressed as a hexidecimal RGB value or a color name	3.0	4.0	
	frameborder=1 OR 0 OR "yes" OR "no"		Sets a border (*1* or *yes*) or omits a border (*0* or *no*) around a frame. (Microsoft's browser uses the numbers, Netscape's the words.)	3.0	3.0	
	marginheight=*n*		The space between frames, in pixels	2.0	3.0	
	marginwidth=*n*		Creates a margin within the frame (specified in pixels)	2.0	3.0	
	name="*name*"		A target name for the frame (used by <A>and <AREA> tags to send linked files to that particular frame)	2.0	3.0	
	noresize		Prevents users from resizing the frame (by omitting the resize box)	2.0	3.0	
	scrolling= "yes" OR "no" OR "auto"		Includes or omits a scrollbar for the frame. By default (or using "auto"), a scroll bar appears if the frame's contents go beyond its borders.	2.0	3.0	
	src="*URL*"		The URL of the file to be placed in the frame	2.0	3.0	
<FRAMESET>		</FRAMESET>	Marks the tags that make up a set of frames. (Replaces the <BODY> tag on frameset pages.)	2.0	3.0	94–7
	border=*n*		The width of the frameset's border, in pixels; *0* means no border	3.0	4.0	
	bordercolor="*#RRGGBB*" OR "*color*"		A color for the frameset's borders, expressed as a hexidecimal RGB value or a color name	3.0	4.0	

START TAG	ATTRIBUTES	END TAG	EXPLANATION	SUPPORT NS	MS	PAGE
	cols="*col1, col2, col3,...*"		Sets up a frameset as a set of "columns." The set of columns is specified by giving a width for each one. Widths can be specified in pixels, as a percentage of the window size, or as an asterisk (*), meaning that the column should take up the remaining space. If more than one column is specified with an asterisk, the space is divided evenly among them.	2.0	3.0	
	frameborder=1 OR 0 OR "yes" OR "no"		Sets a border (*1* or *yes*) or omits a border (*0* or *no*) around a frameset. (Microsoft's browser uses the numbers, Netscape's the words.)	3.0	3.0	
	framespacing=*n*		The space between frames, in pixels		3.0	
	onload="*script*"		A script to be run when the document is loaded into the browser	2.0	3.0	172
	onunload="*script*"		A script to be run when the document is unloaded (i.e., when another page is loaded)	2.0	3.0	172
	rows="*row1, row2, row3,...*"		Sets up a frameset as a set of "rows." The set of rows is specified by giving a height for each one. Heights can be specified in pixels, as a percentage of the window size, or as an asterisk (*), meaning that the row should take up the remaining space. If more than one row is specified with an asterisk, the space is divided evenly among them.	2.0	3.0	
<H1>		**</H1>**	Marks text as a level-1 head (the largest head size)	1.0	1.0	84–5
	align="left" OR "right" OR "center"		The alignment of the heading	1.0	1.0	
<H2>		**</H2>**	Marks text as a level-2 head	1.0	1.0	84–5
	align="left" OR "right" OR "center"		The alignment of the heading	1.0	1.0	
<H3>		**</H3>**	Marks text as a level-3 head	1.0	1.0	84–5
	align="left" OR "right" OR "center"		The alignment of the heading	1.0	1.0	
<H4>		**</H4>**	Marks text as a level-4 head	1.0	1.0	84–5
	align="left" OR "right" OR "center"		The alignment of the heading	1.0	1.0	
<H5>		**</H5>**	Marks text as a level-5 head	1.0	1.0	84–5
	align="left" OR "right" OR "center"		The alignment of the heading	1.0	1.0	
<H6>		**</H6>**	Marks text as a level-6 head	1.0	1.0	84–5
	align="left" OR "right" OR "center"		The alignment of the heading	1.0	1.0	
<HEAD>		**</HEAD>**	Marks the tags in the HTML document's head	1.0	1.0	71

KEY

NS=Netscape

MS=Microsoft

End tags and attributes in **boldface** are required

START TAG	ATTRIBUTES	END TAG	EXPLANATION	SUPPORT NS	MS	PAGE
\<HR>			Creates a horizontal rule	1.0	1.0	88–9
	align= "left" OR "right" OR "center"		The alignment of the rule in the window	1.0	1.0	
	color="#RRGGBB" OR "color"		A color for the rule, specified as RGB values (in hexadecimal) or as a color name		3.0	
	noshade		Omits the default 3D shading for the rule	1.0	1.0	
	size=n		The length of the rule, in pixels	1.0	1.0	
	width=n OR "n%"		The width of the rule, in pixels or as a percentage of the window size	1.0	1.0	
\<HTML>		\</HTML>	Labels the document as an HTML document (introduces all other HTML tags)	1.0	1.0	71
\<I>		**\</I>**	Marks text to be set in italic	1.0	1.0	108
\<IFRAME>		**\</FRAME>**	Specifies the attributes of an individual frame within a frameset		3.0	94–7
	align="left" OR "right" OR "top" OR "middle" OR "bottom"		The alignment of the frame in the browser window		3.0	
	frameborder=1 OR 0 OR "yes" OR "no"		Sets a border (1 or yes) or omits a border (0 or no) around a frame. (Microsoft's browser uses the numbers, Netscape's the words.)		3.0	
	height=n, width=n		The height and width of the inline frame, in pixels		3.0	
	hspace=n, vspace=n		The horizontal and vertical space, in pixels, set between the frame and the surrounding content		3.0	
	marginheight=n		The space between frames, in pixels		3.0	
	marginwidth=n		Creates a margin within the frame (specified in pixels)		3.0	
	name="name"		A target name for the frame (used by \<A>and \<AREA> tags to send linked files to that particular frame)		3.0	
	scrolling= "yes" OR "no" OR "auto"		Includes or omits a scrollbar for the frame. By default (or using "auto"), a scroll bar appears if the frame's contents go beyond its borders.		3.0	
	src="URL"		The URL of the file to be placed in the frame		3.0	
\<ILAYER>		\</ILAYER>	Creates an inline layer: a group of objects that can be manipulated via dynamic HTML	4.0		
	above="layer"		A layer that the current layer should always be displayed above	4.0		
	background="URL"		A graphics file to be used as the background	4.0		
	below="layer"		A layer that the current layer should always be displayed below	4.0		
	bgcolor="#RRGGBB" OR "name"		A background color	4.0		

START TAG	ATTRIBUTES	END TAG	EXPLANATION	SUPPORT NS	MS	PAGE
	clip="*left, top, right, bottom*"		The x-y coordinates for the visible portion of the inline layer	4.0		
	height=*n*, width=*n*		The height and width of the layer, in pixels	4.0		
	left="*coords*"		The position of the left edge of the layer in the window	4.0		
	name="*text*"		A name for the layer, so it can be referred to by scripts or by other layers	4.0		
	onblur="*script*"		A script to be run when the layer loses focus	4.0		
	onfocus="*script*"		A script to be run when the layer gains focus	4.0		
	onload="*script*"		A script to be run when the document is loaded into the browser	4.0		
	pagex=*n*, pagey=*n*		The horizontal and vertical location for the layer in the window	4.0		
	src="*URL*"		The URL for the layer's contents	4.0		
	top="*coords*"		The position of the left edge of the layer in the window	4.0		
	visibility="show" OR "hide" OR "inherit"		Whether or not the layer should be visible; "inherit" (the default) means that the layer will inherit its visibility from its parent element	4.0		
	z-index=*n*		The layering order of the element (a value in x-y-z coordinate space)	4.0		103
<IMG>			Inserts an image file or video clip into the page	1.0	1.0	124–5
	align="top" OR "texttop" OR "middle" OR "absmiddle" OR "bottom" OR "absbottom" OR "baseline" OR "left" OR "right" OR "center"		The alignment of the image or video clip relative to surrounding text	1.1	1.0	88
	alt="*text*"		Alternate text that will be displayed if the image can't be	1.0	1.0	125
	border=*n*		The width of the border, specified in pixels (defaults to *border=1*; *border=0* omits the border)	1.1	1.0	
	controls		Used with *dynsrc=*, displays video controls		2.0	
	dynsrc="*URL*"		Specifies an AVI file to be inserted		2.0	
	height=*n*, width=*n*		The height and width of the image or video clip, in pixels	1.1	1.0	137–8
	hspace=*n*, *vspace=n*		The horizontal and vertical space, in pixels, set between the image or video clip and surrounding text	1.1	1.0	
	ismap		Specifies that the image is a server-side image map	1.0	1.0	126–7
	loop=*n* OR "infinite"		Used with *dynsrc=*, the number of times the video clip will loop		2.0	
	lowsrc="*URL*"		The URL for an image (preferably one with a low resolution or small file size) to be inserted while a larger final image loads	1.0	4.0	138
	name="*text*"		A name for the image, so that it can be manipulated by a script	3.0	3.0	

START TAG	ATTRIBUTES	END TAG	EXPLANATION	SUPPORT NS	MS	PAGE
	src="*URL*"		The URL of the image to be inserted	1.0	1.0	
	start="fileopen" OR "mouseover"		Used with *dynsrc=*, the event that starts the video clip running		2.0	
	usemap="#*name*"		Names the map to be used for a client-side image map. The name is the one specified by the *name=* attribute of the <MAP> tag.	2.0	1.0	126–9
<INPUT>			Creates input controls within a form	1.0	1.0	168–71
	align="left" OR "right" OR "top" OR "texttop" OR "middle" OR "absmiddle" OR baseline" OR "bottom" OR "absbottom"		For *type="image"*, the alignment of the image in the window	1.0	1.0	88
	alt="*text*"		For *type="image"*, alternate text to be displayed if the image can't be	1.0	1.0	125
	accesskey=*x*		A key that can be pressed to access the control		4.0	
	checked		For *type=checkbox* or *type=radio*, specifies that the box or button should be chosen as a default	1.0	1.0	
	disabled		Indicates that the button should be disabled by default		4.0	169
	height=*n*, width=*n*		For *type="button"*, *"reset"*, *"submit"*, or (in later browsers) *"image"*, the height and width of the button	1.0	4.0	
	maxlength="*length*"		For *type=text*, the maximum length of an entry, in characters	1.0	1.0	
	name="*text*"		A name for the control, used as a variable name when input is sent to a script for processing. (Used for all input types.) For *type=radio*, all the radio buttons in a group have the same name.	1.0	1.0	
	onblur="*script*"		A script to be run when the control loses focus		4.0	172
	onchange="*script*"		A script to be run when the control is changed		4.0	172
	onclick="*script*"		A script to be run when the control is clicked		4.0	172
	onfocus="*script*"		A script to be run when the control gains focus		4.0	172
	onselect="script"		A script to be run when the control loses focus		4.0	172
	readonly		Specifies that the control cannot be changed by the user		4.0	
	size="*size*"		For *type=text*, the length of the text box	1.0	1.0	
	src="*URL*"		For *type=image*, names an image to use as a Submit button	1.0	1.0	
	type= "button" OR "checkbox" OR "file" OR		In an HTML form, the type of control to be created: a button a checkbox a file	1.0 1.0 1.0 2.0	1.0 3.0 1.0 4.0	171–2

START TAG	ATTRIBUTES	END TAG	EXPLANATION	NS	MS	PAGE
	"hidden" OR		an invisible, read-only field	1.0	1.0	171-2
	"image" OR		an image (acting as a Submit button)	1.0	1.0	
	"password" OR		a password field (a text field that hides entries)	1.0	1.0	
	"radio" OR		a radio button	1.0	1.0	
	"reset" OR		a Reset button	1.0	1.0	
	"submit" OR		a Submit button	1.0	1.0	
	"text"		a text field	1.0	1.0	
	tabindex=n		The order in which this control will be accessed when the form is navigated using the Tab key		4.0	
	value="*text*"		For *type="checkbox"*, the text displayed next to the button. For *type=text*, the default entry in the text field. For *type=submit*, *type=reset*, or *type=button*, the text displayed on the button. Also, for all, the value sent for the variable named by the control's name in the script that processes the form.	1.0	1.0	
<INS>		**</INS>**	Marks text to be marked as inserted		4.0	108
<KBD>		**</KBD>**	Marks text to be set as keyboard input	1.0	1.0	108
<LABEL>		**</LABEL>**	Provides a label for a form control		4.0	
	accesskey=x		A key that can be pressed to access the control		4.0	
	for="*id*"		Names the control that the label is to be used for (the value is the name given the control with the *id=* attribute		4.0	
	onblur="*script*"		A script to be run when the label loses focus		4.0	
	onfocus="*script*"		A script to be run when the label gains focus		4.0	
<LAYER>		**</LAYER>**	Creates an inline layer: a group of objects that can be manipulated via dynamic HTML	4.0		88
	above="*layer*"		A layer that the current layer should always be displayed above	4.0		
	background="*URL*"		A graphics file to be used as the background	4.0		130
	below="*layer*"		A layer that the current layer should always be displayed below	4.0		
	bgcolor="#*RRGGBB*" OR "*name*"		A background color	4.0		130
	clip="*left, top, right, bottom*"		The x-y coordinates for the visible portion of the inline layer	4.0		
	height=n, width=n		The height and width of the layer, in pixels	4.0		
	left="*coords*"		The position of the left edge of the layer in the window	4.0		
	name="*text*"		A name for the layer, so it can be referred to by scripts or by other layers	4.0		
	onblur="*script*"		A script to be run when the layer loses focus	4.0		

KEY

NS=Netscape

MS=Microsoft

End tags and attributes in **boldface** are required

START TAG	ATTRIBUTES	END TAG	EXPLANATION	SUPPORT NS	SUPPORT MS	PAGE
	onfocus="*script*"		A script to be run when the layer gains focus	4.0		
	onload="*script*"		A script to be run when the document is loaded into the browser	4.0		
	onmouseout="*script*"		A script to be run when the mouse pointer leaves the element	4.0		
	onmouseover="*script*"		A script to be run when the mouse pointer is over the element	4.0		
	pagex=*n*, pagey=*n*		The horizontal and vertical location for the layer in the window	4.0		
	src="*URL*"		The URL for the layer's contents	4.0		
	top="*coords*"		The position of the left edge of the layer in the window	4.0		
	visibility="show" OR "hide" OR "inherit"		Whether or not the layer should be visible; "inherit" (the default) means that the layer will inherit its visibility from its parent element	4.0		
	z-index=*n*		The layering order of the element (a value in x-y-z coordinate space)	4.0		103
<LEGEND>		</LEGEND>	Provides a label for a set of Fields (<FIELDSET>) in a form		4.0	
	accesskey=*x*		A key that can be pressed to access the control		4.0	
	align="top" OR "bottom" OR "left" OR "right" OR "center"		The alignment of the legend		4.0	
<LI>		</LI>	Creates a new item in a list (<DIR>, <MENU>, <OL>, or <UL>)	1.0	1.0	84-6
	type="A" OR "a" OR "I" OR "i" OR "1" OR "disc" OR "circle" OR "square"		Used with <OL> or <UL>, specifies a number or bullet style for the item. (See <OL> and <UL> for explanations of options.)	1.1	1.0	
	value=*n*		Used with <OL>, a number for that item	1.0	1.0	
<LINK>			Links an external document to the current document	4.0	3.0	
	rel="stylesheet" OR "font"		The relationship of the linked content to the file. Theoretically, there can be many more values for this attribute, but these are the most common.	4.0	3.0	99, 116
	disabled		Specifies that the link should be disabled by default			
	href="*URL*"		The URL for the linked material	4.0	3.0	
	media="screen" OR "print" OR "projection" OR "braille" OR "speech" OR "all"		For *rel="stylesheet"*, the type of media the style sheet is for	4.0	3.0	
	type="*MIME-type*"		The MIME type of the linked content	4.0	3.0	
<MAP>		</MAP>	Marks the map code for a client-side image map (referred to by the <IMG> tag's *usemap=* attribute)	2.0	1.0	128-9
	name="*name*" or "*URL*"		Provides a name or URL for the map	2.0	1.0	

START TAG	ATTRIBUTES	END TAG	EXPLANATION	SUPPORT NS	MS	PAGE
<MARQUEE>		**</MARQUEE>**	Marks text that should scroll across the screen		2.0	
	align="top" OR "middle" OR "bottom"		Specifies an alignment of the marquee with the surrounding text		2.0	
	behavior="scroll" OR "slide" OR "alternate"		Specifies a scrolling action: "scroll" (the default) scrolls from one side of the screen and off the other, "slide" scrolls just until it reaches the other side, and "alternate" scrolls back and forth across the window		2.0	
	bgcolor="#RRGGBB" OR "name"		Names a color for the marquee's background, using an RGB value (expressed in hexadecimal) OR a color name		2.0	130
	direction="left" OR "right" OR "down" OR "up"		The direction the marquee will scroll		2.0	
	height=n OR n%, width=n OR n%		The height and width of the marquee, described in pixels or as a percentage of the screen height		2.0	
	hspace=n, vspace=n		The horizontal and vertical space, in pixels, set between the marquee and surrounding text		2.0	
	loop=n OR "infinite"		The number of times the marquee will loop		2.0	
	scrollamount=n		The unit, in pixels, by which the marquee scrolls		2.0	
	scrolldelay=n		The number of milliseconds between scrolls		2.0	
<MENU>		**</MENU>**	Creates a menu list	1.0	1.0	84–5
<META>			Provides general information about the HTML document, usually to provide information to search engines or document management systems	1.1	2.0	
	content="text"		Provides the infomation described in http-equiv=	1.1	2.0	
	http-equiv= "copyright" OR "description" OR "expires" OR "keywords" OR "refresh" OR "reply-to"		Defines how the text supplied with content= should be used	1.1	2.0	
	name="text"		An alternative to http-equiv= for describing the use of the <META> tag			
	url="URL"		The current document's URL	1.1	2.0	
<MULTICOL>		</MULTICOL>	Marks text that should be set in multiple columns	3.0		88–9
	cols=n		The number of columns	3.0		
	gutter=n		The amount of space between columns, in pixels	3.0		
	width=n		The width of the column set, in pixels	3.0		
<NOBR>		**</NOBR>**	Joins elements that should not be separated by a line break	1.0	1.0	

START TAG	ATTRIBUTES	END TAG	EXPLANATION	SUPPORT NS	MS	PAGE
<NOEMBED>		</NOEMBED>	Used with <EMBED>, marks elements that should be displayed in browsers that don't support plug-ins. (Browsers that support plug-ins ignore text marked by <NOEMBED>.)	2.0	3.0	
<NOFRAMES>		</NOFRAMES>	Used with the <FRAMES> tag, marks content that should be displayed in browsers that don't support frames. (The text is ignored by frames-capable browsers.)	2.0	3.0	94–7
<NOLAYER>		</NOLAYER>	Used with the <LAYER> tag, marks content that should be displayed in browsers that don't support layers. (The text is ignored by layers-capable browsers.)	4.0		
<NOSCRIPT>		</NOSCRIPT>	Used with the <SCRIPT> tag, marks material that should be displayed in browsers that don't support the scripting language. (The text is ignored by most script-capable browsers.)	3.0	3.0	186–7
<OBJECT>		</OBJECT>	Inserts an object (e.g., an image, media file, or program)	4.0	3.0	124, 190
	align="left" OR "right" OR "center" OR "top" OR "middle" OR "bottom" OR "baseline" OR "texttop" OR "absmiddle" OR "absbottom"		The alignment of the object in the window	4.0	3.0	
	border=*n*		The width of the border around the object, specified in pixels		3.0	
	classid="*class-identifier*"		A unique identifier for the plug-in or program. (The syntax depends on the type of object being inserted.)	4.0	3.0	
	codebase="*URL*"		The directory that holds the program	4.0	3.0	
	codetype="*MIME-type*"		The MIME type of the program		3.0	
	data="*URL*"		The URL for the object to be inserted into the page	4.0	3.0	
	height=*n* width=*n*		The height and width of the object, in pixels	4.0	3.0	
	hspace=*n*, vspace=*n*		The horizontal and vertical space, in pixels, set between the object and surrounding text		3.0	
	name="*name*"		A name by which other programs can refer to the object		3.0	
	standby="*text*"		Text that displays while the object is loading		3.0	
	tabindex=*n*		The order in which this control will be accessed when the form is navigated using the Tab key		4.0	
	type="*MIME-type*"		The object's MIME type. The browser uses this to determine whether it can display the object.	4.0	3.0	
	usemap="*name*"		Names the map to be used for a client-side image map		3.0	128–9

START TAG	ATTRIBUTES	END TAG	EXPLANATION	SUPPORT NS	SUPPORT MS	PAGE
<OL>		</OL>	Creates an ordered (numbered) list	1.0	1.0	84–6
	type="A" OR "a" OR "I" OR "i"		Specifies alternate numbering styles: capital letters, lowercase letters, uppercase roman numerals, and lowercase roman numerals, respectively. (If no type is specified, the default Arabic numerals are used.)	1.1	1.0	
	start=n		Specifies a starting number	1.1	1.0	
<OPTGROUP>		</OPTGROUP>	For <SELECT>, groups options within the menu			
	disabled		Indicates that the option group should be disabled by default			169
	label="*text*"		A label for the option group			
<OPTION>		**</OPTION>**	Used after the <SELECT> tag to create an option in a menu	1.0	1.0	153
	disabled		Indicates that the option group should be disabled by default			
	label="text"		A label for the option			
	selected		Specifies that the option should be selected by default			
	value="*text*"		The value to be sent if the option is selected	1.0	1.0	
<P>		</P>	Inserts a paragraph break	1.0	1.0	84–5
	align="left" OR "right" OR "center"		The alignment of the paragraph in the window	1.0	1.0	
<PARAM>			Used with the <OBJECT> or <APPLET> tags to pass parameter values to a program	2.0	3.0	
	name="*name*"		Names the parameter the value should be assigned to	2.0	3.0	
	value="value"		Provides a value for the parameter	2.0	3.0	
<PRE>		</PRE>	Marks text that should be laid out exactly as typed, including spaces and carriage returns	1.0	1.0	87
<Q>		</Q>	Marks text that should be set as an inline quote		4.0	108
<S>		</S>	Marks text that should be set as strikeout (same as <STRIKE>)	3.0	1.0	108
<SAMP>		</SAMP>	Marks text that should be set as a sample	1.0	1.0	108
<SCRIPT>		</SCRIPT>	Marks a client-side script	2.0	3.0	186–7
	language="*name*"		Names the language the script is written in	2.0	3.0	
	src="URL"		Names an external script file	3.0	3.01	

KEY

NS=Netscape

MS=Microsoft

End tags and attributes in **boldface** are required

START TAG	ATTRIBUTES	END TAG	EXPLANATION	SUPPORT NS	MS	PAGE
<SELECT>		</SELECT>	Creates a menu of choices, either a pull-down menu (the default) or a scrolling menu, in a form	1.0	1.0	168-71
	accesskey=*x*		A key that can be pressed to access the control		4.0	
	align="left" OR "right" OR "top" OR "middle" OR "bottom"		The alignment of the menu in the browser window		4.0	
	disabled		Indicates that the menu should be disabled by default		4.0	169
	multiple		Allows multiple selections from a scrolling menu	1.0	1.0	
	name="*name*"		Creates a name for the menu, used as a variable name when the input is sent to a script for processing	1.0	1.0	
	onblur="*script*"		A script to be run when the control loses focus	2.0	3.0	172
	onchange="*script*"		A script to be run when the control value is changed	2.0	3.0	172
	onfocus="*script*"		A script to be run when the control gains focus	2.0	3.0	172
	size=*n*		Creates a scrolling menu of the depth specified (in pixels)	1.0	1.0	
	tabindex=*n*		The order in which this control will be accessed when the form is navigated with the Tab key		4.0	
<SMALL>		</SMALL>	Marks text that should be set in a small size	1.1	3.0	108
<SPACER>			Creates a blank space in the page layout	3.0		88-9
	align="left" OR "right" OR "top" OR "texttop" OR middle" OR "absmiddle" "baseline" OR "bottom" OR "absbottom"		For *type=block*, tells the browser how to wrap the adjoining text around the space	3.0		
	height=*n*, width=*n*		For *type=block*, the width and height of the empty space	3.0		
	size=*n*		For *type=horizontal* or *type=vertical*, the size of the empty space, in pixels	3.0		
	type="horizontal" or "vertical" or "block"		Tells the browser to create a space in the current line (horizontal), to create a vertical space above the next item (vertical), or to create a rectangular space (block)	3.0		
<SPAN>		</SPAN>	Groups a set of words so that they can be styled via a style sheet. Styles can be assigned to the <SPAN> element using the generic *style=* attribute with the <SPAN> tag or by giving the <SPAN> element an id or class (via those generic attributes) that are styled via an external style sheet.	4.0	3.0	105
<STRIKE>		</STRIKE>	Marks text that should be set as strikeout (same as <S>)	1.1	1.0	108
<STRONG>		</STRONG>	Marks text that should be emphasized (usually set in bold)	1.0	1.0	108

START TAG	ATTRIBUTES	END TAG	EXPLANATION	SUPPORT NS	MS	PAGE
<STYLE>		</STYLE>	Marks the document's style sheet	4.0	3.0	98–101
	disabled		Indicates that the style sheet should be disabled by default		4.0	169
	media="screen" OR "print" OR "projection" OR "braille" OR "speech" OR "all"		The type of media the style sheet is designed for			
	title="*text*"		A name for the style sheet, to be used in a menu that allows users to select from different style sheets			
	type="*MIME-type*"		The MIME type of the style sheet, usually "text/css"	4.0	3.0	
_{		}	Marks text that should be set subscript	1.1	3.0	108
^{		}	Marks text that should be set superscript	1.1	3.0	108
<TABLE>		**</TABLE>**	Marks the set of elements that make up a table	1.1	2.0	90–3
	align="left" OR "right" OR "center"		The table's alignment in the window	2.0	2.0	
	background="*URL*"		The URL of a background graphic to be used for the table		3.0	130
	bgcolor="*#RRGGBB*" OR "*name*"		The color of the table's background, using the RGB values (expressed in hexadecimal) or a color name	3.0	2.0	130
	border=*n*		A width for the row's border, in pixels; "*border=0*" means no border	1.1	2.0	
	bordercolor="*#RRGGBB*" OR "*name*"		A color for the table's border		2.0	
	cellpadding=*n*		The space between each cell's border and its contents, specified in pixels	1.1	2.0	
	cellspacing=*n*		The space between adjoining cells	1.1	2.0	
	cols=*n*		The number of columns in the table	3.0	3.0	
	frame="void" OR "above" OR "below" OR "hsides" OR "vsides" OR "lhs" OR "rhs" OR "box" OR "border"		How the table will be outlined. Most of the values select particular sides of the table; "box" and "border" both specify a border on all sides.		3.0	
	height=*n*, width=*n* OR "*n*%"		The tables total height and width, specified in pixels or, for width, as a percentage of the table size	1.1	2.0	
	rules="none" OR "groups" OR "rows" OR "cols" OR "all"		How rules will be used to separate table cells		3.0	

KEY

NS=Netscape

MS=Microsoft

End tags and attributes in **boldface** are required

START TAG	ATTRIBUTES	END TAG	EXPLANATION	SUPPORT NS	SUPPORT MS	PAGE
\<TBODY\> **\<TFOOT\>** **\<THEAD\>**		**\</TBODY\>** \</TFOOT\> \</THEAD\>	Separate tables into header, body, and footer areas		3.0	
	align="left" OR "center" OR "right" OR "justify" OR "char"		The alignment of the table header, body, or footer		4.0	
	bgcolor="#RRGGBB" OR "name"		The color of the table's background, using the RGB values (expressed in hexadecimal) or a color name		4.0	130
	valign="top" OR "middle" OR "bottom" OR "baseline"		The vertical alignment of text within the cells		4.0	
\<TD\> **\<TH\>**		**\</TD\>** \</TH\>	Marks the data (\<TD\>) or a heading (\<TH\>) that goes in a table cell	1.1	2.0	90–3
	align="left" OR "right" OR "center"		Specifies the data's alignment in the cell	1.1	2.0	
	background="URL"		The URL of a background graphic to be used for the table cell		3.0	130
	bgcolor="#RRGGBB" OR "name"		A color for the cell's background	3.0	2.0	130
	bordercolor="#RRGGBB" OR "name"		A color for the cell's border		2.0	
	colspan=n		The number of columns the cell spans	1.1	2.0	
	height=n, width=n OR "n%"		The height and width of the table cell, in pixels or, for width, as a percentage of the table size	1.1	2.0	
	nowrap		Disables line-wrapping in the cell	1.1	2.0	
	rowspan=n		The number of rows the cell spans	1.1	2.0	
	valign="top" OR "middle" OR "bottom" OR "baseline"		The vertical alignment of the cell's contents relative to its borders	1.1	2.0	
\<TEXTAREA\>		\</TEXTAREA\>	Creates a multiline text field in a form	1.0	1.0	168–71
	accesskey=x		A key that can be pressed to access the control		4.0	
	cols=n, rows=n		The width (cols) and height (rows) of the text area, in characters	1.0	1.0	
	disabled		Indicates that the control should be disabled by default		4.0	169
	name="name"		A name for the text area, used as a variable name when the input is sent to a script for processing	1.0	1.0	
	onblur="script"		A script to be run when the control loses focus	2.0	3.0	172
	onchange="script"		A script to be run when the control's content is changed	2.0	3.0	172
	onfocus="script"		A script to be run when the control gains focus	2.0	3.0	172
	onselect="script"		A script to be run when the user selects text in the textarea field		4.0	172

START TAG	ATTRIBUTES	END TAG	EXPLANATION	SUPPORT NS	MS	PAGE
	readonly		Indicates that the text cannot be changed by the user		4.0	
	tabindex=*n*		The order in which this control will be accessed when the form is navigated with the Tab key		4.0	
	wrap="off" OR "virtual" OR "physical"		Specifies how text lines wrap in the control. "off" (the default) means no word wrap; "virtual" means the text wraps in the browser window but are sent to the processing script as a single line; "physical" means the text wraps in the window and is sent to the script with line breaks.	2.0		
<TR>		**</TR>**	Creates a new table row	1.1	2.0	90–3
	align="left" OR "right" OR "center"		The alignment of the contents of the row's cells	1.1	2.0	
	background="*URL*"		An image file to be used as the row's background		3.0	
	bgcolor="#*RRGGBB*" OR "*name*"		A color for the table row's background	3.0	2.0	130
	bordercolor="#*RRGGBB*" OR "*name*"		A color for the row's border		2.0	130
	valign="top" OR "middle" OR "bottom" OR "baseline"		The vertical alignment of the row's contents relative to the cell's borders	1.1	2.0	
<TT>		**</TT>**	Marks text that should be set in teletype (monospaced) text	1.0	1.0	108
<U>		**</U>**	Marks text that should be set underlined	3.0	1.0	108
<UL>		**</UL>**	Creates an unordered (bulleted) list	1.0	1.0	84–6
	type="disc" OR "circle" OR "square"		A shape for the bullets	1.0		
<VAR>		**</VAR>**	Marks text that should be set as a variable	1.0	1.0	108
<WBR>			Sets a word break	1.0	1.0	

KEY

NS=Netscape

MS=Microsoft

End tags and attributes in **boldface** are required

Special thanks to Brian Wilson, whose site, Index Dot HTML: The Advanced HTML Reference (http://www.blooberry.com/html/), was the source of much of the browser support information in this table. The site is an exhaustive and invaluable resource for anyone trying to find that important information.

Browser Capabilities

With the following table you can quickly see which capabilities are supported by the two leading web browsers: Netscape Navigator and Microsoft Internet Explorer. Rather than show you only what the latest version can do, we've included all previous versions of the browser, so you can see when a capability was first supported, and how long it has been there.

This reference shows you which capabilities are supported by the two major browsers. We list capabilities down the left hand side, organized by category, and show you the versions of each browser that support them. On the right side of the table is the page number where you will find a description of the capability.

If there is a number listed in the bar graph, it means that a particular capability is not fully supported. These are indicated by numbers which coincide with notes at the bottom of the page; for instance, in Netscape Navigator, "Active X" is available for the PC only, as shown by the number "4".

Browser Capabilities

	NETSCAPE NAVIGATOR					MICROSOFT INTERNET EXPLORER				PAGE
	1.0	1.1	2.0	3.0	4.0	1.0	2.0	3.0	4.0	
HTML SUPPORT										
HTML 2.0 — Basic HTML and forms	●	●	●	●	●	○	○	○	○	74
HTML 3.2 — Style tags, tables, frames		●	●	●	●		○	○	○	74
HTML 4.0 — Style sheets, DHTML					●				○	74
TYPOGRAPHY CONTROLS										
\<FONT\> tag — Specification of type face, size, and color		●	●	●	●		○	○	○	112
Style sheets — Typographic control via style sheets					●			○	○	114
Downloadable fonts — Automatic downloading of nonstandard fonts					● [1]				○ [2]	116
ANIMATION										
Animated GIF — Sequenced playback of GIF89a graphics			●	●	●			○	○	152
DHTML — Animation of HTML elements via JavaScript					●				○	158
Java — Animated interfaces programmed in Java			●	●	●			○	○	156
PROGRAMMING/INTERACTIVITY										
CGI — Communications to server-side processing	●	●	●	●	●	○	○	○	○	183
JavaScript/JScript — Programmable via JavaScript and JScript			●	●	●			○	○	186
Java — Programmable via Java			●	●	●			○	○	188
VBScript — Programmable via VBScript								○ [3]	○ [3]	186
ActiveX — Programmable via ActiveX				● [4]	● [4]			○ [3]	○ [3]	192
ALTERNATE FORMATS										
Plug-in support — Add-in support of additional formats			●	●	●			○	○	11
XML — Custom-created tags									○	142

1 TrueDoc only
2 OpenType only, TrueDoc through ActiveX on PC
3 PC only
4 PC only/through plug-in

Glossary

A

ActiveX
A Microsoft core technology that allows software components to interoperate.

ActiveX control
A program, based on *ActiveX* technology, that adds new features to an ActiveX-compatible program.

adaptive palette
A palette created by choosing the most-used colors in an image.

AIFF
Audio Interchange File Format, a cross-platform digital sound format.

animated GIF
A graphic file, in GIF89a format, that includes multiple frames that can be played in succession to create an animation. See also *GIF*.

anti-alias
To blur the edges of a graphic to reduce the stair-stepping pattern ("jaggies") that often appears on low-resolution output devices such as computer screens.

API
Application programming interface, a method built into servers and other programs that allows external programs to call on special functions of that program.

AppleScript
A scripting language developed by Apple to offer a standard method of automating Macintosh programs.

applet
A *Java* program designed to be distributed over the Net.

ASCII
Stands for American Standard Code for Information Interchange. ASCII files, sometimes called "pure text" files, can contain only information included in that code set, which consists of the 26 letters of the alphabet (both uppercase and lowercase), numbers from 0 to 9, and a few common symbols.

ASF
Advanced Streaming Format, a format for streaming audio and video created by Microsoft and used in its NetShow products.

attribute
A value provided within an HTML tag to supply additional information about how the tagged element should be treated.

.au
A sound file format commonly used on Unix computers.

avatar
In graphics-based *chat* systems, a figure that represents a participant.

AVI
Audio-video interleave, the standard video format for Microsoft Windows.

B

bit depth
The number of bits used to record each pixel of information in an image file. Common formats are 8-bit (256 colors or shades of gray) and 24-bit (16.7 million colors). Also often used to refer to the number of bits per *sample* in a sound file.

bitmap
A graphics format that creates an image using an array of pixels of different colors or shades. See also *object-based graphics*.

block-level tag
In HTML, a tag that names an element that begins a new line. Compare *phrase-markup tag*.

bookmark
A record of a particular page's URL, stored with a user's browser preferences, allowing the user to return to that page by choosing the page's name from a menu.

branching diagram
In Web design, a diagram that shows what pages a Web site contains and how they are related to one another.

browser
Client software designed to communicate with Web servers and interpret the data received from them. Many different browsers are available, each with different features. The most common browsers are Netscape Navigator and Microsoft Internet Explorer.

browser-safe palette
A palette of 216 colors (based on 6-bit color) used by most browser manufacturers to display color on 8-bit (256-color) systems. Mapping graphics to the browser-safe palette before posting them on a Web site avoids the danger that Web graphics will be subject to *dithering* on the viewer's system.

C

cache
An area of memory or disk reserved for holding data that is expected to be used again, making that data faster to retrieve the next time it is used.

cascading style sheets
The most widely supported *style sheet* language for Web publishing.

CGI
Common Gateway Interface, a set of rules by which *browsers* can request the services of programs stored on a *server* and the server can return files based on the program's results.

chat
A system, usually based on *IRC,* that allows Internet users to exchange messages with other visitors to a site in real time.

class
In HTML 4.0, a group of elements defined by the author. You add an element to a class using the *class=* attribute. With *cascading style sheets,* designers can assign layout attributes to all the members of a class.

client
In a *client-server system* such as the Web, the user's computer.

client-server system
A networking system in which processes are split between *server* computers, which hold files for distribution, and *client* computers, which can request files and other services from the servers.

client-side image map
An *image map* for which the map information and the map processing program reside on the client (user's) computer.

client-side processing
Running programs on an Internet *client,* rather than on a *server.*

client software
A term used to describe *browsers,* mail readers, and other software used on the *client* machine to read files obtained over a *client-server system* such as the Web.

code signing
A method of ensuring the safety of downloadable programs, such as *ActiveX controls,* in which the program's creator signs the object, and client systems check for the signature before running it.

common gateway interface
See *CGI.*

content negotiation
A method by which *servers* can check which client software is available on the *client* machine and download a page appropriate to that software.

creative brief
A statement of the goals of a design process.

CSS
See *cascading style sheets.*

CSS1
Version 1 of the specification for *cascading style sheets.*

CSS2
Version 2 of the specification for *cascading style sheets.*

CSS positioning
A method of placing elements in a *browser* window using *cascading style sheet* commands.

D

deprecated
In *HTML,* used to refer to tags that have been superceded by other methods in later versions of the HTML specification.

design specifications
Specifications describing how each element of a document is to be laid out.

design templates
Standard designs that can be reused for a set of similar pages.

dithering
A method of creating a color by combining pixels of two or more other colors.

document object model
A method of addressing the different parts of an HTML document from scripts and other programs. Often abbreviated DOM. Usually refers to the DOM described in a specification under development by the *W3C.*

DOM
See *document object model.*

domain name
A name by which an Internet *server* is known (e.g., "peachpit.com"). The first part of the domain name provides a unique, plain-language identifier for the Internet server. The second part (following the period) is usually a three-letter code signifying the type of site: e.g., *.com* for commercial, *.edu* for educational institution.

downloadable fonts
Fonts that are downloaded along with an *HTML* file. At this writing, there are two different technologies in use for downloadable fonts: Microsoft's and Adobe's *OpenType* and Bitstream's *TrueDoc.*

DSSSL
Document semantics and style specification language, a popular style language for *SGML* publishing.

DTD
Document type description, a file that defines the tags used in an SGML or XML application.

dynamic HTML
Refers to a set of technologies, including *style sheets, CSS positioning,* and *JavaScript,* that let page authors create animated and interactive interfaces with *HTML.*

E

ECMAScript
A scripting standard overseen by the standards organization ECMA. *JavaScript* and *JScript* are based on ECMAScript.

e-mail
A system for exchanging electronic messages over a network.

end tag
In *HTML,* the tag that marks the end of an element. The end tag is usually the same as the *start tag* but preceded by a slash (/) character.

event handler
A command that triggers actions when a certain event occurs—either an interactive event, such as the user clicking a button, or a non-interactive event, such as a page loading. In *HTML 4.0* and recent *browsers,* event handler attributes can be added to many tags and generate scripted actions.

extension
In *HTML,* tags supported by *browsers* that aren't part of the standard *HTML* specification.

F

Flash
See *Shockwave Flash.*

FlashPix
A graphics format, used by LivePix and Microsoft's PIctureIt, that allows for speedy rendering of images at several zoom levels.

forum
A Web site feature that lets users post messages in a public space, where they can be read and responded to by others.

frames
An *HTML* feature that lets designers split the *browser* window into separate areas, each of which can hold a separate *HTML* file and can scroll and be updated separately from the rest of the window.

frameset
The set of *frames* that make up a page. A <FRAMESET> tag defines the number of rows and columns in the window.

Frontier
A scripting language developed by UserLand, used as an alternative to *AppleScript* to script actions in Macintosh programs.

FTP
File transfer protocol, a method for sending files over the Internet.

functional specification
A document that describes the functions a site will offer and the characteristics of each function. The functional specification codifies the expectations for any programmed interaction on a site and should provide all the information the programmers need to begin their work.

G

GIF
Graphics Interchange Format, a compressed *bitmap* format created by CompuServe. The oldest version, called GIF87a or CompuServe GIF, has been superceded by a newer version, called GIF89a, which supports *transparency* and animation. See also *animated GIF, JPEG.*

gopher
A protocol used to create hierarchical menus, allowing users to move through information by moving through the directory structure until they find the information they need.

H

helper application
An application launched by a *browser* to display files it can't read itself. See also *ActiveX control, plug-in.*

hexadecimal
A numbering system using base-16 (rather than the base-10 of the decimal system). In hexadecimal, the numbers from 10 to 16 are indicated by the letters A through F. Hexadecimal numbers are used to specify RGB (red/green/blue) values in *HTML* tags and *style sheets.*

history list
A list of pages that the user has visited during an online session, listed in a *browser* menu so that the user can choose the page's name to return to it.

home page
Sometimes used as a generic name for a Web site, but usually referring to the top page of a site structure, which provides access to all other pages on the site.

HTML
Hypertext Markup Language, a set of tags developed by the creators of the Web to mark the structural elements of text documents. A defining feature of HTML is its inclusion of tags that create *hyperlinks* to other documents on the Internet. HTML is an application of *SGML.*

HTML 2.0
The specification, finalized in September 1995, that codified the first standard set of *HTML* tags.

HTML 3.2
The second official *HTML* recommendation by the *W3C*, adding features such as tables and some style tags.

HTML 4.0
The latest version of the *HTML* specification, which introduces *style sheets* and other advanced features to *HTML.*

HTML filters
Programs that translate an application's files into *HTML*-coded text files.

HTTP
Hypertext transfer protocol, the communications *protocol* on which the *World Wide Web* is based. HTTP sets rules for how information is passed between the *server* and the *browser* software.

hyperlink
In a *hypertext* document, such as a Web page, an electronic link that, when chosen, calls up a piece of linked information.

hypertext
An electronic Information structure through which the reader navigates via *hyperlinks.*

I

Internet Imaging Protocol (IIP)
A method of rendering images that allows the browser or other software to handle an image in discrete sections, allowing for quick rendering.

image map
A type of graphic in which different locations on the image file (specified by pixel coordinates) act as *hyperlinks* to different *URLs.*

indexed color
A photo-editing option that allows you to map an image to a new, usually reduced, color palette.

information architect
For any publishing project, the person responsible for determining how information will be organized. In Web design, the information architect is usually responsible for deciding how the information will be arrayed on the pages of a Web site and how it will be accessed by the user.

inheritance
In *cascading style sheets*, the principle that elements use the same style properties as any element that contains them, unless those properties are specifically overridden.

inline frame
A frame that is not part of a *frameset* but is defined individually.

inline graphic
A graphic loaded into a *browser* window as part of an *HTML* document.

interlacing
A feature of some graphics formats that allows the graphic to be loaded into a Web page in alternate rows and/or columns, allowing visitors to see a rough version of the image before it is completely downloaded.

Internet
A worldwide computer network that links thousands of smaller networks. Financed by the U.S. government, the Internet was originally developed to allow information exchange between academics and scientists around the country.

Internet Relay Chat
An Internet protocol for exchanging text messages in real time among multiple simultaneous users. Abbreviated as IRC.

Internet Service Provider
A company that provides a connection to the Internet.

InterNIC
The service that registers *domain names* for Internet users.

IRC
See *Internet Relay Chat.*

ISP
See *Internet Service Provider.*

J

Java
A cross-platform programming language developed by Sun Micro-systems. Because Java programs can run on any processor, it is often used for programs that are distributed over the Web.

JavaScript
A *scripting language* developed by Netscape, specialized for controlling Web *browser* processes.

Java Virtual Machine
A software layer that executes compiled *Java* code. The existence of the "virtual machine" is the key to Java's cross-platform capabilities.

JPEG
A compressed *bitmap* format, developed by (and named for) the Joint Photographic Experts Group of the International Standards Organization. JPEG is generally used for photographic images. An alternate version, called *Progressive JPEG*, supports *interlacing.*

JScript
A *JavaScript*-compatible scripting language developed by Microsoft and supported in its software.

L

Liquid Audio
An audio format designed to deliver CD-quality sound files over the Web.

lossless compression
A compression scheme, such as that used by *GIF,* that reduces file sizes without discarding any image information.

lossy compression
A compression scheme, such as that used by *JPEG,* that reduces file sizes by discarding nonessential image information.

M

map file
For *server-side image maps,* a file (stored on the *server*) that holds the map information, linking specific regions of the image to specific target *URLs.*

MBONE
The Multimedia Backbone, a virtual network over which Web publishers can *multicast* sound and video transmissions.

MIDI
Musical Instrument Digital Interface, a standard for recording and playing synthesized sounds on electronic instruments.

MIME
Multipurpose Internet Mail Extensions, a method of specifying the format of a file for Internet software such as mail readers and Web *browsers.* The software uses the MIME code to determine how to interpret the file.

monospaced
A term used to describe a typeface in which every character has the same width. Such typefaces are useful for tables, program documentation, or other texts in which vertical alignment is crucial.

MPEG
A compressed video format, created by and named for the Motion Picture Experts Group of the International Standards Organization.

multicasting
On the Web, sending a multimedia stream that can be read by multiple *clients.* (The stream is duplicated by multicast-capable routers along the way.) Client software "listens in" to a particular Internet address to receive the multicast stream. See also *MBONE.*

N

navigation bar
On a Web page, a set of *hyperlinks,* usually in the form of icons or text links, that offers access to a standard set of pages—usually the top pages of the site's main sections.

newsgroup
An *Internet* service that allows users to post comments that can be read by any other user.

Netscape color cube
See *browser-safe palette.*

O

object-based graphics
Graphics created as an assembly of shapes, or "objects." Object-based graphics are suitable only for illustrative (line-based) images. Also often called *vector graphic.*

object detection
A technique used to determine whether or not a specific object, such as a *plug-in,* exists in the *client* software.

OpenType
A font technology, developed by Microsoft and Adobe, that combines the features of Type 1 and TrueType fonts, making the different font formats compatible across different systems and platforms. Microsoft's *downloadable font* technology is based on OpenType.

P

page architecture
In Web design, a plan for the placement of information on a page.

PDF
Portable Document Format, an electronic document format created by Adobe Systems and based on PostScript, used by Adobe's Acrobat program.

perl
Practical Extraction and Report Language, a *scripting language* often used to create server-side *scripts.*

PGML
Precision Graphics Markup Language, a method for describing *vector graphics* based on PostScript and *XML,* proposed by Adobe, Netscape, and Sun Microsystems.

phrase-markup tag
An HTML tag that marks a phrase inside a *block-level tag.* Phrase markup tags do not create a line break.

plug-in
A *helper application* that displays nonstandard formats inside the *browser* window.

PNG
A 24-bit, compressed graphics format that can support multiple levels of *transparency* and two-dimensional *interlacing.*

Progressive JPEG
A version of the *JPEG* graphics format that supports *interlacing.*

protocol
A set of rules for exchanging information between computers over a network or via a modem connection.

Q

QuickTime
A video format created by Apple Computer and supported on the Macintosh and Windows platforms.

QuickTime VR
A technology created by Apple Computer for creating and viewing 3D scenes.

R

RealAudio
A streaming audio format developed by RealNetworks.

RealFlash
A streaming animation format with synchronized graphics developed by Macromedia and RealNetworks.

real-time motion
In digital animation or video, the effect of natural motion achieved by using a frame rate of 24 to 30 frames per second.

RealVideo
A streaming video format developed by RealNetworks.

S

sample
In digital media, a digital recording of sound or visual data, taken and played back at high frequencies to create the illusion of natural sound or motion.

script
A list of instructions to be executed by a piece of software. Unlike full-featured programming languages, scripts are interpreted line by line by the software that executes them, rather than being compiled into quicker-executing machine code. Because they are not compiled, scripts are easy to read and update.

scripting language
A simple programming language, such as *JavaScript* or *PERL,* used to automate the behavior of an application or operating system.

search engine
A program that searches through electronic information. Web search engines such as Lycos and Info-Seek search through indexes of the entire Internet in response to user queries. Search engines can also be set up to search the contents of individual sites.

server
In a *client-server system,* the computer that holds the data to be distributed.

server-side image map
An *image map* for which the *map file* and the map processing program reside on the *server,* and the coordinates of a user's click are sent to the server for processing.

server-side processing
Running programs on an Internet *server* rather than on the *client.*

SGML
Standard Generalized Markup Language, a language, widely used by government and educational institutions, used to mark the structural elements of text documents so that the documents can be read and displayed appropriately by a variety of software. *HTML* is one application of SGML. SGML is codified by the International Standards Organization as ISO 8879.

Shockwave
Macromedia's technologies for playing files from its multimedia authoring programs on the Web. Shockwave tools, including authoring programs and players, are available for Macromedia's Director, Flash, and FreeHand applications.

Shockwave Audio
A streaming sound format that can be played through Macromedia's Shockwave player.

Shockwave Flash
An interactive, animated vector graphics format from Macromedia, supported as part of its *Shockwave* suite of technologies.

staging server
A *server* that has the same directory structure and software as the server that will be used to publish Internet files, used to test Web pages before they are made publicly available.

start tag
In *HTML,* the tag that marks the beginning of an element. Many tags also require *end tags* to mark the element's end.

storyboard
A document that shows the planned sequence of frames for a video or any other time-based storytelling form.

streaming
Describes technologies that feed media files to a player progressively, so that a file can begin playing as it is being downloaded.

structural tag
In *HTML,* a tag that describes a document element. Compare *style tag.*

style sheet
Layout instructions added to an *HTML* file via a style sheet language such as *cascading style sheets.*

style tag
In *HTML,* a tag that describes the layout of an element. Compare *structural tag.*

subsetting
With *downloadable fonts,* creating a font file that includes only the characters that are actually used on the *HTML* page. Subsetting results in smaller font files.

T

TCP/IP
Stands for Transmission Control Protocol/Internet Protocol, the *protocol* developed for communication over the Internet and now supported by most computer systems.

Telnet
A *protocol* that allows an Internet user to run programs stored on another Internet computer, or a program that uses the protocol.

tile
To arrange an object or graphic across an area by repeating it in contiguous, adjacent areas. On the Web, small background graphics are tiled to fill the *browser* window.

transparency
A feature of an image file in which certain colors can be made invisible against a background. *GIF* and *PNG* graphics support transparency.

TrueDoc
A technology created by Bitstream that creates font outlines that match an electronic document's original fonts. Netscape uses TrueDoc for its *downloadable font* technology.

U

URL
Uniform Resource Locator, a standard method of naming files on the World Wide Web. Sometimes referred to as URI (Universal Resource Identifier) or URN (Universal Resource Name).

V

validate
For *SGML* or *XML,* to verify that a document's content is valid according to the rules specified in the *DTD.*

variable
In programming, a placeholder for a value that can be reassigned based on user input or other changing conditions.

vector graphics
Another name for *object-based graphics,* reflecting the fact that the objects that make up the images are created from mathematical splines, or vectors, rather than described as individual pixels. EPS and FreeHand files are common vector graphics formats.

VBScript
See *Visual Basic Scripting Edition.*

videoconferencing
An online conferencing system in which video images of the participants are displayed on the other participants' screens. Conversations may be held via text or audio, depending on the system and the available bandwidth.

Visual Basic
A programming language developed by Microsoft especially for creating Windows programs.

Visual Basic Script
See *Visual Basic Scripting Edition.*

Visual Basic Scripting Edition
A *scripting language* based on Microsoft's Visual Basic programming language, specialized for controlling Web processes and *ActiveX controls* and passing information to *Java* programs. Sometimes referred to as *Visual Basic Script* or *VBScript.*

VRML
Virtual Reality Modeling Language, a *scripting language* used to define 3D shapes for use on the Web. VRML (often pronounced "ver´-mul") supports *hyperlinking* and programmed behaviors.

VRMLScript
A scripting language specialized for controlling *VRML worlds.*

W

W3C
See *World Wide Web Consortium.*

WAIS
Wide Area Information Service, a protocol used to build indexes of text documents, including Internet pages, allowing quick searches for information.

.wav
The native sound format for Microsoft Windows.

webmaster
The person in charge of managing a Web site. The name is used for a variety of functions, including but not limited to the role of head editor, lead producer, or site engineer.

world
The word used for a *VRML 3D* environment, to differentiate it from the "page" interface of 2-D formats.

World Wide Web
An *Internet* service, based on the *HTTP protocol,* that allows publishers to post data in richly formatted pages and users to navigate information on *servers* around the world through a system of *hyperlinks.*

World Wide Web Consortium
A group, composed of volunteers from Internet software companies, academics, and other interested parties, that oversees the development of technologies for the World Wide Web.

WYSIWYG
Stands for "what you see is what you get," a phrase used to describe HTML editors that let authors edit pages in a graphic format that mimics the appearance of the page as it will be displayed in a browser.

X

XML
Extensible Markup Language, a system, based on *SGML,* for creating markup languages for the Web.

XSL
Extensible Style Language, a *style sheet* language being developed for use with XML.

Z

z-index
In css positioning, the layering order of an element. The term refers to the element's position in an x-y-z Cartesian coordinate system.

Index

Q

<Q> tag. 219
QuickTime, 151, 160–1
    online resources for, 165
    for sound, 164
QuickTime VR, 133
    online resources for, 139

R

RDF (Resource Description Format), 144
    online resources for, 149
RealAudio, RealNetworks, 155, 160, 161, 165, 198
    online resources for, 165
RealNetworks, 160, 165. *See also* RealAudio, RealFlash,
    RealPlayer, RealVideo
    online resources for, 165
RealFlash, 155, 160
RealPlayer, RealNetworks, 155, 161
RealVideo, RealNetworks, 160–1, 164
roles, 38–51
rollovers, 172

S

<S> tag, 108, 219
<SAMP> tag, 108, 219
<SCRIPT> tag, 172, 186, 219
scripting languages, 148, 182, 184, 186–7. *See also*
    individual languages
    vs. programming languages, 182
scripts, 47, 48, 185. *See also* APIs, CGI, client-side processing,
    programming, scripting languages, server-side processing
    client, 186–7
    prebuilt, 163
    vs. programs, 182
    with VRML, 148
    with XML, 143–4
search engines, 51, 110
    coding for (online resources), 53
    site-specific, 60
security for client-side processing, 188
Seidler, Peter, 15, 31, 44, 61, 182, 198
<SELECT> tag, 171, 220
server push, 162

servers, 9, 49, 53
    statistics analysis, 200, 203
server-side processing, 180–5
SGML, 72, 140
    as basis of HTML, 70
    as basis of XML, 142
    online resources for, 81
Shedroff, Nathan, 37, 146, 201
Shockwave, 12, 57, 64, 153, 158, 164, 198
    See also Shockwave Audio, Shockwave Flash
    animation, 153–5
    for FreeHand graphics, 123
    interactivity with, 174
    online resources for, 165, 179
    sound, 164–5
Shockwave Audio, 165
Shockwave Flash, 153–5, 157, 161, 198
    for interactivity, 174
SimpleText, 80
<SMALL> tag, 108, 220
smart quotes, 109
Sotherland, Fred, 25, 27, 32, 95, 112, 199
sound, 164–5
SoundEdit 16, Macromedia, 165
<SPACER> tag, 88–9, 220
<SPAN> tag, 104, 105, 220
    id= attribute, 105
special characters, 109
    online resources for, 119
specifications, design, 201
staging server, 49
start tag, 73
statistics, server, 200
    online resources for, 203
storyboard, 43
streaming, 151
    animated GIF, 152
    Shockwave, 154
    sound, 164–5
    video, 160–2
StreamWorks, Xing Technology, 160
    online resources for, 165
<STRIKE> tag, 108, 220
<STRONG> tag, 108, 220
structural tags, 71–2, 83, 88, 108
    design specifications for, 84–5, 108
    layout with, 84–6
    with style sheets, 98
structure, site, 42–5, 54–67. *See also* information architecture
Studio Archetype, 36. *See also* Grotting, John; Merholz, Peter

style sheets, 21, 23, 72, 76, 82, 83, 85, 158. *See also*
    cascading style sheets, CSS1, CSS1
    HTML tags for, 99
    online resources for, 119
    for page layout, 98–105
    pseudo-classes, 115
    syntax for, 98
    type controls in, 114–6
    for XML, 142, 145
<STYLE> tag, 77, 99, 114, 221
style tags, 72, 88, 108
    design specifications for, 108
style= attribute, 99, 205
<SUB> tag, 108, 221
subsetting for downloadable fonts, 117
Sun Microsystems, 168
<SUP> tag, 108, 221
symbols, escape codes for, 109

T

<TABLE> tag, 92, 221
    height= attribute, 93
    width= attribute, 93
tables, 75, 88, 90–3
    online resources for, 105
<TBODY> tag, 92, 222
TCP/IP, 6, 9
<TD> tag, 92, 93, 222
technical specification. *See* functional specification
technologies timeline, 198
Telnet, 8, 9
templates, 201
testing
    color, 135
    HTML results, 48, 77
    hyperlinks, 48, 49
    interface design (user testing), 63
<TEXTAREA> tag, 171, 222–3
text-only systems, 21, 64, 125
<TFOOT> tag, 222
<TH> tag, 92, 93, 222
<THEAD> tag, 222
Times typeface, 107
    as default, 85
<TR> tag, 92, 92, 223
transparency in graphics, 88, 122, 139
TrueDoc, Bitstream, 116, 117
    online resources for, 119
<TT> tag, 108, 223

DARCY DINUCCI (darcy@tothepoint.com) has written about design and technology for over a decade, as an editor for *PC World, NeXTworld,* and *Publish* magazines, as a contributor to *MacWeek, Print,* and *U&lc,* and as editor of *The Little PC Book* and *The Macintosh Bible, 5th edition,* for Peachpit Press. She runs To the Point Publishing (http://www.tothepoint.com), a publishing services company in San Francisco.

MARIA GIUDICE (maria@hotstudio.com) is the creative director for HOT, a multiple media design agency in San Francisco. Formerly a partner in YO, Maria has been specializing in information design for over 10 years. Her clients include Agfa, Netscape, Narrowline, Apple, and Microsoft. Her work has been featured in *Information Architects* (Graphis Press, 1996). She teaches and lectures regularly about designing for print and the Web, and has been profiled in *Communication Arts, Print*, and *Publish.* Visit http://www.hotstudio.com/ for more information.

LYNNE STILES (lynne@chezhank.com) is an information designer in San Francisco. Projects include publications for Addison-Wesley, HarperCollins, Peachpit Press, Publish magazine and the Digital Color Prepress series for Agfa Corporation. Web design work includes sites for Peachpit Press, Big Book and Match.com. Her work has been reproduced and profiled in *Print, Communication Arts*, and *Information Architects* (Graphis Press, 1996.)